Celebrations

READ-ALOUD HOLIDAY

AND THEME BOOK

PROGRAMS

Other Books by Caroline Feller Bauer

HANDBOOK FOR STORYTELLERS

MY MOM TRAVELS A LOT

THIS WAY TO BOOKS

TOO MANY BOOKS!

Celebrations

READ-ALOUD HOLIDAY AND THEME BOOK PROGRAMS

BY

CAROLINE FELLER BAUER

Drawings by Lynn Gates Bredeson

THE H. W. WILSON COMPANY

1985

FOR PETER
Every day is a celebration with you.

Library of Congress Cataloging in Publication Data

Bauer, Caroline Feller.
   Celebrations: read-aloud holiday and theme book programs.

   bibliography: p.
   Includes index.
   1. Children — Books and reading. 2. Libraries,
Children's — Activity programs. 3. Activity programs in
education. 4. Holidays. I. Title.
Z1037.A1B3 1985   808.06'8   85-714
ISBN 0-8242-0708-4

Printed in the United States of America

Acknowledgments

I wish to thank the many authors, literary agents, and publishers who kindly granted permission to include the following works, which are listed below:

Absolute Zero (pages 139-141) by Helen Cresswell. Reprinted with permission of Macmillan Publishing Company. Copyright © 1978 by Helen Cresswell.

"Analysis of Baseball" from *New & Selected Things Taking Place* by May Swenson. Copyright © 1971 by May Swenson. Reprinted by permission of Little, Brown and Company in association with the Atlantic Monthly Press.

"The Base Stealer" by Robert Francis. Copyright © 1948. Reprinted from *The Orb Weaver* by permission of Wesleyan University Press.

"Beowulf Against Grendel" excerpted from the book *Beowulf: A New Telling* by Robert Nye. Copyright © 1968 by Robert Nye. Reprinted by permission of Dell Publishing Co., Inc. and the author.

"Boa Constrictor" from *Where the Sidewalk Ends: The Poems and Drawings of Shel Silverstein*. Copyright © 1974 by Snake Eye Music, Inc. Reprinted by permission of Harper & Row, Publishers, Inc.

"The Bogeyman" from *Nightmares* by Jack Prelutsky. Copyright © 1976 by Jack Prelutsky. By permission of Greenwillow Books (A Division of William Morrow & Company).

"Borders" from *All the Colors of the Race* by Arnold Adoff. Copyright © 1982 by Arnold Adoff. By permission of Lothrop, Lee & Shepard Books (A Division of William Morrow & Company).

"Calendar" from *Wide Awake and Other Poems* by Myra Cohn Livingston. Copyright © 1959 by Myra Cohn Livingston. Reprinted by permission of Marian Reiner.

"The Chinese Checker Players" excerpted from *The Pill Versus the Springhill Mine Disaster* by Richard Brautigan. Copyright © 1968 by Richard Brautigan. Reprinted by permission of Delacorte Press/Seymour Lawrence.

"A Chinese Fairy Tale" from *The Rat-Catcher's Daughter* by Laurence Housman. Copyright © 1974 by Atheneum Publishers (A Margaret K. McElderry Book). Reprinted with permission of Atheneum Publishers, The Executors of the Laurence Housman Estate, and Jonathan Cape Ltd. (publishers of *Moonshine and Clover*, a collection of stories by Laurence Housman, in which "A Chinese Fairy Tale" can also be found).

"The Christmas Apple" (pages 53-63) from *This Way to Christmas* by Ruth Sawyer. Copyright © 1916, 1924 by Harper & Row, Publishers, Inc. Copyright © 1944 by Ruth Sawyer Durand. Reprinted by permission of Harper & Row, Publishers, Inc.

"The Christmas Roast" from *The Silver Touch and Other Christmas Stories* by Margret Rettich. Copyright © 1976 by Annette Betz Verlag Munchen. Translation copyright © 1978 by William Morrow & Company, Inc. By permission of William Morrow & Company.

"A City Pet" from *City Sandwich* by Frank Asch. Copyright © 1978 by Frank Asch. By permission of Greenwillow Books (A Division of William Morrow & Company).

"A Commercial for Spring" from *It Doesn't Always Have to Rhyme* by Eve Merriam. Copyright © 1964 by Eve Merriam. Reprinted by permission of the author.

"Country Christmas" from *Skip Around the Year* by Aileen Fisher. Copyright © 1967 by Aileen Fisher. Reprinted by permission of Harper & Row, Publishers, Inc.

"Crayons" from *Rhymes About Us*, copyright © 1974 by Marchette Chute. Reprinted by permission of the publisher, E. P. Dutton, Inc.

"The Day the T.V. Broke" by Gerald Jonas. Copyright © 1967 by Saturday Review Magazine Co. Reprinted by permission.

"The Fight of the Year" by Roger McGough from *Watchwords*. Reprinted by permission of the author, A. D. Peters & Co. Ltd., and Jonathan Cape Ltd.

"Fish Committing Suicide" from *Droodles* by Roger Price. Reprinted by permission of Price/Stern/Sloan Publishers, Inc., Los Angeles. Copyright © 1953 by Roger Price. All rights reserved.

"Fish Fishing" and "Rich Sardine With Private Can" from *Oodles of Droodles* by Roger Price. Reprinted by permission of Price/Stern/

Contents

Introduction

When I was 10, my fourth grade class took a trip to Washington, D.C., to observe the House of Representatives in session. After so many years, I've forgotten most of what was discussed — probably important issues like the national defense and new taxation. What I do remember best about our visit was the thing that seemed so funny to me: the morning when several representatives stood up to read into the Congressional Record suggestions from their constituents for new holidays. I still laugh when I think of all those serious, grown-up people suggesting that we have a National Carrot Day, or a National Grass Seed Week!

It's true, though, that ever since then I've loved the idea that we can create our own holidays. Just think: every day of the year can be a celebration. "Real" holidays are important, of course, but I personally like those celebrations I've dreamed up myself, especially when I can share them with a group of children.

The first year I worked as a children's librarian at the New York Public Library, I discovered that people begin asking for Christmas and Chanukah books as early as September. (It seems that the same people who do their Christmas shopping in October begin planning their holiday book programs early as well!) All fall I blithely checked the books out, until suddenly it was December: time for my own holiday program, and not a single Christmas or Chanukah book remained on the shelves. It was then that I invented "Snow Day", and my young audiences seemed to enjoy the program just as much as they would have enjoyed one on Chrismas. After all, I thought later, what difference would it make which event we were celebrating, as long as we were celebrating something fun, and the festivities involved primarily books?

And that is how, these many years later, I came to put together *Celebrations: Read-Aloud Holiday and Theme Book Programs.* And that is why you won't be surprised that the book contains some events you haven't heard of before (how about National Nothing Day?) and others that have no exact date but can be celebrated just about any time you feel like it (Grandparents' Day). I certainly haven't excluded traditional dates, but with the exception of Christmas, I've tried to use these holidays to promote a larger concept. For instance, in dealing with Thanksgiving, I've left the pilgrims and turkeys for another time and am instead using this uniquely American holiday for a program on the theme of "Thank you, America," with emphasis on recent immigrants and multi-ethnic understanding. And for Valentine's Day, I've used the theme of friends and friendship.

Although some of the programs in this book can be used on a specific date, don't feel trapped by the calendar. A program can be put on whenever you are in the mood for monsters, friends, baseball or television. As an example, baseball can be celebrated in the spring when the season opens or in October when the World Series rolls around or on both occasions. February 14th is Valentine's Day but you can give a program on friends and friendship any day of the year. I'm sure you will be able to think of other ways to use these programs to suit your individual needs or your calendar.

This book is meant for all those adults who work with children, particularly middle-grade children, in order to promote the lifelong good habit: reading. These holiday programs are pre-packaged and ready-to-go; no defrosting or cooking needed! Obviously you will want to adapt the book to your own needs, but I like to use an entire chapter as a program. The first step is to gather together as many books from the booklist as you can find and arrange them on a convenient table. Then look through the activities or recipes and see if something there might appeal to your students. Depending on what you select, you might also need to collect some supplies.

The material that is meant to be read aloud is the most important segment of these chapters. Don't rush through the story or poems just so you can get to a craft item or a writing project. Each reading should be thought of as the performance of your life. Imagine that your mother-in-law is in the room or the President of the World has come to listen to your story. When the reading is over you can turn to the activities, crafts or writing ideas. Make sure that you leave time for your group to browse through the book exhibit.

Please notice and admire Lynn Gates Bredeson's art work. I want you to use it, too. The opening page of each program contains a marginal drawing designed to reproduce as a bookmark. Just duplicate it directly from the book to pass out as a souvenir of the program theme. The other drawings can be used on promotion material for the program.

Let me tell you how *Celebrations* is organized. Each chapter, or program, follows the same general order: prose selections, poems, activities (crafts, treats, creative writing, etc.) and a booklist.

PROSE SELECTIONS. I chose some of my favorite short stories, folk tales or book excerpts for each program in *Celebrations*. They are all short enough to read in a single sitting, but long enough to give the listener a memorable listening experience. I'm delighted to have all these stories gathered in one volume. Some of the stories have been out of print, and others were "lost" because I couldn't remember in what collection the story had appeared or, worse, where I had shelved the book in my own library. The stories have been tested on audiences in schools, public libraries, and other group situations, such as overnight camping trips. I hesitate to tell you the age of the groups with which I worked for fear of limiting your use of this collection. Maybe your group is young in years but mature in listening skills, or perhaps the reverse is true. Let me give you a hint, however: most of the groups I read these stories to were from the fourth to seventh grades. Another thing to keep in mind is that even the selections within one chapter vary in style and maturity. You might find a rather sophisticated story followed by a very young one. Choose one or share both depending on your situation.

Do read these selections aloud to yourself before you try them on your audience so that you are aware of whether to adopt a light or sober tone. I hope that you will enjoy some of the selections enough to re-read them to your group.

POETRY. The poems were, of course, selected to fit the theme of each program, but they were also chosen to create balance among them. You will find light and even silly verse side by side with more thoughtful poetry. In all cases, I tried to choose poems that read well aloud. As with the prose selections, you should certainly read the poems aloud to yourself before you present them to an audience so that you won't be tripping over your words. My approach is not to say "Now I'm going to read a poem" —I just launch right into the reading by announcing the title. I believe your children will be as enthralled with the poetry as they are with the stories.

Poems usually become better appreciated with repeated readings as the audience begins to understand the words and images. So do re-read the poems.

All the poems in a chapter have been grouped together so that you will be able to find them easily and read them one after another. However, you may wish to present some before and some after the prose selection, or you may want to share one poem one day and another the next— stretching the program over several days.

BULLETIN BOARDS. Almost every classroom or library has a bulletin board. The ideas suggested for bulletin boards are ultra-simple. Anyone can duplicate the idea, even if you're not in the least bit craft-oriented. The idea of the bulletin board display is to bring people up to the board to read the message. Meanwhile, close to or under the bulletin board, you will already have placed a display table that holds the books from the booklists. The closer the children get to the books the more likely they will be to pick them up and read them.

TREATS. At our house it's not a holiday or a celebration unless there is food involved, which accounts for the inclusion of recipes in this book.

I tried to find something edible that fit into the theme of the chapter, was relatively easy to make, and was appealing to children without being highly caloric. All the recipes have been tested on my own family, and if you meet my husband or my dog you will see that I didn't always succeed in finding something that was not fattening.

ACTIVITIES, JOKES, CRAFTS. The activities are for those people who enjoy integrating activities into the reading program. Since the primary objective of this collection is to introduce children to literature these activities are extras, but I personally enjoy playing with the books as well as reading them.

CREATIVE WRITING. The ideas presented under "Creative Writing" are to be used as imaginative exercises, not as graded assignments. If you have fifteen minutes to allow children to stretch their imaginations, let them try their writing skills with some of the theme-oriented ideas. Children can also share their creations orally on a volunteer-only basis.

BOOKLISTS. Since the major thrust of these programs is to get your audience involved with books, the booklists at the end of each chapter are an integral part of each program and are meant to be used. When planning a program, take the list directly to the card catalog in your library and pull out as many of the books as you can find from the shelves to make a book exhibit. Be sure to add to the exhibit any titles on the same theme that you have enjoyed but are not on the list.

If you are not close to a library you may want to duplicate the booklists to distribute to your audience so that they may have a list in hand to take to the library or bookstore.

Notice that the lists contain books for various age groups: picture books and young adult selections are listed along with middle grade reading. I find that many adults who work with older children tend to discard the picture books as too young for their group. As it happens, however, there are some books that have the format of a book for pre-school or primary children but are actually intended for a much older audience, even adults. So, even if a book on your program's theme looks as if it had been produced for a younger audience, so long as it is well written and beautifully illustrated, it might very well be worth considering for your group. The same is true of books that appear to be too difficult for your group: the characters, plot or theme may make a book just right for one of your readers. So exhibit all the books you can find, and let the children decide which ones they would like to read.

General age groupings are given for each group. These are to be used as guides only:

> P = pre-school through primary
> M = fourth through sixth grades
> U = upper grades; seventh grade and above.

ENJOY! Any day is a holiday if you have a good book to read.

> Caroline Feller Bauer
> Huntington Beach, California

The Art of Art

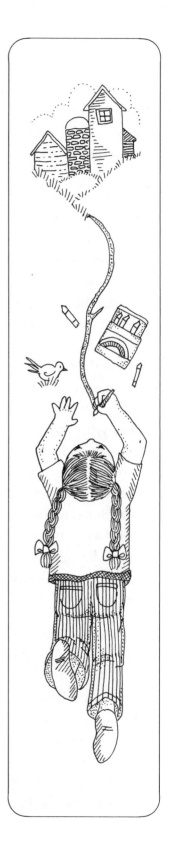

"First we see the hills in the painting, then we see the painting in the hills." —LI LI-WĒNG, 17th century Chinese poet

Take a day or a week or a month to celebrate art. Begin with a story and poems and extend your activities into an exploration of color, book illustrations, the fine arts, photography, and art application. This program is meant as an introduction to—and an appreciation of—art. The activities emphasize seeing what you are looking at, but they include some ideas for exploring the properties of color and design.

The Addison-Wesley series of self-portraits by book illustrators is an excellent introduction to the art of book illustration. If you use this series, collect as many of the artists' books as you can find so that your group can have an opportunity to examine their work. The most efficient way of finding books by a particular illustrator is to look for the listing in the illustrators section in the annual *Children's Books In Print* (R. R. Bowker). This large reference volume, available in many children's libraries and bookstores, is used as a selection and reference tool.

1

A simple way to begin this program is to have all the children close their eyes and imagine a world with no color, or a world of only one color. A piece of colored cellophane handed out as a souvenir will give everyone an opportunity to see a new world of one color.

Many of the books in the bibliography are picture books in which an artist experiments with color. Make sure that you give your group time to browse through these books. Add any books that you feel you would like to introduce in order to give the reader an appreciation for fine art.

Some books explore the role of the artist in society on a picture-book level, and these too should be shared with your group. Please exhibit as many of these books as you can, regardless of the recommended age level. Most of the picture books will be appropriate for an older age-group as well as for a younger one.

The program offers two stories. Use both, or use the Housman story with more sophisticated students and the Hough story with younger children.

The Art of Art is appropriate to use at any time during the year. The third week in March is set aside as Art Week and is sponsored by Richard R. Falk Associates, 147 West 42nd Street, New York, New York 10036. Its purpose is to "focus attention on art and the artists and their achievements in society." If you are looking for a specific occasion to celebrate Art Week, use an illustrator's or artist's birthday. Here's a list of some:

Mitsumasa Anno	March 20, 1926
Martha Alexander	May 25, 1920
Frank Asch	August 6, 1946
Marcia Brown	July 13, 1918
Nancy Ekholm Burkert	February 16, 1933
Eric Carle	June 25, 1929
Kay Chorao	January 7, 1937
Barbara Cooney	August 6, 1917
Tomi de Paola	September 15, 1934

Diane Dillon	March 13, 1933
Leo Dillon	March 2, 1933
William Pène DuBois	May 9, 1916
Wanda Gág	March 11, 1893
Paul Goble	September 27, 1933
M. B. Goffstein	December 20, 1940
Nonny Hogrogian	May 7, 1932
Pat Hutchins	June 18, 1942
Ezra Jack Keats	March 11, 1916
Steven Kellogg	October 6, 1941
Hilary Knight	November 1, 1926
Leo Lionni	May 5, 1910
Arnold Lobel	May 22, 1933
James Marshall	October 10, 1942
Mercer Mayer	December 30, 1943
Nancy Winslow Parker	October 18, 1930
Alice Provensen	August 14, 1918
Martin Provensen	July 10, 1916
Arthur Rackham	September 19, 1867
Maurice Sendak	June 10, 1928
Dr. Seuss	March 2, 1904
Ernest H. Shepard	December 10, 1879
Uri Shulevitz	February 27, 1935
Peter Spier	June 6, 1927
William Steig	November 14, 1907
John Tenniel	February 28, 1820
Tomi Ungerer	November 28, 1931
Margot Zemach	November 30, 1931

Prose Selections

A Chinese Fairy Tale

by LAURENCE HOUSMAN

Tiki-Pu was a small grub of a thing; but he had a true love of Art deep down in his soul. There it hung mewing and complaining, struggling to work its way out through the raw exterior that bound it.

Tiki-Pu's master professed to be an artist: he had apprentices and students, who came daily to work under him, and a large studio littered about with the performances of himself and his pupils. On the walls hung also a few real works by the older men, all long since dead.

This studio Tiki-Pu swept; for those who worked in it he ground colors, washed brushes, and ran errands, bringing them their dog chops and bird's-nest soup from the nearest eating house whenever they were too busy to go out for it themselves. He himself had to feed mainly on the bread crumbs that the students screwed into pellets for their drawings and then threw about on the floor. It was on the floor, also, that he had to sleep at night.

Tiki-Pu looked after the blinds and mended the windowpanes, which were often broken when the apprentices threw their brushes and mahlsticks at him. Also he strained rice paper over the linen-stretchers, ready for the painters to work on; and for a treat, now and then, a lazy one would allow him to mix a color for him. Then it was that Tiki-Pu's soul came down into his fingertips, and his heart beat so that he gasped for joy. Oh, the yellows and the greens, and the lakes and the cobalts, and the purples that sprang from the blending of them! Sometimes it was all he could do to keep himself from crying out.

Tiki-Pu, while he squatted and ground at the color powders, would listen to his master lecturing to the students. He knew by heart the names of all the painters and their schools, and the name of the great leader of them all who had lived and passed from their midst more than three hundred years ago; he knew that too, a name like the sound of the wind, Wio-Wani. The big picture at the end of the studio was by him.

That picture! To Tiki-Pu it seemed worth all the rest of the world put together. He knew, too, the story that was told of it, making it as holy to his eyes as the tombs of his own ancestors. The apprentices joked over it, calling it, "Wio-Wani's back door," "Wio-Wani's night cap," and many other nicknames; but Tiki-Pu was quite sure, since the picture was so beautiful, that the story must be true.

Wio-Wani, at the end of a long life, had painted it; a garden full of trees and sunlight, with high-standing flowers and green paths, and in their midst a palace. "The place where I would like to rest," said Wio-Wani, when it was finished.

So beautiful was it then, that the emperor himself had come to see it and, gazing enviously at those peaceful walks and the palace nestling among the trees, had sighed and owned that he too would be glad of such a resting-place. Then Wio-Wani stepped into the picture and walked away along a path till he came, looking quite small and far-off, to a low door in the palace wall. Opening it, he turned and beckoned to the emperor; but the emperor did not follow; so Wio-Wani went in by himself and shut the door between himself and the world for ever.

That happened three hundred years ago; but for Tiki-Pu the story was as fresh and true as if it had happened yesterday. When he was left to himself in the studio, all alone and locked up for the night, Tiki-Pu used to go and stare at the picture till it was too dark to see, and at the little palace with the door in its wall by which Wio-Wani had disappeared out of life. Then his soul would go down into his fingertips, and he would knock softly and fearfully at the beautifully painted door, saying, "Wio-Wani, are you there?"

Little by little, in the long-thinking nights and the slow early mornings when light began to creep back through the papered windows of the studio, Tiki-Pu's soul became too much for him. He who could strain paper and grind colors and wash brushes had everything within reach for becoming an artist, if it was the will of Fate that he should be one.

He began timidly at first, but in a little while he grew bold. With the first wash of light he was up from his couch on the hard floor and was daubing his soul out on scraps and odds-and-ends and stolen pieces of rice paper.

Before long the short spell of daylight that lay between dawn and the arrival of the apprentices at their work did not suffice him. It took him so long to hide all traces of his doings, to wash out the brushes and rinse clean the paintpots he had used, and on the top of that to get the studio swept and dusted, that there was hardly time left him in which to indulge the itching of his fingers.

Driven by necessity, he became a pilferer of candle ends, picking them from their sockets in the lanterns that the students carried on dark nights. Now and then one of these would remember that, when last used, his lantern had had a candle in it and would accuse Tiki-Pu of having stolen it. "It is true," he would confess, "I was hungry—I have eaten it." The lie was so probable, he was believed easily and was well beaten accordingly. Down in the ragged linings of his coat Tiki-Pu could hear the candle ends rattling as the buffeting and chastisement fell upon him, and often he trembled lest his hoard should be discovered. But the truth of the matter never leaked out; and at night, as soon as he guessed that all the world outside was in bed, Tiki-Pu would mount one of his candles on a wooden stand and paint by the light of it, blinding himself over the task, till the dawn came and gave a better and cheaper light to work by.

Tiki-Pu quite hugged himself over the results; he believed he was doing very well. If only Wio-Wani were here to teach me, thought he, I would be on the way to becoming a great painter!

The resolution came to him one night that Wio-Wani *should* teach him. So he took a large piece of rice paper and strained it, and

6

sitting down opposite "Wio-Wani's back door," began painting. He had never set himself so big a task as this; by the dim stumbling light of his candle he strained his eyes nearly blind over the difficulties of it and at last was almost driven to despair. How the trees stood row behind row, with air and sunlight between, and how the path went in and out, winding its way up to the little door in the palace wall were mysteries he could not fathom. He peered and peered and dropped tears into his paintpots; but the secret of the mystery of such painting was far beyond him.

The door in the palace wall opened; out came a little old man and began walking down the pathway towards him.

The soul of Tiki-Pu gave a sharp leap in his grubby little body. "That must be Wio-Wani himself and no other!" cried his soul.

Tiki-Pu pulled off his cap and threw himself down on the floor with reverent grovelings. When he dared to look up again Wio-Wani stood over him big and fine; just within the edge of the canvas he stood and reached out a hand.

"Come along with me, Tiki-Pu!" said the great one. "If you want to know how to paint, I will teach you."

"Oh, Wio-Wani, were you there all the while?" cried Tiki-Pu ecstatically, leaping up and clutching with his smeary little puds the hand that the old man extended to him.

"I was there," said Wio-Wani, "looking at you out of my little window. Come along in!"

Tiki-Pu took a heave and swung himself into the picture and fairly capered when he found his feet among the flowers of Wio-Wani's beautiful garden. Wio-Wani had turned and was ambling gently back to the door of his palace, beckoning to the small one to follow him; and there stood Tiki-Pu, opening his mouth like a fish to all the wonders that surrounded him. "Celestiality, may I speak?" he said suddenly.

"Speak," replied Wio-Wani; "what is it?"

"The emperor, was he not the very flower of fools not to follow when you told him?"

7

"I cannot say," answered Wio-Wani, "but he certainly was no artist."

Then he opened the door, that door he had so beautifully painted, and led Tiki-Pu in. Outside the little candle end sat and guttered by itself, till the wick fell overboard, and the flame kicked itself out, leaving the studio in darkness and solitude to wait for the growings of another dawn.

It was full day before Tiki-Pu reappeared; he came running down the green path in great haste, jumped out of the frame onto the studio floor, and began tidying up his own messes of the night and the apprentices' of the previous day. Only just in time did he have things ready by the hour when his master and the others returned to their work.

All that day they kept scratching their left ears and could not think why; but Tiki-Pu knew, for he was saying over to himself all the things that Wio-Wani, the great painter, had been saying about them and their precious productions. And as he ground their colors for them and washed their brushes and filled his famished little body with the bread crumbs they threw away, little they guessed from what an immeasurable distance he looked down upon them all and had Wio-Wani's word for it tickling his right ear all the day long.

Now before long Tiki-Pu's master noticed a change in him; and though he bullied him and thrashed him and did all that a careful master should do, he could not get the change out of him. So in a short while he grew suspicious. "What is the boy up to?" he wondered. "I have my eye on him all day. It must be at night that he gets into mischief."

It did not take Tiki-Pu's master a night's watching to find that something surreptitious was certainly going on. When it was dark he took up his post outside the studio, to see whether by any chance Tiki-Pu had some way of getting out; and before long he saw a faint light showing through the window. So he came and thrust his finger softly through one of the panes and put his eye to the hole.

There inside was a candle burning on a stand, and Tiki-Pu squatting with paintpots and brush in front of Wio-Wani's last masterpiece.

"What fine piece of burglary is this?" thought he. "What serpent have I been harboring in my bosom? Is this beast of a grub of a boy thinking to make himself a painter and cut me out of my reputation and prosperity?" For even at that distance he could plainly perceive that the work of this boy went head and shoulders beyond his, or that of any painter living.

Presently Wio-Wani opened his door and came down the path, as was his habit now each night, to call Tiki-Pu to his lesson. He advanced to the front of the picture and beckoned for Tiki-Pu to come in with him; and Tiki-Pu's master grew clammy at the knees as he beheld Tiki-Pu catch hold of Wio-Wani's hand and jump into the picture, and skip up the green path by Wio-Wani's side, and in through the little door that Wio-Wani had painted so beautifully in the end wall of his palace!

For a time Tiki-Pu's master stood glued to the spot with grief and horror. "Oh, you deadly little underling! Oh, you poisonous little caretaker, you parasite, you vampire, you fly in amber!" cried he. "Is that where you get your training? Is it there that you dare to go trespassing; into a picture that I purchased for my own pleasure and profit, and not at all for yours? Very soon we will see whom it really belongs to!"

He ripped out the paper of the largest windowpane and pushed his way through into the studio. Then in great haste he took up paintpot and brush and sacrilegiously set himself to work upon Wio-Wani's last masterpiece. In the place of the doorway by which Tiki-Pu had entered he painted a solid brick wall; twice over he painted it, and mortared every brick to its place. And when he had quite finished, he laughed, and called, "Good night, Tiki-Pu!" and went home to be quite happy.

The next day all the apprentices were wondering what had become of Tiki-Pu; but as the master himself said nothing, and as another boy came to act as color-grinder and brush-washer to the establishment, they very soon forgot all about him.

In the studio the master used to sit at work with his students all about him and a mind full of ease and contentment. Now and then he would throw a glance across to the bricked-up doorway of

9

Wio-Wani's palace and laugh to himself, thinking how well he had served out Tiki-Pu for his treachery and presumption.

One day—it was five years after the disappearance of Tiki-Pu—he was giving his apprentices a lecture on the glories and the beauties and the wonders of Wio-Wani's painting—how nothing for color could excel, or for mystery could equal it. To add point to his eloquence, he stood waving his hands before Wio-Wani's last master-piece, and all his students and apprentices sat round him and looked.

Suddenly he stopped at mid-word, and broke off in the full flight of his eloquence, as he saw something like a hand come and take down the top brick from the face of paint that he had laid over the little door that Wio-Wani had so beautifully painted in the palace wall. In another moment there was no doubt about it; brick by brick the wall was being pulled down, in spite of its double thickness.

The lecturer was altogether too dumbfounded and terrified to utter a word. He and all his apprentices stood round and stared while the demolition of the wall proceeded. Before long he recognized Wio-Wani with his flowing white beard; it was his handiwork, this pulling down of the wall! He still had a brick in his hand when he stepped through the opening that he had made, and close after him stepped Tiki-Pu!

Tiki-Pu had grown tall and strong—he was even handsome; but for all that his old master recognized him, and saw with an envious foreboding that under his arms he carried many rolls and stretchers and portfolios and other belongings of his craft. Clearly Tiki-Pu was coming back into the world and was going to be a great painter.

Down the garden path came Wio-Wani, and Tiki-Pu walked after him; Tiki-Pu was so tall that his head stood well over Wio-Wani's shoulders—old man and young man together made a handsome pair.

How big Wio-Wani grew as he walked down the avenues of his garden and into the foreground of his picture! And how big the brick in his hand! And ah, how angry he seemed!

Wio-Wani came right down to the edge of the picture frame and held up the brick. "What did you do that for?" he asked.

"I...didn't!" Tiki-Pu's old master was beginning to reply; and the lie was still rolling on his tongue when the weight of the brickbat, hurled by the stout arm of Wio-Wani, felled him. After that he never spoke again. That brickbat, which he himself had reared, became his own tombstone.

Just inside the picture frame stood Tiki-Pu, kissing the wonderful hands of Wio-Wani, which had taught him all their skill. "Good-bye, Tiki-Pu!" said Wio-Wani, embracing him tenderly. "Now I am sending my second self into the world. When you are tired and want rest, come back to me: old Wio-Wani will take you in."

Tiki-Pu was sobbing and the tears were running down his cheeks as he stepped out of Wio-Wani's wonderfully painted garden and stood once more upon earth. Turning, he saw the old man walking away along the path towards the little door under the palace wall. At the door Wio-Wani turned and waved his hand for the last time. Tiki-Pu still stood watching him. Then the door opened and shut, and Wio-Wani was gone. Softly as a flower the picture seemed to have folded its leaves over him.

Tiki-Pu leaned a wet face against the picture and kissed the door in the palace wall that Wio-Wani had painted so beautifully. "O Wio-Wani, dear master," he cried, "are you there?"

He waited and called again, but no voice answered him.

The Magic Pencil
by CHARLOTTE HOUGH

One day when Annabel was throwing sticks for her dog in the woods near her home she found a magic pencil in the bracken. She knew it was magic because when she happened to draw a cat with it in her drawing book that evening, the drawing faded away from the page and a dear little real tabby cat appeared instead and settled itself down on the mat in front of the fire. So then Annabel drew a saucer of cream and that appeared, too, and the little cat lapped it up with a proper little real pink tongue.

After that Annabel's mother called her down to supper and she hadn't really got a chance to be by herself again until the next day after breakfast. It was nearly Christmastime, so Annabel went up to her bedroom and drew a fur coat for her mother and hung it up at the back of her wardrobe so that it would be a secret. Then she drew a motorcar for her father and she looked out of the window and saw it come purring up to the front door all by itself. It was rather an old-fashioned one because that was the only sort that Annabel knew how to draw, but it was beautifully black and shiny, with red leather seats and a big rubber horn. Then Annabel drew the car again, but all hidden by trees this time, and she looked out of the window and watched while it started itself up and drove itself into the woods so that it should be a secret.

Then Annabel got very excited, and she was just about to draw a lot more things when she heard her mother calling her from down-stairs asking her to take the dog out for a walk because it was a nice day and her mother thought it might cloud over later on.

So Annabel, who was a good obedient child, put her drawing book

12

away in a drawer and took the dog out for a walk in the woods, and when she reached the place where she had found the pencil, there was a goblin with a very worried expression on his face, walking round and round in circles looking for something.

As soon as Annabel saw him she guessed that he was looking for the magic pencil, but when the goblin asked her if she had seen it Annabel said "No," and added under her breath "not before yesterday," so that it would not be quite so untrue, but not so that the goblin could hear her.

The goblin looked so disappointed that Annabel felt sorry for him, but all the same she couldn't bear to give it back to him before she had drawn some presents for herself. So she said she was in rather a hurry and she called her dog and ran back home as quickly as she could and she went up to her bedroom and drew herself a big box of chocolates and ate them nearly all. Then she drew a picture of herself with very thick eyelashes and long hair that came right down below her waist, and a beautiful party frock that was a proper, long, grown-up one with a sash that tied in a bow, and when she looked at herself in the mirror she looked so pretty that she could hardly believe it.

Then Annabel thought she would have a party to go with the party frock and she thought what fun it would be to draw all the things she liked best at parties: crackers and prizes and cakes and trifles and balloons and ices and little baby sausages and sandwiches and flags sticking out of them to say what they were. But the more Annabel thought about these things, the more she thought that she would do it in a little while but not yet, because she had eaten so many chocolates just lately, so she decided to go and call on her friend Jane and show her the dress and the eyelashes and the hair and perhaps let her do one little drawing for herself with the pencil.

Jane lived in a house on the other side of the wood, and when Annabel came to the part where the goblin was, she looked the other way because it made her feel so guilty to see him looking for his pencil.

But the goblin saw her and he called out: "That's a fine new party dress you've got on today."

"Yes," said Annabel, turning round. "My mother made it," and she added under her breath, "my breakfast, I mean," so as to make it be not quite so untrue, but she went rather red.

But as soon as the goblin saw her face he realized that her hair and her eyelashes were quite different from yesterday and that she must have got hold of some magic because she was quite an ordinary little girl and not a fairy, and he shouted out in a terrible voice: "YOU'VE GOT MY PENCIL!" and he started to run after her and Annabel started to run away because she was frightened of the goblin when he was so angry, even though he was smaller than she was. But she couldn't run nearly as fast as usual because her dress was so long it kept catching in the branches, and she couldn't see properly because she had so many eyelashes, and presently she fell flat on her face and the magic pencil rolled out of her pocket and the goblin pounced on it and picked it up. He pointed it at her and shouted at once:

"Magic pencil take away
The things she's drawn for herself today!"

Then the goblin ran off into the bracken clutching his pencil and leaving Annabel sitting there in her vest and knickers, with her ordinary hair and ordinary eyelashes.

When she got home her mother was very cross with her for going out-of-doors in her underclothes. When Annabel tried to explain about the goblin and the magic pencil, her mother wouldn't believe her and said she must have been dreaming, and when Annabel showed her the tabby kitten, she said it must be a little stray cat who had come in through the window.

But Annabel knew she hadn't been dreaming, because why should she have been feeling so sick if she hadn't just eaten nearly a whole box of chocolates?

And *they'll* know, won't they, on the twenty-fifth of December!

Poetry Selections

The Paint Box

by E. V. RIEU

"Cobalt and umber and ultra-
    marine,
Ivory black and emerald green —
What shall I paint to give pleasure
    to you?"
"Paint for me somebody utterly
    new."

"I have painted you tigers in
    crimson and white."
"The colors were good and you
    painted aright."
"I have painted the cook and a
    camel in blue
And a panther in purple." "You
    painted them true.

Now mix me a color that nobody
    knows,
And paint me a country where
    nobody goes,
And put in it people a little like you,
Watching a unicorn drinking the
    dew."

Magical Eraser

by SHEL SILVERSTEIN

She wouldn't believe
This pencil has
A magical eraser.
She said I was a silly moo,
She said I was a liar too,
She dared me prove that it was true,
And so what could I do —
I erased her!

Rhinos Purple,
Hippos Green

by MICHAEL PATRICK HEARN

My sister says
I shouldn't color
Rhinos purple,
Hippos green.
She says
I shouldn't be so stupid;
Those are things
She's never seen.
But I don't care
What my sister says,
I don't care
What my sister's seen
I will color
What I want to —
Rhinos purple,
Hippos green.

Just For A Change
by WILLIAM COLE

I wish that things didn't all have
   to be
The colors you always *expect*
   to see:

Just imagine a sky of green,
A sky that's never, ever seen;
And from it shines on everyone
A great big cheerful purple sun!

Over the grass of bright, bright red
Orange flowers and black are
   spread;
One other thing not seen before—
A silver house, a golden door....

I know it sounds silly, crazy, and
   strange,
But *I'd* like to see it just for a
   change.

Crayons
by MARCHETTE CHUTE

I've colored a picture with crayons.
   I'm not very pleased with the
      sun.
I'd like it much stronger and
   brighter
   And more like the actual one.
I've tried with the crayon that's
   yellow,
   I've tried with the crayon that's
      red.
But none of it looks like the
   sunlight
   I carry around in my head.

Souvenirs

Make yellow paper hats to wear while reading Frank Asch's *Yellow Yellow* (McGraw, 1971).

Give children a piece of blue cellophane and a piece of yellow to use while reading Leo Lionni's *Little Blue and Little Yellow* (Obolensky, 1959).

Any color cellophane, gelatin, or acetate that children can look through to change the color of their world makes an exciting souvenir.

Treats

Finger Painting: Use chocolate pudding as finger paint.

Sculpture: Sculpt with peanut butter play dough.

YOU NEED: peanut butter

a few spoonfuls of honey

powdered milk

HOW TO: Mix with hands (clean!). Add powdered milk until it makes a dough that pleases you. Mold the dough or roll it out and use cookie cutters to create shapes. Use nuts, raisins, or sprinkles.

HINT: Use cocoa powder to make chocolate peanut-butter dough. Don't eat too much—it's fattening!

Coloring: Use food color to give ordinary food an out-of-the-ordinary color. Ask the children if the food tastes different because it looks different.

Try coloring butter red, bread blue, milk green.

Eating: Eat colored fruit—yellow bananas, purple grapes, green pears, and red apples—to remember Charlotte Zolotow's *Mr. Rabbit and the Lovely Present* (Harper, 1962).

Bulletin Board

Write a heading in red crayon: Magical Drawings in Books.

Below list the books in your exhibit.

Provide a piece of red cellophane (if it will get a lot of use, enclose it in a carboard frame) so children can make the sign disappear. Red on red will make the sign vanish.

Put up as many sheets of colored paper as there are colors (at least six).

Let the children list anything they can think of that is associated with that color. Examples:

Red	*Blue*	*Yellow*	*Green*	*Orange*
apples	sky	daffodils	lime Jello	orange slices
roses	unhappiness	sun	lettuce	carrots
nail polish	sapphires	lemons	peas	cheese
watermelon	forget-me-nots	cowardice	green grapes	cheese crackers
excitement			pickles	orange juice

Creative Drawing/Activities

Have the children read William Cole's "Just For A Change." Ask them to draw a picture of a world with new colors.

Set aside a few minutes a day to look at and talk about one painting in your favorite art book or from among art prints. This takes only a few minutes, and your students will have a chance to learn about some of the world's great works of art.

Set aside a bulletin board on which you place art prints, art post-cards, or reproductions of art cut from magazines. Change your at-home or library art exhibit at least once a month.

Read aloud a chapter from an art book each day.

Decorate a door or playroom wall with a collage of art prints. Shellac them for a finished effect.

Cut a circular piece of cardboard about four inches in diameter. Put a pinhole in the center. Put another hole near the edge so that a cord can be attached to hang the cardboard circle around the neck. Have the children use their pinhole circle viewers to see objects and scenes as they might be seen by an insect or through the lens of a camera. This will help them become more perceptive of the world around them by concentrating their field of view.

Collect art prints or photographs and have the children try to match them as illustrations to books they've read. A picture of a bear and her cub, for instance, might suggest Robert McCloskey's *Blueberries for Sal* (Viking, 1948); or two hippopotami might suggest James Marshall's *George and Martha* (Houghton, 1972).

Make a miniature art gallery. Cut away one side of a large cardboard box. Cover the walls of the art gallery with solid-colored contact paper. Frame several postcard reproductions of art with cardboard or paper and hang them on the walls of the gallery. If possible, populate the gallery with paper dolls or doll visitors. Small sculpture (precious knickknacks) can be exhibited in tiny boxes.

Field Trips

To the local art museum. If you live in an area where there is no art museum, plan a bus trip to the nearest community that has one. If you are taking a group, call in advance so a tour can be planned especially for them.

To homes in the area that contain original art or reproductions of merit. Does your town have artists or an art group? If so, why not contact them. They may be able to help you view some interesting art in the area.

In your own home. Examine each decoration in your home with your children. Why did you choose it? Does it have a particular significance for you? Where did it come from? If you could own any painting or piece of sculpture in the world, which would you choose? Show them a picture of it in a book.

1. Books about Art and Artists:

Anno, Mitsumasa, and Masaichiro Anno. *Anno's Magical ABC: An Anamorphic Alphabet.* Il. by Mitsumasa Anno. Philomel, 1981. All ages.

The letters of the alphabet appear distorted until viewed with a silver tube, supplied with the book.

Arnosky, Jim. *Drawing from Nature.* Il. by author. Lothrop, 1982. M, U.

Short text gives nature facts that make drawing from life easier and more perceptive.

Asch, Frank. *Yellow Yellow.* Il. by Mark Alan Stamaty. McGraw, 1971. P.

A little boy walks through detailed black-and-white drawings wearing a yellow hat.

Baker, Alan. *Benjamin's Book.* Il. by author. Lothrop, 1983. All ages.

A hamster tries to rectify a smudge on a nice clean page.

Baker, Betty. *Dupper.* Il. by Chuck Eckart. Greenwillow, 1976. M.

Dupper is a prairie dog who is an artist and dares to be different.

Baylor, Byrd. *Guess Who My Favorite Person Is.* Il. by Robert Andrew Parker. Scribner, 1977. P, M.

Two friends tell about their favorite things including color; creative and imaginative.

Bester, Roger. *Guess What?* Photographs by author. Crown, 1980. All ages.

Photographic animal portraits are presented as riddles. The reader sees parts of an animal, then its habitat, and finally the animal.

Blegvad, Erik. *Self-Portrait: Erik Blegvad.* Il. by author. Addison-Wesley, 1979. M, U.

A short autobiography of the illustrator.

Branley, Franklyn Mansfield. *Color: From Rainbows to Lasers.* Il. by Henry Roth. Crowell, 1978. M.

Explores theories about light, the color spectrum, color printing, etc.

Brown, Osa. *The Metropolitan Museum of Art Activity Book.* Random, 1983.

Crafts, toys and puzzles based on art in the museum's collection.

Bulla, Clyde Robert. *Daniel's Duck.* Il. by Joan Sandin. Harper, 1979. P.

In this I-Can-Read book, a boy discovers that art is personal expression.

Cohen, Miriam. *No Good in Art.* Il. by Lillian Hoban. Greenwillow, 1980. P.

A young boy finds out that his drawing is not so bad after all.

Crews, Donald. *Freight Train.* Il. by author. Greenwillow, 1978. P.

The cars of a train are each painted in a brilliant, clear color.

Cumming, Robert. *Just Look...a Book about Paintings.* Scribner, 1979. M, U.

Color, light, perspective, and mood are discussed in a relaxed way.

Davidson, Marshall B. *A History of Art.* Il. with paintings. Random, 1984. M, U.

Survey of art history.

Drescher, Henrik. *Simon's Book.* Il. by author. Lothrop, 1983. P.

Simon's drawing pad is alive with a "madcap chase."

DuBois, William Pène. *Lion.* Il. by author. Viking, 1981. P.

Artist Foreman creates LION in the Animal Factory. A classic picture book.

Emberley, Edward R. *Ed Emberley's Big Green Drawing Book.* Little, 1979. M.

Step-by-step drawings show how to draw snakes, alligators, and cars.

Fair, Sylvia. *The Bedspread.* Il. by author. Morrow, 1982. All ages.

Two elderly sisters appliqué differing views of their childhood on a bedspread.

40 Fun Chalk-Talk Gags. (Ed Harris, 5901 Drew Avenue South, Minneapolis, Minnesota 55410). M.

Start with an outline drawing. Add a few lines and you have a new picture.

Freeman, Don. *The Chalk Box Story.* Il. by author. Lippincott, 1976. P.

Pieces of colored chalk draw a story.

Glubok, Shirley. *The Art of Egypt Under the Pharaohs.* Macmillan, 1980. M, U.

Glubok has written over thirty art books for children. This is just one of her introductory books.

Goffstein, M. B. *Lives of the Artists.* Illustrated. Farrar, 1981. M.

> Short, cryptic biographies of Rembrandt, Guardi, Van Gogh, Bonnard, and Nevelson.

Grillone, Lisa, and Joseph Gennaro. *Small Worlds Close Up.* Crown, 1978. All ages.

> Familiar objects are seen through a scanning electron microscope. A new perspective.

Haskins, Ilma. *Color Seems.* Il. by author. Vanguard, 1973. P.

> A picture book that demonstrates how colors seem "cool," "warm," "moving," or "hidden."

Hirsh, Marilyn. *How the World Got Its Color.* Il. by author. Crown, 1972. P.

> A little girl uses a paint set to give the world color.

Hoban, Tana. *A, B, See!* Photographs by author. Greenwillow, 1982. P.

> Photographs show objects beginning with each letter in the alphabet.

————. *Is It Red? Is It Yellow? Is It Blue?* Photographs by author. Greenwillow, 1978. P.

> Full-color photographs emphasize objects and scenes in color.

————. *Take Another Look.* Photographs by author. Greenwillow, 1981. All ages.

> Cut-out overlays show a small portion of a photograph. Underneath is revealed the entire object. See also *Look. Again!* (Macmillan, 1971.)

Hochman, Shirley. *Identifying Art.* Sterling, 1974. M.

> An activity approach to the study of art. Short paragraphs describe a painting and an artist. Gives easy-to-do art-related activities. See also *Invitation to Art* (Sterling, 1974).

Holme, Bryan. *Enchanted World: The Magic of Pictures.* Oxford, 1979. M, U.

> A survey of the fine arts. Each picture is accompanied by a short explanatory paragraph. Emphasis is on the art object rather than the artist. See also *Creatures of Paradise: Pictures to Grow Up With* (Oxford, 1980).

Hutchins, Pat. *The Mona Lisa Mystery.* Il. by Laurence Hutchins. Greenwillow, 1981. M.

> A class trip to Paris is a slapstick comedy involving the stealing and forging of the Mona Lisa.

Hyman, Trina Schart. *Self-Portrait: Trina Schart Hyman.* Il. by author. Addison-Wesley, 1981. M, U.

> A short autobiography of the illustrator.

Jeschke, Susan. *Angela and Bear.* Il. by author. Holt, 1979. P.

> A little girl draws a bear that comes to life.

Johnson, Crockett. *Harold and the Purple Crayon.* Il. by author. Harper, 1955. P.

> A little boy draws himself in and out of adventures with a purple crayon. See also *Harold's Circus* (Harper, 1959) and *Harold's Trip to the Sky* (Harper, 1957).

Jonas, Ann. *Round Trip.* Il. by author. Greenwillow, 1983. P.

> Turn this book upside down. The pictures work both ways for a black-and-white story of a trip.

Kennet, Frances, and Terry Measham. *Looking at Paintings.* Il. by Malcolm Livingstone. Van Nostrand, 1978. M, U.

> Explores how painters see and paint subjects differently. Pictures of fashion, horses, and nature are covered. Short narratives are designed to expand fine-art senses. Easy-to-do projects included.

Kent, Jack. *The Scribble Monster.* Il. by author. Harcourt, 1981. P.

> A little boy draws a monster on a wall and it chases him and his friend all over town.

Kesselman, Wendy. *Emma.* Il. by Barbara Cooney. Doubleday, 1980. All ages.

> The perfect picture book to introduce the value of art. In this simple text, a seventy-two-year-old grandmother begins to paint pictures and finds that art makes a wonderful companion and friend.

Kherdian, David. *The Animal.* Il. by Nonny Hogrogian. Knopf, 1984. All ages.
The animal sees the world with love.

Konigsburg, E. L. *The Dragon in the Ghetto Caper.* Il. by author. Atheneum, 1974. M.
Andrew only draws dragons, but he wants to be a detective.

_____. *The Second Mrs. Giaconda.* Atheneum, 1975. U.
A fictional account of Leonardo da Vinci's painting of the Mona Lisa.

Lionni, Leo. *A Color of his Own.* Il. by author. Pantheon, 1976. P.
A chameleon finds a friend. Wherever they go they change color together.

_____. *Little Blue and Little Yellow.* Il. by author. Obolensky, 1959. All ages.
Two blobs of color hug and become green in the perfect color adventure.

Lobel, Arnold. *The Frog and Toad Coloring Book.* Il. by author. Harper, 1981. All ages.
Outline drawings to color.

_____. *The Great Blueness and Other Predicaments.* Il. by author. Harper, 1968. P.
How the world, once only gray, black, and white, becomes a world of color.

Macaulay, David. *Cathedral: The Story of Its Construction.* Il. by author. Houghton, 1973. M, U.
Detailed pen-and-ink drawings describe the construction of a Gothic cathedral.

Merrill, Jean. *Maria's House.* Il. by Frances Gruse Scott. Atheneum, 1974. M.
Maria doesn't want to draw a picture of her own poor house for art class, but when she does, she is surprised that Miss Lindstrom likes it.

Nikly, Michelle. *The Emperor's Plum Tree.* Trans. by Elizabeth Shub. Il. by author. Greenwillow, 1982. All ages.
No garden can last forever, but a painting is a lasting reminder of a garden's perfection.

Oakley, Graham. *Graham Oakley's Magical Changes.* Il. by author. Atheneum, 1980. All ages.
Split pages create hundreds of surrealistic paintings.

O'Neill, Mary. *Hailstones and Halibut Bones.* Il. by Leonard Weisgard. Doubleday, 1961. M.
Each of the poems in this collection celebrates a different color.

Paterson, Katherine. *Bridge to Terabithia.* Il. by Donna Diamond. Crowell, 1977. M.
Jess is interested in art and is befriended by his teacher.

Pinkwater, Daniel. *Bear's Picture.* Il. by author. Dutton, 1984. All ages.
Two proper gentlemen disapprove of Bear's painting, but he loves it.

Provensen, Alice and Martin. *Leonardi Da Vinci.* Il. by authors. Viking, 1984. P.
A pop-up of the life of the great artist.

Raskin, Ellen. *The Tattooed Potato and Other Clues.* Il. by author. Dutton, 1975. M.
A detective spoof that involves an artist, Garson, who is able to solve crimes.

Rauch, Hans-Georg. *The Lines Are Coming: A Book about Drawing.* Scribner, 1978. M, U.
How lines form pictures. Picture-book presentation.

Robbins, Ruth. *How the First Rainbow Was Made.* Il. by author. Parnassus, 1980. P.
An Indian legend tells about the first rainbow and explains why spiders are entitled to their own private rainbows.

Sadler, Catherine Edwards, reteller. "The Magic Brush" in *Treasure Mountain: Folktales from Southern China.* Il. by Cheng Mung Yn. Atheneum, 1982.
Ma Liang's painted objects come alive.

Say, Allen. *The Ink-Keeper's Apprentice.* Harper, 1979. M, U.
Kiyoi is a thirteen-year-old apprentice to Noro Shinpei, a famous Japanese cartoonist.

Schaaf, Peter. *The Violin Close Up.* Photographs by author. Four Winds, 1980. All ages.
Clear photographs explore each part of the violin...close up.

Scheffer, Victor B. *The Seeing Eye.* Il. with photographs. Scribner, 1971. M, U.
Form, color, and texture in nature are described through color photography.

Schwartz, Amy. *Begin at the Beginning.* Il. by author. Harper, 1983.
Sara tries to paint a picture of the entire world and learns to "begin at the beginning."

Simon, Hilda. *The Magic of Color.* Il. by author. Lothrop, 1981. M.
The basic concepts of color are examined. An excellent introduction to the world of color.

Spier, Peter. *Oh, Were They Ever Happy!* Il. by author. Doubleday, 1978. P.
Three children paint a barn in their mother's absence. The results are a colorful mess.

Sutcliff, Rosemary. *Sun Horse, Moon Horse.* Il. by Shirley Felts. Dutton, 1978. M, U.
A fictional account of the people who created the White Horse of Uffington 2,000 years ago.

Tison, Annette, and Talus Taylor. *The Adventures of the Three Colors.* World, 1971. P.
Acetate overlays show how primary colors mix to make other colors.

Travers, P. L. "The Day Out" in *Mary Poppins.* Il. by Mary Shepard. Harcourt, 1962. M.
In this chapter, Mary walks into a chalk drawing for an adventure.

Ward, Winifred. "The Nuremberg Stove" in *Tell It Again: Great Tales from around the World.* Ed. by Margaret Hodges. Il. by Joan Berg. Dial, 1963. M.
A young boy, interested in art, hides in a stove when it is sold to the king.

Zelinsky, Paul. *The Maid and the Mouse and the Odd-Shaped House.* Il. by author. Dodd, 1981. All ages.
A drawing story in full color.

Zemach, Margot. *Self-Portrait: Margot Zemach.* Il. by author. Addison-Wesley, 1978. M, U.
A short autobiography of the artist.

Zolotow, Charlotte. *Mr. Rabbit and the Lovely Present.* Il. by Maurice Sendak. Harper, 1962. P.
In searching for the perfect birthday present for her mother, a little girl finds colorful fruit to fill a basket.

2. Books whose only relationship to art is that there is color in the title:

Alexander, Lloyd. *The Black Cauldron.* Holt, 1965. M, U.
One of the books of the Prydain series.

Benchley, Nathaniel. *Red Fox and His Canoe.* Il. by Arnold Lobel. Harper, 1964. P.
Red Fox invites one too many animals into his canoe. An I-Can-Read Book.

Cameron, Eleanor. *To the Green Mountains.* Dutton, 1975. U.
Kath remembers the green mountains during World War I.

Childress, Alice. *Rainbow Jordan.* Coward, 1981. U.
Rainbow Jordan tries to understand the people that influence her life.

Christopher, John. *The White Mountains.* Macmillan, 1967. M.
The first in a science-fiction series that tells of the horror of the Tripods.

Cooper, Susan. *The Silver Cow.* Il. by Warwick Hutton. McElderry, 1983. M.
Huw finds a silver cow, a present from the Tylwyth Teg.

Gates, Doris. *Blue Willow.* Il. by Paul Lantz. Viking, 1966. M.
Janey Larkin and her family keep moving, but her family always cherishes the blue willow plate.

Kerr, M. E. *Is That You, Miss Blue?* Harper, 1975. U.
Flanders finds life in a boarding school is different and strange.

Lang, Andrew. *Red Fairy Book.* Ed. by Brian Alderson. Il. by Faith Jaques. Kestrel, 1976. M.
A classic collection of fairy tales.

Mazer, Norma Fox, and Harry Mazer. *The Solid Gold Kid.* Delacorte, 1977. U.
Two young people are kidnapped and held for ransom.

McHargue, Georgess. *The Turquoise Toad Mystery.* Delacorte, 1982. M.

Ben spends Christmas vacation on an archaeological dig in Arizona and finds himself involved in a mystery.

O'Dell, Scott. *The Black Pearl.* Il. by Milton Johnson. Houghton, 1967. U.
A black pearl brings trouble to a family in La Paz in Baja California.

———. *Island of the Blue Dolphins.* Houghton, 1960. M.
Karana spends eighteen years of her life alone on an island in the Pacific.

Peck, Robert Newton. *Trig Sees Red.* Il. by Pamela Johnson. Little, 1978. M.
Trig leads a campaign to save Pop the Cop's job.

Roche, P. K. *Plaid Bear and the Rude Rabbit Gang.* Il. by author. Dial, 1982. P.
Plaid Bear leads his friends against the rabbits.

Scher, Paula. *The Brownstone.* Il. by Stan Mack. Pantheon, 1973. P.
The animals in a brownstone apartment house switch apartments until everyone is satisfied.

Snyder, Zilpha Keatley. *Black and Blue Magic.* Il. by Gene Holtan. Atheneum, 1966. M.
Harry gets magic and learns to fly.

Sobol, Donald J. *Encyclopedia Brown Takes the Case.* Il. by Leonard Shortall. Nelson, 1973. M.
A ten-year-old boy solves a number of mysteries in the town of Idaville. See also other titles in the Encyclopedia Brown series.

Thiele, Colin. *Blue Fin.* Il. by Roger Haldane. Harper, 1974. U.
Snook Pascoe would like to work on his father's boat, but he seems to bring bad luck.

Waldron, Ann. *The Bluebury Collection.* Dutton, 1981. M.
Bessie Hightower tries to crack a numbers racket all by herself.

Williams, Vera B. *Three Days on a River in a Red Canoe.* Il. by author. Greenwillow, 1981. All ages.
A picture journal of a camping trip with Mother, Aunt Rosie, and three children.

Zolotow, Charlotte. *The White Marble.* Il. by Deborah Kogan Ray. Crowell, 1982. P, M.
A boy and a girl appreciate the mood of the night in a city park.

B Is for Baseball

"A home run by your team is great and one by the other team is terrible." — LAWRENCE S. RITTER

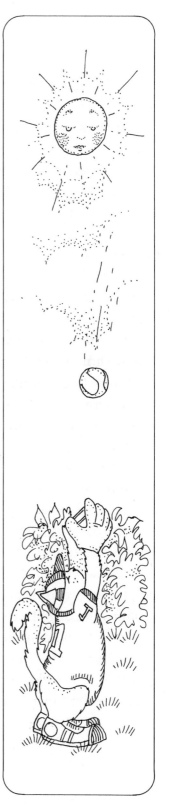

Y ou will have to invent your own holiday celebrating baseball. The season opens in April and ends in October, so you have a choice of a spring, summer, or fall holiday. Those adults who grew up in the forties and fifties might feel that those years were the Golden Age of Baseball, when the Brooklyn Dodgers and the New York Yankees were fierce rivals. When the Brooklyn Dodgers finally won the World Series in 1955, the fans celebrated for days, and when the Dodgers left Brooklyn for the sunny California climate, something went out of the sport for us old-timers.

Apparently the game's popularity continues stronger than ever among boys and girls, men and women. Quoting batting averages and other game statistics is a form of conversation. Baseball is played in backyards and school playing fields; professional teams play in city stadiums. The game was invented and is most often played here in the United States, but enthusiastic teams also play in Latin America and the Far East, especially in Japan.

25

Thousands of boys and girls play as part of nationally organized Little League teams. Divided by age, children from eight to seventeen years old can play on teams as part of this Little League system, or on one of the American Legion baseball teams. Most children in the United States are at least exposed to the game as part of their physical education program. From spring through fall, baseball is given lots of media coverage, and baseball's many fans have maintained the game as America's national sport.

The present game of baseball evolved from the British game of cricket. In 1839, Abner Doubleday, who lived in Cooperstown, New York, laid out a diamond-shaped field with four bases and called the game baseball. In 1845, Alexander J. Cartwright, a surveyor, developed the rules that are used to play the game today. The team he organized was called the Knickerbocker Baseball Club of New York. The Knicks first game was played against the New York Nine. The Knicks lost, 23 to 1. The National Baseball Hall of Fame and Museum is located in Cooperstown, New York.

Today professional baseball is organized into the American and National Leagues. Teams play all summer for first place and a pennant. The two first-place teams then compete against each other for the yearly national championship World Series in the fall.

Baseball spectators are almost as active as the players, constantly comparing the players and arguing about which team is better. Who won when and where, batting averages, and pitching records are discussed.

Leisure reading about baseball can be directed to novels, which are often concerned with personal growth or interaction between teammates, to biographies of baseball players, and to compilations of statistics and anecdotes. The bibliography offered in this book includes books about other sports as well. Use the baseball program as a celebration of team sports in general.

Prose Selection

Here is a favorite story. It's about Sam Greene's best friend, a sixty-year-old black man who works at his mother's inn. Davy shares Sam's intense interest in the Brooklyn Dodgers. When Davy has a heart attack, Sam is determined to get him a baseball signed by Jackie Robinson, one of the greatest stars of American baseball.

Thank You, Jackie Robinson

by BARBARA COHEN

"Hey, Jackie," I called, "Hey, Jackie," in a voice as loud as a thunderbolt. I mean, there were two airplanes flying overhead right that minute and Jackie Robinson heard me anyway.

He glanced over in the direction he could tell my voice was coming from, and I began to wave frantically, still calling "Jackie, hey, Jackie."

He lifted up his hand, gave one wide wave, and smiled. "Hey, kid," he called, and continued on his way to the batting cage. In another instant he'd have been too busy with batting practice to pay any attention to me.

"Sign my ball," I screamed. "Sign my ball."

He seemed to hesitate briefly, I took this as a good omen. "You gotta," I went on frantically. "Please, please, you gotta."

"He don't gotta do nothing," the usher said. "That's Jackie Robinson, and everyone knows that he don't gotta do nothing."

I went right on screaming.

"Come on, kid," the usher said, "we're getting out of here." He was a big, hulking usher, who must have weighed about eight hundred pounds, and he began pulling on me. Even though I gripped the cement with my sneakers and held onto the rail with my hand, he managed to pull me loose. But he couldn't shut me up.

"Please, Jackie, please," I went right on screaming.

It worked. Or something worked. If not my screaming, then maybe the sight of that monster usher trying to pull me up the aisle and scrungy old me pulling against him for dear life.

27

"Let the kid go," Jackie Robinson said when he got to the railing. "All he wants is an autograph."

"He's a fresh kid," the usher said, but he let me go.

"Kids are supposed to be fresh," Jackie Robinson said.

I thrust my ball into Jackie's Robinson's face. "Gee, thanks, Mr. Robinson," I said. "Sign it, please."

"You got a pen?" he asked.

"A pen?" I could have kicked myself. "A pen?" I'd forgotten a pen! I turned to the usher. "You got a pen?"

"If I had," the usher said triumphantly, "I certainly wouldn't lend it to you!"

"Oh, come on," Jackie Robinson said, "don't be so vindictive. What harm did the kid do, after all?"

"Well, as it happens, I don't have one," the usher replied smugly.

"Wait here," I said. "Wait right here, Mr. Robinson. I'll go find one."

Jackie Robinson laughed. "Sorry, kid, but I've got work to do. Another time, maybe."

"Please, Mr. Robinson," I said. "It's for my friend. My friend, Davy."

"Well, let Davy come and get his own autographs," he said. "Why should you do his dirty work for him?"

"He can't come," I said. The words came rushing out of me, tumbling one on top of the other. I had to tell Jackie Robinson all about it, before he went away. "Davy can't come because he's sick. He had a heart attack."

"A heart attack?" Jackie Robinson asked. "A kid had a heart attack?"

"He's not a kid," I explained. "He's sixty years old. He's my best friend. He's a colored man, like you. He's always loved the Dodgers, but lately he's loved them more than ever."

Now that I think about it, what I said could have annoyed Jackie Robinson very much. But at the time, it didn't. I guess he could tell how serious I was about what I was saying. "How did this Davy get to be your best friend?" he asked.

So I told him. I told him everything, or as near to everything as I could tell in five minutes. I told him how Davy worked for my mother, and how I had no father, so it was Davy who took me to my first ball game. I told him how they wouldn't let me into the hospital to see Davy, and how we had always talked about catching a ball that was hit into the stands and getting it autographed.

Jackie listened silently, nodding every once in a while. When I was done at last, he said, "Well, now, kid, I'll tell you what. You keep this ball you brought with you. Keep it to play with. And borrow a pen from someone. Come back to the dugout the minute, the very second, the game is over, and I'll get you a real ball, one we played with, and I'll get all the guys to autograph it for you."

"Make sure it's one you hit," I said.

What nerve. I should have fainted dead away just because Jackie Robinson had deigned to speak to me. But here he was, making me an offer beyond my wildest dreams, and for me it wasn't enough. I had to have more. However, he didn't seem to care.

"O.K.," he said, "*if* I hit one." He had been in a little slump lately.

"You will," I said, "you will."

And he did. He broke the ball game wide open in the sixth inning when he hit a double to left field, scoring Rackley and Duke Snider. He scored himself when the Cubs pitcher, Warren Hacker, tried to pick him off second base. But Hacker overthrew, and Jackie, with that incredible speed he had, ran all the way home. Besides, he worked two double plays with Preacher Roe and Gil Hodges. On consecutive pitches, Carl Furillo and Billy Cox both hit home runs, shattering the 1930 Brooklyn home-run record of 122 for a season. The Dodgers scored six runs, and they scored them all in the sixth inning. They beat the Cubs, 6-1. They were hot, really hot, that day and that year.

But I really didn't watch the game as closely as I had all the others I'd been to see. I couldn't. My mind was on too many other things — on Jackie Robinson, on what was going to happen after the game was over, on that monster usher, who I feared would yet find some way of spoiling things for me, but above all on Davy and the fact that he was missing all of the excitement.

And then I had to worry about getting hold of a pen. You could

29

buy little pencils at the ball park for keeping box scores, but no pens. It was the first—and last—time in my life I walked into a ball park without something to write with. And I didn't see how I could borrow one from someone, since in all that mess of humanity I'd never find the person after the game to return it to him. Unless I took the guy's name and address and mailed it back to him later.

It didn't look to me like the guys in the bleachers where I was sitting had pens with them anyway. Most of them had on tee shirts, and tee shirts don't have pockets in them for pens. I decided to walk over to the seats along the first-base line to see if any of those fans looked more like pen owners. I had to go in that direction any-way to make sure I was at the dugout the second the ball game ended. I took with me my ball in its box.

On my way over I ran into this guy hawking cokes and I decided to buy one in order to wash down the two egg-salad sandwiches I had eaten during the third inning.

This guy had a pen in his pocket. As a matter of fact he had two of them. "Look," I said to him, as I paid him for my soda, "could I borrow one of those pens?"

"Sure," he said, handing it to me after he had put my money into his change machine. He stood there, waiting, like he expected me to hand it back to him after I was done with it.

"Look," I said again, "maybe I could sort of buy it from you."

"Buy it from me? You mean the pen?"

"Yeah."

"What do you want my pen for?"

"I need it because Jackie Robinson promised me that after the game he and all the other guys would autograph a ball for me." Get-ting involved in all these explanations was really a pain in the neck.

"You don't say," the hawker remarked. I could tell he didn't believe me.

"It's true," I said. "Anyway, are you going to sell me your pen?"

"Sure. For a dollar."

I didn't have a dollar. Not anymore. I'd have to try something else. I started to walk away.

"Oh, don't be silly, kid," he called to me. "Here, take the darn pen. Keep it." It was a nice pen. It was shaped like a bat, and on it, it said, "Ebbets Field, Home of the Brooklyn Dodgers."

"Hey, mister, thanks," I said. "That's real nice of you." It seemed to me I ought to do something for him, so I added, "I think I'd like another coke." He sold me another coke, and between sipping first from one and then from the other and trying to watch the game, I made very slow progress down to the dugout. I got there just before the game ended in the top of the ninth. The Dodgers didn't have to come up to bat at all in that final inning, and I was only afraid that they'd all have disappeared into the clubhouse by the time I got there. I should have come down at the end of the eighth. But Jackie Robinson had said the end of the game. Although my nerve had grown by about seven thousand per cent that day, I still didn't have enough to interrupt Jackie Robinson during a game.

I stood at the railing near the dugout, waiting, and sure enough, Jackie Robinson appeared around the corner of the building only a minute or two after Preacher Roe pitched that final out. All around me people were getting up to leave the ball park, but a lot of them stopped when they saw Jackie Robinson come to the rail to talk to me. Roy Campanella, Pee Wee Reese, and Gil Hodges were with him.

"Hi, kid," Jackie Robinson said. He was carrying a ball. It was covered with signatures. "Pee Wee here had a pen."

"And a good thing, too," Pee Wee said, "because most of the other guys left the field already."

"But these guys wanted to meet Davy's friend," Jackie Robinson said.

By that time, Preacher Roe had joined us at the railing. Jackie handed him the ball. "Hey, Preacher," he said, "got enough strength left in that arm to sign this ball for Davy's friend here?"

"Got a pen?" Preacher Roe asked.

I handed him the pen the hawker had given me. I was glad I hadn't gone through all the trouble of getting it for nothing.

"Not much room left on this ball," Roe said. He squirmed his signature into a little empty space beneath Duke Snider's and then he handed me both the pen and the ball. Everybody was waving programs and pens in the faces of the ballplayers who stood by the railing. But before they signed any of them, they all shook my hand. So did Jackie Robinson. I stood there, clutching Davy's ball and watching while those guys signed the programs of the other fans. Finally, though, they'd had enough. They smiled and waved their hands and walked away, five big men in white uniforms, etched sharply against the bright green grass. Jackie Robinson was the last one into the dugout and before he disappeared around the corner, he turned and waved to me.

I waved back. "Thank you, Jackie Robinson," I called. "Thanks for everything." He nodded and smiled. I guess he heard me. I'm glad I remembered my manners before it was too late.

When everyone was gone, I looked down at the ball in my hands. Right between the rows of red seaming Jackie Robinson had written, above his own signature, "For Davy. Get well soon." Then all the others had put their names around that.

I took the ball I had bought out of the box and put it in my pocket. I put the ball Jackie Robinson had given me in the box. Then I went home.

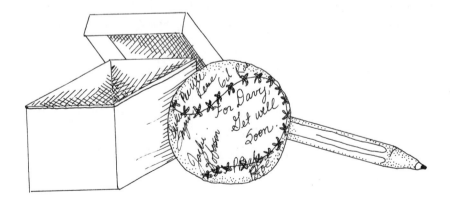

Poetry Selections

Analysis of Baseball

by MAY SWENSON

It's about
the ball,
the bat,
and the mitt.
Ball hits
bat, or it
hits mitt.
Bat doesn't
hit ball, bat
meets it.
Ball bounces
off bat, flies
air, or thuds
ground (dud)
or it
fits mitt.

Bat waits
for ball
to mate.
Ball hates
to take bat's
bait. Ball
flirts, bat's
late, don't
keep the date.
Ball goes in
(thwack) to mitt,
and goes out
(thwack) back
to mitt.

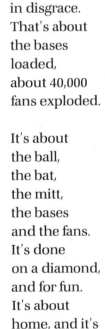

Ball fits
mitt, but
not all
the time.
Sometimes
ball gets hit
(pow) when bat
meets it,
and sails
to a place
where mitt
has to quit
in disgrace.
That's about
the bases
loaded,
about 40,000
fans exploded.

It's about
the ball,
the bat,
the mitt,
the bases
and the fans.
It's done
on a diamond,
and for fun.
It's about
home, and it's
about run.

33

OUTside

by ARNOLD ADOFF

i am standing at home plate   watching that fast ball
leave the pitcher
s

hand

and travel in a straight
line into the   catcher
s

mitt

while the umpire
yells
strike three

out

The Base Stealer

by ROBERT FRANCIS

Poised between going on and back, pulled
Both ways taut like a tightrope-walker,
Fingertips pointing the opposites,
Now bouncing tiptoe like a dropped ball
Or a kid skipping rope, come on, come on,
Running a scattering of steps sidewise,
How he teeters, skitters, tingles, teases,
Taunts them, hovers like an ecstatic bird,
He's only flirting, crowd him, crowd him,
Delicate, delicate, delicate, delicate—now!

34

Casey at the Bat

by ERNEST LAWRENCE THAYER

The outlook wasn't brilliant for the Mudville nine that day;
The score stood four to two with but one inning more to play.
And then, when Cooney died at first, and Barrows did the same,
A sickly silence fell upon the patrons of the game.

A straggling few got up to go in deep despair. The rest
Clung to that hope which springs eternal in the human breast;
They thought, If only Casey could but get a whack at that
We'd put up even money now, with Casey at the bat.

But Flynn preceded Casey, as did also Jimmy Blake,
And the former was a lulu and the latter was a cake;
So upon the stricken multitude grim melancholy sat,
For there seemed but little chance of Casey's getting to the bat.

But Flynn let drive a single, to the wonderment of all,
And Blake, the much despised, tore the cover off the ball;
And when the dust had lifted, and men saw what had occurred,
There was Jimmy safe at second, and Flynn a-hugging third.

Then from five thousand throats and more there rose a lusty yell;
It rumbled through the valley, it rattled in the dell;
It knocked upon the mountain and recoiled upon the flat,
For Casey, mighty Casey, was advancing to the bat.

There was ease in Casey's manner as he stepped into his place;
There was pride in Casey's bearing and a smile on Casey's face.
And when, responding to the cheers, he lightly doffed his hat,
No stranger in the crowd could doubt 'twas Casey at the bat.

Ten thousand eyes were on him as he rubbed his hands with dirt,
Five thousand tongues applauded when he wiped them on his shirt;
Then while the writhing pitcher ground the ball into his hip,
Defiance gleamed from Casey's eye, a sneer curled Casey's lip.

And now the leather-covered sphere came hurtling through the air,
And Casey stood a-watching it in haughty grandeur there.
Close by the sturdy batsman the ball unheeded sped;
"That ain't my style," said Casey. "Strike one," the umpire said.

From the benches, black with people, there went up a muffled roar,
Like the beating of the storm waves on a stern and distant shore.
"Kill him! Kill the umpire!" shouted someone on the stand;
And it's likely they'd have killed him had not Casey raised his hand.

With a smile of Christian charity great Casey's visage shone;
He stilled the rising tumult, he bade the game go on;
He signaled to the pitcher, and once more the spheroid flew;
But Casey still ignored it, and the umpire said, "Strike two."

"Fraud!" cried the maddened thousands, and echo answered "Fraud!"
But one scornful look from Casey and the audience was awed;
They saw his face grow stern and cold, they saw his muscles strain,
And they knew that Casey wouldn't let that ball go by again.

The sneer is gone from Casey's lip, his teeth are clenched in hate,
He pounds with cruel violence his bat upon the plate;
And now the pitcher holds the ball, and now he lets it go,
And now the air is shattered by the force of Casey's blow.

Oh, somewhere in this favored land the sun is shining bright,
The band is playing somewhere, and somewhere hearts are light;
And somewhere men are laughing, and somewhere children shout,
But there is no joy in Mudville—mighty Casey has struck out.

Treat

A no-cook treat to enjoy while watching a baseball game.

Baseball Cookies

YOU NEED: ½ cup wheat germ

1½ cups peanut butter

1½ cups honey

3 cups dried milk

¾ cup graham cracker crumbs

HOW TO: Mix all ingredients together. Form into balls about the roll of large marbles. Roll in confectioner's sugar.

Baseball Riddles

by JOSEPH ROSENBLOOM

What animals do you find at every baseball game? *Bats*

What insect is found on the grass in ball parks? *A ground fly*

Why was the baseball player arrested? *He stole bases*

Why was the baseball player taken along on the camping trip?
They needed someone to pitch the tent

Where do catchers eat their meals? *On home plates*

Why is the ball park the coolest place in warm weather?
There are fans in the stands

37

Bulletin Board

Do you speak baseball?

Duplicate this list of baseball terms and place it on the bulletin board. If your children are baseball addicts, you can mix up the definitions and the words and have the children match the word with the definition. (Or they could use the reference tools in the library to look up the correct answers.)

Ball: A pitch at which the batter does not swing and which the umpire rules did not cross home plate in the strike zone (usually between the batter's armpits and the top of his knees).

Bean ball: A pitch thrown at a hitter's head.

Bench warmer: A player who seldom plays in a game.

Bunt: When the batter taps the ball with his bat instead of swinging at it.

Change-up: A slow pitch, also known as "letup."

Cleanup: The fourth batter position in the lineup.

Clutch hitter: A hitter who bats well when it counts.

Double play: When two runners are put out on one play.

Force play: A situation in which a base runner must attempt to reach the next base. On a force play, the fielder has only to touch the base for the runner to be out.

Full count: Three balls and two strikes on the batter.

Grand slam: A bases-loaded homerun.

Hit and run: A play in which the runner on first base breaks for second base the moment the ball is pitched while the batter then tries to hit the pitch into the "hole" between first and second base.

Hook: A curve ball.

Leg hitter: A runner who beats out many hits because of good running speed.

Pop fly: A high fly ball within or just beyond the infield.

Pulling a rock: Making a dumb mistake.

Rookie: A first-year player.

Run: A run is scored when a player advances around the bases and touches home plate without being put out.

Run batted in (RBI): A run that scores as a direct result of offensive action (a base hit, base on balls, sacrifice fly, etc.) by the batter.

Shutout: No runs scored, a blank job.

Steal: When there is no hit but a base runner advances safely by running to the next base before he is thrown out.

Strike: Any pitch that the batter swings at but misses or any pitch not swung at that the umpire rules crossed the plate in the strike zone (usually between the batter's armpits and the top of his knees).

Strike out: Three strikes counts as an out.

Walk: A batter automatically goes to first base—gets a "walk"—if a pitcher throws four balls to him.

Wild pitch: A pitch thrown past the catcher that permits a base runner to advance.

Woodman: A good batter.

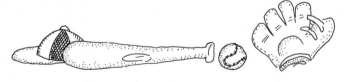

Creative Writing

Have your students describe the day their team won or lost the BIG game.

Books about Baseball:

Adler, David A. *Jeffrey's Ghost.* Il. by Jean Jenkins. Holt, 1984. M.
> A ghost helps a baseball team to victory.

Adoff, Arnold. *Outside Inside Poems.* Il. by John Steptoe. Lothrop, 1981. M.
> How a young baseball player feels inside and outside.

Christopher, Matt. *The Fox Steals Home.* Il. by Larry Johnson. Little, 1978. M.
> Bobby tries to keep his mind on baseball even though his parents are getting a divorce and his father will be moving away.

Clark, Steve. *Complete Book of Baseball Cards.* Grosset, 1976. M.
> The history of baseball cards from the 1880's to the present. Descriptions of collections, black-and-white photographs plus color photo insert.

Cohen, Barbara. *Benny.* Lothrop, 1977. M.
> Twelve-year-old Benny would rather play baseball than work in the family store, but then he befriends a German refugee and he finds new priorities.

_____. *Thank You, Jackie Robinson.* Il. by Richard Cuffari. Lothrop, 1974. M.
> Sam's closest friend is a sixty-year-old black man who is also a Dodger fan.

Companis, Al. *Play Ball with Roger the Dodger.* Il. by Syd Hoff. Putnam, 1980. P, M.
> Cartoons and brief text help improve your baseball game.

Dyer, Mike. *Getting Into Pro Baseball.* Watts, 1979. M.
> Advice on how to break into major league baseball.

Earle, Vana. *The Big League Book of Baseball Fun.* Il. by Marc Nadel. Collier Books, 1982. M.
> Crossword puzzles, word finds, mazes, all based on current baseball facts.

Fisher, Leonard Everett. *Noonan. A Novel about Baseball, ESP, and Time Warps.* Il. by the author. Doubleday, 1978. M, U.
> Johnny goes 100 years into the future and comes back to the present with a magic pitching talent.

Gemme, Leila Boyle. *T-Ball Is Our Game.* Photographs by Richard Marshall. Children's Press, 1978. P.
> A photo essay about baseball for beginning readers.

Hoff, Syd. *Baseball Mouse.* Il. by author. Putnam, 1979. P.
> Bernard is a field mouse who longs to be a baseball star.

Honig, Donald. *Way to Go, Teddy.* Watts, 1973. M.
> Ted's father thinks he is a star baseball player. The truth is that Ted is going back to the Class D team.

Hurwitz, Johanna. *Baseball Fever.* Il. by Ray Cruz. Morrow, 1981. M.
> Ezra's father does not understand his obsession with baseball.

Isadora, Rachel. *Max.* Il. by author. Macmillan, 1976. All ages.
> Max joins his sister's ballet class and finds it helps his baseball game.

Kalb, Jonah. *The Easy Baseball Book.* Il. by Sandy Kossin. Houghton, 1976. P.
> Cartoon drawings and easy-to-read text give hints on hitting, throwing, and field practice.

_____. *The Goof That Won the Pennant.* Il. by Sandy Kossin. Houghton, 1976. M.
> The Blazers, born losers, find out that winning is more fun than losing.

Kessler, Leonard. *Old Turtle's Baseball Stories.* Il. by author. Greenwillow, 1982. P.
> Old Turtle tells stories about Cleo Octopus, Melvin Moose, and Carla Kangaroo, great baseball players in the old days. A Read-Alone book.

Knudson, R. R. *Zanboomer.* Harper, 1978. M.
> Zan, a devoted baseball player, is injured and finds that running can bring equal satisfaction.

Konigsburg, Elaine L. *About the B'nai Bagels.* Il. by author. Atheneum, 1969. M.
> Mack's mother is the manager of his Little League team and his brother is the coach. He discovers that "sometimes it takes a guy a whole Little League season" to grow up.

Liss, Howard. *More Strange but True Baseball Stories.* Random, 1972. M.
> Short incidents from baseball history are described, such as the wrong-way runner and the one-pitch victory.

Parish, Peggy. *Play Ball, Amelia Bedelia.* Il. by Wallace Tripp. Harper, 1972. P.
> Amelia takes the directions for playing ball seriously and "puts Dick out" and tries to keep a player from "stealing" the base.

Peck, Robert Newton. *Last Sunday.* Il. by Ben Stahl. Doubleday, 1977. M.
> The mascot of the Canby Catfish baseball team tells about "Vermont's open-air insane asylum."

Ritter, Lawrence S. *The Story of Baseball.* Morrow, 1983. M, U.
> Historical presentation of the game of baseball.

Rubin, Robert. *Ty Cobb: The Greatest.* Putnam, 1978. M.
> One of the Putnam sports-shelf series about the man who holds more records in baseball than anyone else.

Shoemaker, Robert H. *The Best in Baseball,* rev. ed. Crowell, 1974. M, U.
> Collective biographies of some of the baseball greats.

Slote, Alfred. *Hang Tough, Paul Mather.* Lippincott, 1973. M.
> A former Little League star has leukemia, and he and his family cope with this circumstance.

———. *Matt Gargan's Boy.* Lippincott, 1975. M.
> Danny hopes that his major-league-baseball-playing father will remarry his mother.

Smith, Doris Buchanan. *Last Was Lloyd.* Viking, 1981. M.
> Lloyd is the worst baseball player in school, but in the park he's a home-run king.

Sperling, Dan. *A Spectator's Guide to Baseball.* Avon, 1983. M, U.
> A dictionary of baseball.

Stadler, John. *Hooray for Snail!* Il. by author. Crowell, 1984. P.
> Snail plays baseball. Little text, bright pictures.

Thayer, Ernest Lawrence. *Casey at the Bat; A Ballad of the Republic Sung in the Year 1888.* Il. by Wallace Tripp. Coward, 1978. All ages.
> Lively drawings accompany the sad story of the day Casey struck out in Mudville.

Tolle, Jean Bashor. *The Great Pete Penney.* McElderry, 1979. M.
> A leprechaun gives a Little League player a ring that enables her to pitch unhittable curve balls.

Willard, Nancy. *The Highest Hit.* Harcourt, 1978. M.
> Kate gives her uncoordinated mother baseball lessons for her birthday. A broken chapel window is one result.

Books about Some Other Sports:

Avi. *S.O.R. Losers.* Bradbury, 1984. M, U.
> Really funny account of a seventh grade soccer team of losers. The score of their first game is 32-0.

Blessing, Richard. *A Passing Season.* Little, 1982. U.
> "In Oiltown, almost nothing's more important than football."

Dygard, Thomas J. *Winning Kicker*. Morrow, 1978. M.
> Coach Earlingham's last year as a high school football coach turns out to be memorable when a girl tries out for the team.

Knudson, R. R. *Zan Hagen's Marathon*. Farrar, 1984. U.
> Zan tries out for the Olympic Marathon.

Knudson, R. R., and P. K. Ebert, eds. *Sports Poems*. Dell, 1971. M. U.
> Over 100 poems featuring major and minor sports.

Levy, Elizabeth. *The Tryouts*. Il. by Jacquie Hann. Four winds, 1979. M.
> It looks as though girls are going to make the eighth grade basketball team.

Okimoto, Jean Davies. *Norman Schnurman, Average Person*. Putnam, 1982. M.
> A "C" person is urged by his dad to join the Junior Football League.

Rules of the Game: The Complete Illustrated Encyclopedia of All the Sports of the World. Diagram Visual Information (2 Continents, 30 East 42 Street, New York, New York 10017), 1974. M. U.
> Details rules for over 150 sports and 400 events.

Savitt, Sam. *A Horse to Remember*. Il. by author. Viking, 1984. M.
> Mike Benson trains a skittish horse for the Maryland Hunt Club Race.

Scioscia, Mary. *Bicycle Rider*. Il. by Ed Young. Harper, 1983. M.
> Marshall Taylor wins his first race in this short, beautifully illustrated book.

Voight, Cunthia. *Tell Me if the Lovers Are Losers*. Atheneum, 1982. U.
> Three girls join the Stanton volleyball team and become friends despite their disparate backgrounds.

Wells, Rosemary. *When No One Was Looking*. Dial, 1980. U.
> For Kathy, winning at tennis becomes an obsession.

Calendar Day

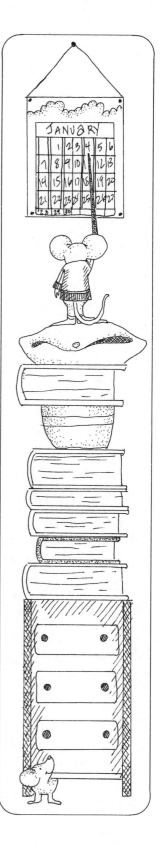

Use this program on any day that you discuss time, or you are explaining a moveable feast such as Chinese New Year or Easter, to welcome a new month, to say good-bye to a week, or to greet any date of the year, perhaps the first and last time it will ever be May 12, 1988.

Most of us think of the year in terms of landmarks: Christmas, Valentine's Day, Dad's birthday. These are fixed celebrations that come every year at the same time. When we look back at an event we might use one of these festivals as an anchor date. "Ah yes, the big snowstorm was just after New Year's."

Who decided that our year starts in January, when any school child knows that the year—the real year—starts at the end of summer in the fall when school begins? Our calendar has a long history. The Egyptians invented the seven-day week. The Babylonians were probably the first people to divide a day into twenty-four equal hours. The

43

length of the year is actually 365 days, 5 hours, 48 minutes, and 46 seconds. This is the reason we need to have an extra day every fourth year, which we call leap year.

Although some major religions still use calendars that were developed hundreds of years ago, most of the world governments use the Gregorian calendar, developed in the 1580's by Pope Gregory XIII. Not every country adopted this calendar immediately. The British had used the Julian calendar, established by Julius Caesar in 46 B.C., until 1752, when King George II proclaimed that henceforth Britain and the American colonies would use the Gregorian calendar. To make the change, eleven days had to be deleted from the present calendar. September 3 became September 14. Pope Gregory XIII had done the same thing earlier when he changed October 5, 1582, to October 15. This trick corrected the Julian calendar.

A nineteenth-century French philosopher, Auguste Comte, proposed a thirteen-month calendar. Each month would have twenty-eight days. There are still some reformers who support this change in our present system. However, the likelihood of getting all the nations of the world to agree to such a change is remote. We might just as well resign ourselves to our unwieldly but familiar calendar.

The calendar that we use today is awkward because months differ in length. Luckily, we all know the traditional rhyme:

Thirty days hath September,   February twenty-eight alone —
April, June and November;   Except in leap year, at which time
All the rest have thirty-one —   February's days are twenty-nine.

Wherever and whenever your private year begins or ends, life does go on. The first booklist at the end of the program is made up of books that feature this continuing feeling of time passing. The incidents in each book remind the reader of the rhythm of daily life marked by anniversaries, holidays, births, and death. One of the most popular examples of this type is the Little House series by Laura Ingalls Wilder. The second booklist contains books of fantasy that deal with visits to the past or the future and factual books about the concept of time.

Prose Selection

Why do we have a calendar? Does it matter if February follows January, or that Wednesday comes after Tuesday? This is what happened to the king and the queen of Sundimundee before the calendar was invented.

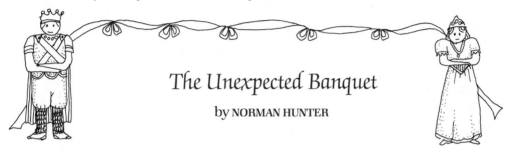

The Unexpected Banquet

by NORMAN HUNTER

There were no calendars in the kingdom of Sundimundee, because printing hadn't been invented. So a man used to go round with a different-colored ribbon tied round his arm according to what day it was. He had a red ribbon for Mondays, a green one for Tuesdays, a blue one for Wednesdays, and so on. And everybody had only to look at his ribbon to know at once whether it was early closing day, or half-holiday, or bath night, or the day for cleaning out the spare room, and so on.

And, of course, the man with the ribbon was a most important and valuable official. In fact he was really one of the weather clerk's assistants, who had been lent to the king for the purpose.*

"There's an awful lot of illness about just now, my dear," said the king to the queen. "We ought to send the man who wears the day ribbons down to be vaccinated. It would be awful if he caught anything. Nobody would know where they were or whether they had passed it or if it was too late or much too early or even if everything was anything."

"Yes, yes," said the queen, hoping the king wasn't going on talking muddly sort of things like that because it made her forget where she was with the lace piano cover she was making.

---

*This part of the story isn't so extreme as it sounds. In Siam the people really did wear a sort of sash the color of which was different for each day of the week. But, of course, that doesn't account for what happens next.

So the days' man was sent along to the court physician and vaccinated that very day.

But, oh dear, the silly, not-thinking sort of person, whatever must he go and do but tie a red ribbon round his vaccinated arm so people shouldn't bump into it and hurt him. Yes, and a red ribbon meant Monday and this was Wednesday. There! Everything the king had said might happen if he was ill looked like happening because he wasn't.

"Monday already," said everyone, scratching their heads or their noses or their chins, according to what sort of people they were. "This has been a most short week." Which, of course, it was, but there was the days' man strutting about with a red Monday ribbon on his arm, so Monday it had to be and no use arguing.

So all the shopkeepers who'd thought it was Wednesday and shut their shops for early closing had to open them again. And all the school children who'd got all ready to stay at home for half-holiday had to go to school again. And extra bath nights were got ready for and spare rooms were cleaned out again, though they didn't need it.

But none of that would really have mattered so frightfully much if it hadn't been that the king and queen were giving a magnificent banquet to all the important people in the kingdom on the Monday that was still to come, but which everyone thought was here already. So, of course, all those important people put on their most important clothes and hung their important jewels round their important selves and all got delivered in coaches and things at the royal palace.

"Agnes, Agnes, quick, come here!" cried the king, when he caught sight of them through the throne-room window.

"People arriving for the banquet. Is it Monday? Can't be. Monday was the other day. What shall we do?"

"What's this? What's this?" cried the queen, rushing in with her nose only half powdered and with ten maids following her down the stairs trying to do her dress up as she ran but not managing to do it. "Banquet! Tonight! Impossible! What day is it?"

She threw a glance out of the window looking for the days' man, but as he wasn't there, the glance went right round the garden and came back to her again without doing any good.

"Quick!" she cried, grasping the situation with her womanly intuition and her queenly brain and her royal readiness all at once. "Go and tell them funny stories, Kingy, while I get something started," and she dashed off to the kitchen, with the maids still following, but not bothering about trying to do up her dress anymore as she was pulling it off in order to put on a nice big apron.

"Cook," she cried, "guests have arrived for the banquet. It's Monday and nobody told us."

"Heavens, mum, I mean, Majesty," said the cook, going all pale and shutting the book she was reading without marking the place. "There's nothing in the house, I should say palace, mum — er — Majesty. Nothing except a tin of sardines or so."

"Bring out your sardines," said the queen, flourishing a rolling pin. "There's got to be a banquet tonight by hook or by crook, or by anything else you like. Some sort of a banquet, any sort of a banquet, but a banquet." She lit the gas oven, which went bang right in her face, dropped the rolling pin on the cook's toe, turned on both the water taps, and grabbed the biggest bowl.

"Bring out everything eatable and anything that looks as if it might be eatable," she commanded, tying a yellow duster round her hair. And the maids, who weren't kitchen maids at all but dressing-boudoir-bedroom sort of maids, had to tie tea cloths round their middles and get things out and put them away again and rush about helping, though they didn't help much because they weren't used to making banquets but only beds.

While all this was going on the king had gone to greet the noble and noticeable visitors and was trying to keep them amused with funny stories until the queen could let him know that the banquet was ready by ringing a bell.

"I wonder," said the king in his best telling-a-story manner, "if you know the story of the man who — er that is to say the lady from — or rather I should say the way in which...." But nobody knew that one and as the king couldn't remember it either, they didn't hear it.

Then the king talked a lot and was just going to have a shot at singing a song when a bell rang.

"Thank goodness," breathed the king inside his beard, "the banquet's ready." But it wasn't. The bell was a muffin man's, but the king didn't discover it till too late and everyone was sitting round the table waiting for something to happen. So he had to have yet another shot at a story and this time he'd nearly finished it when he remembered he'd forgotten the last bit where it makes you laugh. But it didn't matter for just then Br-r-r-r-ing went a bell and in came the queen.

"We've made a sort of a banquet out of the most unlikely kind of scraps," whispered the queen to the king as she sat down. "Goodness knows what everyone will think, but let's hope they won't. Whatever you do, don't eat a crumb or there won't be enough to go round."

Then in came the servants carrying the first course. Everyone got something different. One duke got a sardine-and-a-half on a biscuit-and-a-half and started doing sums to see how much more he'd have if he'd had twice as much as half of what was missing. A duchess got one pickle, one top half of a slice of a cottage loaf, and three assorted peanuts. The prime minister received a lettuce leaf wrapped daintily round a piece of orange with a dab of mustard on it, and the lord chief justice had the pink icing off an almond finger laid carefully on top of a stewed plum. One of the marchionesses was given ten little dog biscuits by mistake through one of the maids having taken the queen's dog's breakfast, which he hadn't eaten, thinking it was part of the banquet, and the lord chancellor had a very generous portion of damp tea cloth that the cook had left on a plate and which oughtn't to have been brought in at all.

"Charming weather, don't you think, and so much of it," said the king, clattering his knife and fork about ever so much on an empty plate because he hadn't been given anything to eat.

"You must let me give you the pattern of a simply too sweet jumper, my dear," said the queen to the most important duchess, who was doing her best with a brazil nut and half a cold sausage and trying to look as if she liked them.

Then the servants came and cleared away the plates for the next course. All the guests had left something on their plates just for manners and several of them had left everything, either because they didn't like it or because they couldn't eat it, or because they were so astonished at having such unlikely food served at a royal banquet that they hadn't time to start before their plates were taken away again.

"Whatever are you going to do for the next course?" whispered the king.

"Shush," said the queen. "You wait."

Presently in came the next course, and what do you think it was? Why, the servants had taken all the leftover bits from the first course and mixed them up and served them out again and brought them in for the second course. Everyone got something different from what they'd had before, only not quite so much, except the lord chancellor who got the damp tea cloth again.

Then the king, who'd just been served with another plate full of nothing, stood up and said, "My Lords, Ladies, and Gentlemen, let us drink to the kingdom of Sundimundee," so of course everyone had to stand up to drink the toast, and immediately as they stood up the servants whisked round ever so quickly and took all the plates away again with hardly anything eaten.

"This is more like a game of cards than a banquet," said the cook, splitting a bean left by a marquis into three and giving one piece each to a duchess, a baronet, and a bishop.

Then in came the third course, made of what had been left of the second one, mixed up and dealt out differently again. And once more everyone got something different and still less of it than before. The lord chancellor got the damp tea cloth again.

Then up popped the queen to propose the health of the guests and as soon as everyone had sat down after drinking that, the king jumped up and said, "Here's to absent friends," meaning those

49

who hadn't been invited. So the servants were able to clear the plates again and get away with nearly everything they had brought in.

And all through the fourth and fifth and sixth courses that unreasonable sort of bewildering banquet went on. Each time the cook mixed up what was left and shuffled it round again. Each time everyone got a little bit less until some of them were being given half a split pea or one end of a lentil. And all the time the king and queen kept popping up and proposing the most extreme sort of toasts like "Here's to the fire brigade," and "Let us drink the toast of the royal baker," which sounded the most awful nonsense but was the best they could do on the spur of the moment. Anyway it made the guests keep popping up too and gave the servants a chance to snatch their plates away with bits of food still on them, so as to make the banquet go another course or so.

But everyone was getting most alarmingly hungry. The king and queen had been served with seven empty plates and had nothing on the eighth, none of which was very satisfying. Still they were too anxious to feel that they were hungry. But the guests who either didn't like what they got or weren't given time to eat it if they did, felt positively hollow inside themselves.

"Next time I go to a royal banquet I shall take sandwiches with me," whispered a duke who'd just managed to swallow half an inch of macaroni before his plate was whisked away.

"Me, too," said a marchioness, forgetting to speak correctly because she was so hungry.

"Gr-mph-mph-g-g-g," said the lord chancellor, who'd had the damp tea cloth every time and at last had got so hungry he'd cut a piece off with his pocket scissors and was trying ever so desperately to eat it, but finding it rather a job.

Things were getting awful. The king and queen couldn't think of any more toasts to propose and several guests had actually managed to eat something. Then the butler sidled up to the queen and whispered, "There isn't anything more left to eat, Your Majesty, except half a teaspoonful of cold gravy and three haricot beans, one

50

with a piece missing, and they won't go round."

Ooer, thought the queen, but she was regal enough not to say it. "Whatever can we do? A royal banquet has to last at least fourteen courses and we've only had nine."

"Think of another toast, quick," whispered the king, but they couldn't think of one, and some of the less noble guests were beginning to tap slightly on the table with their fingertips. If they didn't get something to eat soon they might start banging their spoons and forks about and that would be awful at a royal banquet.

Then all of a sudden there was a commotion at the doors and in rushed the days' man with a blue Wednesday ribbon round his arm and holding up the red Monday one.

"Your Majesties!" he cried. "Oh, forgive me. Oh dear, oh dear." And he told them all about how he'd tied the red ribbon round his vaccinated arm and everything.

"Then it *is* Wednesday," said the queen. "I thought it was because my doggie never likes to have breakfast on Wednesdays and he didn't have any this morning."

Hum, thought the marchioness who'd been given the ten little dog biscuits for the first course, but she was too polite to say anything and even if she hadn't been she wouldn't have had the chance to say it because the king jumped up and everyone grabbed their glasses and stood up too, thinking it was to be another toast. But it wasn't.

"My Lords, Ladies, and Gentlemen," said His Majesty, "we're awfully sorry about this funny sort of banquet, but there's been a mistake. It isn't Monday, it's only Wednesday, and we weren't ready." He told them how it had happened and everyone stood up and cheered, partly because they thought the king and queen should be congratulated for trying so hard to give them a banquet, although it was the wrong day, and partly because the king said there would be a proper banquet on Monday as arranged.

"And now I think someone had better invent printing," said the king, "so that we can have calendars." So someone did and they had them, so that sort of confusion isn't likely to happen anymore.

Poetry Selections

How Far

by MARY ANN HOBERMAN

How far
How far
How far is today
When tomorrow has come
And it's yesterday?

Far
And far
And far away.

How To Get There

by BONNIE NIMS

I go
through Sunday's tunnel, hushed
    and deep;
up Monday's mountain, craggy
    and steep;
along Tuesday's trail, winding and
    slow;
into Wednesday's woods, still
    halfway to go;
over Thursday's bridge, shaky and
    tall;
through the hidden gate in Friday's
    wall
to get to
SATURDAY.

I wish there were a shorter way.

No

by WILLIAM COLE

No birds, no flowers,
No sunshiny hours,
No days without rain
Or frost on the pane;
No fresh fruit is sold,
No weather but cold —
Please, Nature, remember:
Next year, skip November!

I Must Remember

by SHEL SILVERSTEIN

I must remember...
Turkey on Thanksgiving,
Pudding on Christmas,
Eggs on Easter,
Chicken on Sunday,
Fish on Friday,
Leftovers, Monday.
But ah, me — I'm such a dunce.
I went and ate them all at once.

Calendar

by MYRA COHN LIVINGSTON

January shivers,
February shines,
March blows off the winter ice,
April makes the mornings nice,
May is hopscotch lines.

June is deep blue swimming,
Picnics are July,
August is my birthday,
September whistles by.

October is for roller skates,
November is the fireplace,
December is the best because
of sleds
and snow
and Santa Claus.

The Fight of the Year

by ROGER McGOUGH

"And there goes the bell for the
   third month
and Winter comes out of its corner
   looking groggy
Spring leads with a left to the head
followed by a sharp right to the
   body
     daffodils
     primroses
     crocuses
     snowdrops
     lilacs
     violets
     pussywillow
Winter can't take much more
   punishment
and Spring shows no signs of tiring
   tadpoles
   squirrels
   baalambs
   badgers
   bunny rabbits
   mad march hares
   horses and hounds

Spring is merciless
Winter won't go the full twelve
   rounds
     bobtail clouds
     scallywaggy winds
     the sun
     a pavement artist
     in every town
A left to the chin
and Winter's down!
   1 tomatoes
   2 radish
   3 cucumber
   4 onions
   5 beetroot
   6 celery
   7 and any
   8 amount
   9 of lettuce
   10 for dinner
Winter's out for the count
Spring is the winner!"

The Months

by RICHARD B. SHERIDAN

January snowy, February flowy,
   March blowy;
April showery, May flowery, June
   bowery;
July moppy, August croppy,
   September poppy;
October breezy, November wheezy,
   December freezy.

Calendar Book Souvenir

Give everyone a book calendar. Ask your local print shop for paper end cuts. These are the leftovers after paper has been sized for invitations, advertisements, or notices. They vary in size from long and skinny to fat and squat. Take 5 or 6 sheets and fasten at one end with a stapler. This will make a little mini-book. Children may list books they read for one week or one month. For each book have them give author and title, a quote from the book, a sketch of a character or scene, and a recommendation: "Great book," or "Not worth reading." At the end of the time period, post the booklets on bulletin boards so others can profit from their classmates' reading.

Read-a-Thon

A more organized listing of books can be accomplished as a charity drive for the Multiple Sclerosis Society. Each year this organization runs Read-a-Thons to raise money for research. Your local chapter will supply you with a reading kit.

Inquiries can be directed to National Multiple Sclerosis Society, 205 East 42nd Street, New York City, N.Y. 10017.

Joke

If you were locked in a room that had only a bed and a calendar, what would you do for food?

Get water from the bedsprings and dates from the calendar.

Bulletin Board

Make or buy a year's school calendar. Mark fixed dates, vacations, band concerts, holidays on the calendar. Throughout the year, in a different color (red!), write Read A Book, A Good Day To Read, or write the title of a recommended book. Mark birthdays of children's authors and illustrators.

Creative Writing/Activities

Diary

Have children keep a diary to show their personal thoughts as the year passes. Have them list the books they read with personal comments.

Prose Poem

As a class project, list items that symbolize the seasons and create a prose poem.

Spring	Summer	Fall	Winter
strawberries	baseball	school	Christmas
flowers	swimming	football	snow
Easter	vacations	Thanksgiving	rain
new green	heat	apples	cold

Speculation

Pose this question and ask children to write about it: If you could choose any historical time to live in, which would you choose? Why?

Preferences

Ask children to write a story, essay, or poem about their favorite or least favorite month of the year, telling what makes it special to them or what they don't like about it.

A Time Capsule

In order to show future generations what our present civilization was like in 1940, Oglethorpe College in Atlanta, Georgia, buried a number of objects that are to be unearthed in the year 8113. Time capsules were also buried at the New York World's Fairs of 1939-40 and 1964-65. Children can make and bury their own time capsule.

YOU NEED: An airtight, watertight container—a metal box would be good. Some of the materials you collect could include: newspapers, advertisements for food and household appliances, pictures of current hairstyles, pictures of automobiles, words and music of this year's most popular songs, names of best-selling books, lists of favorite books, photographs of the winners of the World Series as well as of the current president of the United States. Personal data could include photographs of homes, pets, and family, the children themselves, a list of their likes and dislikes, secret ambitions, etc.

HOW TO: Place everything in the metal box and seal it. Put today's date on it and the date it will be opened—ten years (or fifteen, or twenty) ahead. On that day the children (and they won't be children by then) can open their own private time capsules and see how they used to live and think.

HINT: If this is a school, library, or city project, make sure the folks in the future know the "open" date.

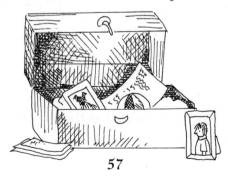

A Perpetual Calendar

YOU NEED: a board
(I used a breadboard)
64 1-inch nails
spray paint
hammer
stick-on letters
cards of various shapes
a key tag or a washer

JANUARY

SUN	MON	TUES	WED	THUR	FRI	SAT
				1	2	3	4	5	6	7

2	3	4	5	6	7	8	9	10	11	12	13	14
9	10	11	12	13	14	15	16	17	18	19	20	21
16	17	18	19	20	21	22	23	24	25	26	27	28
23	24	25	26	27	28	29	30	31			(85)	

HOW TO: Hammer one nail at the top of the board. This will hold a card with the name of the month on it. Below it, hammer a row of seven nails, positioned as in the diagram. These will alternately hold a card with the days of the week printed on it. The third row will have seven nails also and the next three rows will each have thirteen. The last row will have nine. These nails will represent the days of the month. (Be sure to leave ample room between the second and third rows to hang the days of the week card.) One nail on the bottom will be for the year. Spray-paint the whole board (nails too) and let it dry. Next, write the days of the week on a card (see illustration). Then, using stick-on numbers, label the days of the month directly on the board. The days card will be moved along the second row of nails, to correspond correctly to the proper week. Write the months of the year on small cards. Those not in use can be stored behind the one for the current month. Write cards for several years and place the one for the current year on the nail at the bottom. Use a key tag or a washer to indicate the current date.

Books about the Calendar

1. Books that capture the cycle and rhythm of everyday life:

Aliki. *The Twelve Months: A Greek Folktale.* Il. by author. Greenwillow, 1978. All ages.
The twelve months are appreciated by a widow and she is rewarded. An excellent picture book to share with all audiences.

————.*The Two of Them.* Greenwillow, 1979. P.
The seasons and the years pass for a little girl and her grandfather.

Angell, Judie. *Dear Lola or How to Build Your Own Family.* Bradbury, 1980. M.
Six children living without adults almost get caught on Halloween when a newspaper photographer arrives.

Baylor, Byrd. *The Best Town in the World.* Il. by Ronald Himler. Scribners, 1983. M, U.
Poetic descriptions and realistic art about life in a small town when father was growing up.

Blos, Joan W. *A Gathering of Days: A New England Girl's Journal, 1830-32.* Scribner, 1979. M, U.
Daily life on a New England farm.

Blume, Judy. *Superfudge.* Dutton, 1980. M.
Letters to Santa from Peter, who doesn't believe in Santa, and Fudge, who does…or does he?

Bridgers, Sue Ellen. *All Together Now.* Knopf, 1979. U.
Casey Flanagan spends a summer with her grandparents and learns that people are interesting and full of love.

Burningham, John. *Seasons.* Il. by author. Jonathan Cape, 1969. All ages.
Large, colorful pictures and minimal text feature the four seasons.

Cartlidge, Michelle. *A Mouse's Diary.* Il. by author. Lothrop, 1982. P, M.
A week of summer school, written as a diary with detailed illustrations.

Ehrlich, Amy. *Zeek Silver Moon.* Il. by Robert Andrew Parker. Dial, 1972. P.
Everyday events in a child's life are chronicled in a gentle text.

Ellison, Lucile Watkins. *Butter on Both Sides.* Il. by Judith Gwyn Brown. Scribner, 1979. M.
Christmas in July with fresh flowers on the tree.

Esbensen, Barbara Juster. *Cold Stars and Fireflies; Poems of the Four Seasons.* Il. by Susan Bonners. Crowell, 1984. M.
Woolly Bear, Caterpillar, Mittens, Spring Cleaning, and *At the Pool* are titles of some of these thoughtful poems.

Geras, Adele. *The Girls in the Velvet Frame.* Atheneum, 1979. M.
The day-to-day excitements of a family of five girls in pre-World-War-1 Palestine.

Greene, Constance C. *Beat the Turtle Drum.* Il. by Donna Diamond. Viking, 1976. M.
Four months change Kate's life.

Hall, Donald. *Ox-Cart Man.* Il. by Barbara Cooney. Viking, 1979. P.
A picture-book journey through the seasons in New England.

Hopkins, Lee Bennett. *Mama.* Knopf, 1977. U.
The boys would like a pretty Christmas tree this year and Mama wants to get it for them, even if it means stealing.

Hurmence, Belinda. *Tough Tiffany.* Doubleday, 1980. M.
At the annual family reunion, there is all you can eat, plus a few quarrels with relatives.

Hurwitz, Johanna. *Once I Was a Plum Tree.* Il. by Ingrid Fetz. Morrow, 1980. M.
Gerry and her sister are invited to a Passover seder.

Lowry, Lois. *A Summer to Die.* Il. by Jenni Oliver. Houghton, 1977. M.

Meg copes with her sister's illness, the birth of a baby, and death.

Marshak, Samuel. *The Month-Brothers: A Slavic Tale.* Trans. by Thomas P. Whitney. Il. by Diane Stanley. Morrow, 1983. M, U.

This large picture book tells the folk story of two sisters who meet the twelve months.

O'Kelley, Mattie Lou. *From the Hills of Georgia: An Autobiography of Paintings.* Il. by author. Atlantic/Little, 1983. M, U.

Native paintings illustrate vignettes of a year in Georgia.

Pellowski, Anne. *Willow Wind Farm: Betsy's Story.* Il. by Wendy Watson. Philomel, 1981. M.

Ten children have fun all through the year, particularly at Christmas when the lights go out.

Provensen, Alice and Martin. *The Year at Maple Hill Farm.* Il. by authors. Atheneum, 1978. P.

Month by month this book explores the seasonal changes on a farm.

Smith, Doris Buchanan. *Laura Upside Down.* Viking, 1984. M.

Laura and her friends give parties all year long.

Steig, William. *Sylvester and the Magic Pebble.* Il. by author. Windmill, 1969. P.

A donkey is turned into a rock and remains immobile throughout the seasons.

Steinmetz, Leon. *Clocks in the Woods.* Il. by author. Harper, 1979. P.

The porcupine sells every animal a watch, but do animals need to tell time?

Tafuri, Nancy. *All Year Long.* Il by author. Greenwillow, 1983. All ages.

Large, full-color drawings illustrate the months of the year as well as the days of the week.

Von Canon, Claudia. *The Moonclock.* Houghton, 1979. U.

The letters to and from a young Viennese bride of the seventeenth century.

Wilder, Laura Ingalls. *Little Town on the Prairie.* Il. by Garth Williams. Harper, 1953. M.

The fourth of July, Christmas, and a birthday party are all chapter headings in this classic family story.

Wittman, Sally. *A Special Trade.* Il. by Karen Gundersheimer. Harper, 1978. P.

A little girl and an older man get older and change. Nelly ends up helping Bartholomew the way he once helped her.

2. These books feature time in fact and fantasy:

Aiken, Joan. *The Shadow Guests.* Delacorte, 1980. U.

Cosmo, visiting in England, is confronted by strangers from the past who are out for revenge.

Alexander, Lloyd. *Time Cat: The Remarkable Journeys of Jason and Gareth.* Il. by Bill Sokol. Avon, 1982. M.

A cat is transported back into eight periods in which he previously lived. He visits ancient Egypt, Rome, and Revolutionary America.

Anderson, Margaret J. *In the Keep of Time.* Knopf, 1977. M.

In an abandoned tower, three children go back to fifteenth-century Scotland and forward to the twenty-second century. *In the Circle of Time* (Knopf, 1979) is a sequel.

Babbitt, Natalie. *Tuck Everlasting.* Farrar, 1975. M.

The Tuck family accidentally drinks from the spring of eternal life and is doomed to roam the earth unchanged forever.

Bond, Nancy. *A String in the Harp*. McElderry, 1976. M.

> Morgan, living in Wales, uses an ancient harp tuning key to reach the sixth century.

Bosse, Malcolm J. *Cave Beyond Time*. Crowell, 1980. M.

> Fifteen-year-old Ben visits several periods in the past while recovering from an injury.

Boston, Lucy. *The Treasure of Green Knowe*. Il. by Peter Boston. Harcourt, 1958. M.

> Tolly visits his great-grandmother and meets children who grew up in the house in generations past.

Burns, Marilyn. *This Book Is about Time*. Il. by Martha Weston. Little, 1978. M.

> Time facts in an attractive format.

Cameron, Eleanor. *The Court of Stone Children*. Dutton, 1973. M, U.

> Nini, playing in a museum. meets Dominique, a girl from Napoleonic France.

Cresswell, Helen. *A Game of Catch*. Macmillan, 1977. M.

> While playing tag in a castle, two children meet two eighteenth-century children from an old painting.

Curry, Jane. *Poor Tom's Ghost*. McElderry 1977. M, U.

> A hidden staircase, ghostly sobbings, and sinister footsteps are part of this time fantasy that involves a seventeenth-century actor and a modern family.

Engdahl, Sylvia Louise. *Enchantress from the Stars*. Il. by Rodney Shackell. Atheneum, 1970. M, U.

> Three civilizations in different stages of development meet on the planet Andreia in a science-fiction fantasy.

Farmer, Penelope. *Charlotte Sometimes*. Il. by Chris Connor. Harcourt, 1969. U.

> Awakening on her second day at boarding school to find her surroundings slightly different, Charlotte finds that she has changed places with a girl who had been there forty years before.

Fisher, Leonard E. *Noonan: A Novel about Baseball, ESP, and Time Warps*. Il. by author. Doubleday, 1978. M.

> A baseball pitcher is hit on the head by a foul ball and propelled one hundred years into the future.

Houghton, Eric. *Steps Out of Time*. Lothrop, 1980. M.

> Jonathon unlocks the door of his house and steps into the future.

Huddy, Delia. *Time Piper*. Greenwillow, 1979. U.

> A twelfth-century legend haunts a twentieth-century girl and an inventor of a time machine.

Hurmence, Belinda. *A Girl Called Boy*. Clarion, 1982. M.

> A ten-year-old black girl finds herself back in the 1850's as a slave.

Lively, Penelope. *The House in Norham Gardens*. Dutton, 1974. U.

> A ceremonial shield transports Clare from present-day England to the primitive jungles of New Guinea.

Lobel, Arnold. *Frog and Toad Are Friends*. Harper, 1972. P.

> Frog tears the winter months from the calendar to make Spring come more quickly.

Marzollo, Jean. *Halfway Down Paddy Lane*. Dial, 1981. U.

> Kate is transported back in time to the New England of 1850 and finds herself falling in love with her own "brother."

Mayne, William. *Earthfasts*. Dutton, 1967. U.

> A cold-flamed candle reverses time and brings King Arthur and his knights back to life.

Mazer, Norma Fox. *Saturday, the Twelfth of October*. Delacorte, 1975. U.

> Ian Ford crosses the river of time and is adopted by a tribe of cave dwellers in the Stone Age.

Norton, André. *Lavender-Green Magic.* Il. by Judith Gwyn Brown. Crowell, 1974. M.

Three children get lost in a maze and travel back into time where they meet two witches.

Ormondroyd, Edward. *Time at the Top.* Il. by Peggie Bach. Parnassus, 1963. M.

A young girl takes the elevator to the top floor of her apartment house and steps out into the world of 1881.

Park, Ruth. *Playing Beatie Bow.* Atheneum, 1982. U.

A contemporary Australian girl slips through time to the slums of Sydney 100 years ago.

Pascal, Francine. *Hangin' Out with Cici.* Viking, 1977. M.

A bump on the head transports Victoria back to 1944 where she makes friends with her own mother.

St. George, Judith. *The Mysterious Girl in the Garden.* Il. by Margot Tomes. Putnam, 1981. M.

Terrie is bored with her summer in England until she meets a girl who claims to be Princess Charlotte, who lived two hundred years ago.

Sauer, Julia Lina. *Fog Magic.* Viking, 1943. M, U.

Greta wanders through the fog in Nova Scotia and enters a village that existed 100 years in the past.

Stolz, Mary. *Cat in the Mirror.* Harper, 1975. M, U.

Erin exists in New York City and ancient Egypt.

Twain, Mark. *A Connecticut Yankee in King Arthur's Court.* Harper, 1889. U.

The classic time fantasy in which Hank Morgan is sent back 1300 years to King Arthur's court, where he replaces Merlin, the court magician.

Voigt, Cynthia. *Building Blocks.* Atheneum, 1984. U.

Brann crawls into a structure he built of wooden blocks and finds himself transported back in time — 37 years into the past where he meets his father.

Walsh, Jill Paton. *A Chance Child.* Farrar, 1978. U.

Creep enters the nineteenth century where he and two runaways work to survive before the existence of child labor laws.

Grandparents' Day

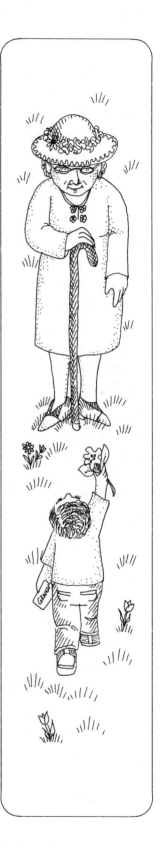

In many foreign cultures, older people are revered for their wisdom and are cherished by their children and grandchildren. In America, youth has traditionally been celebrated. In the 1960's it was even suggested that people over thirty should be considered too old to participate in decision making.

Our views of old age have greatly changed in the last decade. The terms *old age*, *elderly*, and *senior citizen* are being replaced with more active adjectives. The stereotype of old people as nonproductive burdens on society is rapidly changing as the nation sees them participating in every aspect of American life including the presidency of the United States. With the retirement age moving from sixty-five to seventy years of age, a new attitude is seen to be taking over the country. People are living longer and they are remaining vigorous and active well into their seventies and beyond. By the year 2020, more than 28 percent of the American population will be made up

63

of people over fifty-five years of age. In the next forty years, the proportion of over-fifty-fives will climb from 1 out of every 5 to 1 in every 3½ Americans.

Although many children do not have close contacts with older people, books can help introduce them. Recent children's books featuring older people show that segment of our society in a positive fashion. The image of active, vital elderly is vigorously portrayed in many children's books. Children should read several books featuring older people that will give them a balanced view of aging. The books show the advantages of age—maturity, experience, wisdom, and leisure time—balanced against the disadvantages, such as loneliness, rejection, and senility.

One way to make children aware of the elderly is to have them explore their own family's or community's past with older people. Tracing a family's heritage is an exercise in collecting authentic historical data. It will give children a personal perspective on the past, which will make future studies in history more meaningful.

Several books listed in the booklist will help you to get started on your own collection of family history, using grandparents as informants. Not all children will have easy access to their own grandparents. The teacher or librarian initiating this project should be ready to guide the children to older people in the community who will provide articulate stories and comments about their own family or community history.

Grandparent's Day is observed nationally on the first Sunday after Labor Day. The purpose of the day is "to visit grandparents or elderly shut-ins, giving them recognition and showing our appreciation of them." The country of Bulgaria officially celebrates *Babin Den*, or Grandmother's Day, on January 20. Celebrate on the day most convenient for you. My daughter's school honors grandparents and older guests by inviting them to attend classes the day before Thanksgiving vacation. No doubt that day is chosen because a good lunch (turkey dinner) is served.

A Grandparent's Day can be extended to become a celebration of all older people.

Prose Selections

String Beans

by JOHANNA HURWITZ

It was Sunday, and Grandma and Grandpa had come for a visit. Everyone sat around the dinner table smiling as Daddy sliced the roast beef and Mommy passed the mashed potatoes and gravy. There was also a large serving bowl filled with string beans.

"I don't want any beans," said Teddy, pouting and pushing his plate away.

"Teddy," said Mommy. "Eat your food."

"I like string beans," said Nora, proudly biting into one of her beans.

"Of course you do," said Daddy. "Everyone likes string beans."

"No!" said Teddy. "Not me!"

"Well," said Grandpa. "I can remember a time when I had to eat too many beans. It was a long time ago, when I was a little boy about your age.

"I lived in the country then. Next door to my house there was a woman and her son. You may have heard about him. His name was Jack."

"Jack? I don't know anyone named Jack," said Teddy.

"Well," said Grandpa. "He was a lazy, unpleasant fellow. I never liked him too much. In the winter he always threw snowballs at everyone. But let me tell you what happened one day. Jack's mother needed money to buy some food, so she told Jack to take their cow to town and sell it. Only instead of selling it, he traded it away to a man in exchange for a handful of colored beans."

"*That* Jack!" shouted Teddy and Nora. "Grandpa, did you really know *that* Jack who had the beanstalk?"

"I sure did," answered Grandpa. "I thought you might have heard about him. He got awfully famous for being so foolish. He brought those colored beans home, and his mother just threw them out the window and sent Jack upstairs to bed. Then she came over to our house, and we shared our supper with her. We even sent a sandwich back for that boy Jack. They don't tell about it in any of the stories.

"In the morning, when I was leaving for school, I saw an enormous thing growing outside of Jack's house."

"The beanstalk!" cried Teddy and Nora with delight.

"Yes, that's right," said Grandpa. "I knocked on Jack's door and asked if he wanted to walk to school with me. But that boy said he was going to stay home and climb to the top of his beanstalk."

"To the giant!" shouted Nora.

"Fee-fi-fo-fum!" called out Daddy, as he passed the meat platter.

"What happened next?" asked Teddy.

"Well," said Grandpa. "The teacher was furious with Jack. He was a bad student. He never paid attention in class or did his homework. And now he was playing hooky as well."

"Is that like playing hockey?" asked Nora.

"Hooky is when you stay home from school and you aren't sick," explained Mommy.

"Right," said Grandpa. "There we all were studying away and that naughty boy Jack was playing hooky. I was sure he would get into trouble. But when I came home from school that afternoon, there was Jack holding a hen that could lay golden eggs, which he had found at the top of the beanstalk. Everyone thought he was wonderful! When the teacher came to complain to Jack's mother, Jack gave her a golden egg.

"And the next day Jack stayed home from school again and climbed the beanstalk a second time, and he brought back—"

"A bag of gold!" shouted Teddy.

"Right!" said Grandpa. "And the next day he stayed home from school again. This time he got a golden harp, only this time the giant started to follow him down the beanstalk. So when he reached the bottom, he shouted to his mother to bring him an axe."

"And she did, and he chopped down the beanstalk," said Nora.

"Wrong!" said Grandpa. "All those books are wrong! Jack's mother wasn't home. She was out spending the gold pieces. But luckily I had just returned from school. I ran and got my axe, and I chopped the beanstalk down for him."

"Oh, Grandpa. That's wonderful!" breathed Nora.

"Did you see the giant fall?" asked Teddy.

"Of course," said Grandpa. "They may not write about me in the story, but I was there."

"Then what happened?" asked Nora.

"Well, we buried the giant. He made an enormous hole where he landed, and we filled it in with dirt. As for the beanstalk, it had so many beans on it that we picked for three weeks without stopping. Even Jack stopped being lazy and helped to pick. We had string beans for dinner every night for a month. And string-bean soup for lunch and even string-bean cereal for breakfast in the morning.

"That was a long, long time ago, but I still think of it whenever I have string beans for dinner," said Grandpa.

"Teddy, where are your beans?" asked Grandma.

"Did you throw them on the floor?" asked Nora.

Teddy looked down at his plate. He looked under the table. Then he smiled. "I guess I ate them," he said.

The Wooden Bowl

adapted by DOMENICO VITTORINI

Once upon a time in far-off Italy, there was a little boy whose name was Robertino, who loved his grandfather very much. The little boy and the old man were great friends and spent much time together. Robertino loved to sit at his grandfather's knee and listen, his gray eyes wide open, to the stories that he told him. Grandfather was a wonderful storyteller. And oh, the tales he told! Fairy tales and hero tales and exciting hunting stories, like the one in which Grandfather himself had once caught an eagle. Often Robertino and his grandfather would journey together to the land of make-believe to hunt imaginary lions and tigers. No matter how fantastic the stories or the games they played, the tie between these two was real enough, the only tie that kept the old man attached to his life. Grandfather had come to live with Robertino's parents when Grandmother had died three years before. Robertino's mother was a capable woman who took good care of her husband and her little son, but she did not understand the loneliness of the old man. Sometimes she was very impatient with him, especially these days when his hands trembled and every so often he would drop what he was holding in them.

One night at supper, Grandfather picked up his cup to drink his coffee but his poor old hands shook so that the coffee spilled on the clean white tablecloth, and the cup, falling from his hands, shattered into many pieces on the floor. Robertino's mother was angry and spoke harshly to the old man. Grandfather never said a word in reply but only looked at her with hurt in his eyes. Robertino did not say anything either, but he couldn't eat any more supper, for his heart seemed ready to burst with sadness. Poor and dear grandfather!

After that, grandfather had to eat all by himself at a little table in the kitchen. He did not say anything when he was told about this new arrangement, but there was sadness in his eyes, and sadness in the gentle smile he gave his grandchild.

From that evening on, as soon as Robertino finished his supper, he would ask to be excused and he would run into the kitchen to be with the old man he loved very much. Grandfather would take him on his knee and begin a story, and as the magic words began to weave their spell, the bare little kitchen became a beautiful land where there was no pain and no sadness and where an old man and a little boy could roam happily hand in hand.

As time went on and Grandfather grew older, he became weaker and his hands shook more and more. One night as he sat all alone in the kitchen, his hands trembled so that he dropped his bowl of porridge. The porridge spilled all over the kitchen floor and the bowl broke into many pieces. Robertino's father and mother, followed by the child, left the dining room where they had been eating and hastened to the kitchen. As they reached the door they saw the spilled porridge on the spotless floor.

Robertino was very much upset, not only by the indignation of his parents, but especially by the consternation of his grandfather. The old man was confused and crushed. Robertino's mother spoke more harshly than she had ever done before, scolded, and said the only thing to do was to give the old man a wooden bowl. She could not, she said, have her dishes broken just because he had become so careless. She made a big fuss over cleaning up the floor. Robertino stood silently by as she mopped and polished until it was spotless again, scolding and mumbling resentfully all the while.

Suddenly the child went over to the fireplace where his mother had swept the fragments of the bowl. He picked the pieces out carefully and began to put them together. He worked so earnestly that soon the bowl seemed to be whole. Then he took from the side of the hearth a small piece of wood and began to whittle it, keeping his eyes on the earthen bowl as though it were a model. After a while his parents, curious to see what he was doing, went over to him.

"What are you making, Robertino?" asked his mother fondly. She always spoke kindly to her little son.

"I'm making a wooden bowl for you, to have when you grow old," answered Robertino.

Robertino's mother and father looked at each other. They were too ashamed to meet Robertino's eyes. Then the mother took Grandfather's arm and led him back to the table in the dining room and stood near him and helped him as he ate.

From that time on Grandfather never ate all alone in the kitchen again. He sat in his usual place, next to Robertino, in the dining room.

And Robertino was happy again, oh so happy! His grandfather was loved and cared for, and as Robertino watched his parents he realized that they too were experiencing a new and wonderful happiness — for loving-kindness brings true, lasting happiness.

Poetry Selections

A Grandfather Poem
by WILLIAM J. HARRIS

A grandfather poem
must use words of great dignity.

It cannot
contain words like:
Ubangi
rolling pin
popsicle,

but words like:
Supreme Court
graceful
wise.

The Nice Old Couple
by DOROTHY ALDIS

When walking, they waddle,
    a little bit
Like friendly ducks in the rain;
She holds the umbrella, twirling it,
And he points at things with
    his cane.

He laughs when she says some-
    thing, offers his arm,
As he leads her through the
    dripping weather.
They like it out in the April storm
Being cozy and old together.

How Does It Feel to Be Old?

by NORMA FARBER

Open my album — you'll see the
    years and years and years.
How I looked as I grew:
a baby, a bride, a mother of four.
Then holding a new
granddaughter. There's more
to an old, old woman than what
    appears.
There's all that she's been before.
Before and after, both.
Well, who
am I being right now, exactly?
    The mirror's blurred.
Will you rub it true?
Here's a chamois cloth.

71

The Chinese Checker Players

by RICHARD BRAUTIGAN

When I was six years old
I played Chinese checkers with
   a woman
who was ninety-three
   years old.
She lived by herself
in an apartment down the hall
   from ours.
We played Chinese checkers
every Monday and Thursday
   nights.
While we played she usually talked
about her husband
who had been dead for seventy
   years,
and we drank tea and ate cookies
   and cheated.

Norman Moskowitz

by MEL GLENN

My grandfather's picture sits on
   my desk
While I do my homework.
My father spent money on me.
My grandfather spent time.
As I struggle with trig and other
   responsibilities
I remember how my grandfather
   would
Take me for walks in the park,
Explain how a screwball was
   thrown,
Encourage me to think well
   of myself.
I really don't want to wrestle
   with world history,
The gross national product and
   Nathaniel Hawthorne.
I just want to go to the park with
   you again, Grandpa.

Creative Writing/Activity

Grandma, Grandpa, Who Are You?

This program will give you a good opportunity to develop oral history skills.

Ask the children to interview a grandparent — or any other older person — about his or her childhood. Using a tape recorder will enable the interviewer to record accurately and in many cases will be less inhibiting to the interviewee than a pad and pencil. After the interview children should write in notebooks a summary and outline of the information they gained.

Some people are naturally more talkative than others. Some talk too much and stray away from the point. It is best to have a written set of questions that will start a conversation. These questions should be as open-ended as possible.

Alert the interviewers to the fact that patience must be one of the major strengths of a good interviewer. They may want to pursue a point about the educational curriculum of Grandma's day, while she may want to tell them in great detail about her best friend. If they are patient and listen, they may still be able to find out what they'd like to know.

Children should collectively decide what it is they would like to know about the past and write their own questions, but these sample questions may start them in the direction of learning about Grandpa's or Aunt Gert's childhood.

SCHOOL: Where did you go to school? Can you remember your favorite teacher? What was she or he like? What did you dislike about school? What was your favorite subject? What did you hate about school?

FAMILY: Did you have a big family? What did you eat for breakfast, dinner? What kind of parties did you have?

CLOTHES: Do you remember your clothes? Was there one outfit you loved or hated to wear?

VACATIONS: Did you travel anywhere? How did you get there? Did you stay in a hotel? What was it like?

ENTERTAINMENT: What books did you read? What radio or television shows did you listen to or watch?

WORK: What do/did you do for a living? Have there been changes in your profession since you started work?

NAMES: Where did your name come from? Does it mean anything? Are there traditional names in your family?

DATING AND MARRIAGE: How did you meet your wife or husband? Where did you go and what did you do while dating?

BEHAVIOR: Was there anything your parents wouldn't let you do...or made you do, so that you said to yourself, "When I'm a parent I won't do that?" Did you?

FRIENDS: Did you have a best friend? What did you do together?

HOLIDAYS: Describe your favorite holiday. Did you celebrate birthdays or Christmas in a special way?

FOOD: What is your favorite food? Describe a family meal when you were a child. Do you have a favorite recipe you would like to share?

PETS: Did you have a pet? What was something funny it did?

Treat

Ask children to collect favorite recipes from their grandparents and older friends. Reproduce them in a Grandparent's Cookbook.

Children can bring to the celebration a family recipe for a potluck grandparent's snack.

Grandma Mary's Walnut Delights

YOU NEED: *Dough*

　　1 pint cottage cheese
　　½ pound butter
　　2 cups flour

　　Filling
　　¾ cup walnuts
　　¾ cup brown sugar
　　4 tablespoons melted butter

HOW TO:　Mix butter, cottage cheese, and flour. Chill dough until firm enough to handle. Divide dough in half. Roll on floured surface to ⅛ inch thick. Spread with melted butter, brown sugar, and nuts. Cut into triangles and roll from wide end of triangle to small. Repeat with other half of dough. Bake at 400° for twenty minutes.

Bulletin Board

Collect pictures of children's grandparents. Post them with pictures of the children.

Books about Grandparents and Older People:

Aliki. *The Two of Them.* Il. by author. Greenwillow, 1979. P.
> Grandfather and grandchild rely on each other as each changes and gets older.

Ancona, George. *Growing Older.* Il. with photographs. Dutton, 1978. All ages.
> Adults reminisce about their childhood and discuss their thoughts about getting older.

Berger, Terry. *Special Friends.* Photographs by David Hechtlinger. Messner, 1979. M.
> A photo essay showing a young girl visiting her elderly neighbors.

Blue, Rose. *Grandma Didn't Wave Back.* Il. by Ted Lewin. Watts, 1972. M.
> Grandma begins to act strangely, forgetting important things, and it worries Debbie and her family.

Bosse, Malcolm J. *The 79 Squares.* Crowell, 1979. U.
> Old Mister Beck commands Eric to discover the minute details in his garden.

Branscum, Robbie. *Spud Tackett and the Angel of Doom.* Viking, 1983. M.
> Grandma mediates between Spud and and his cousin Leroy in the hills of Arkansas.

Burch, Robert. *Two That Were Tough.* Il. by Richard Cuffari. Viking, 1976. M.
> Mr. Hilton and his rooster, Wild Wings, wish to retain their independence.

Byars, Betsy. *After the Goat Man.* Il. by Ronald Himler. Viking, 1974. M.
> Harold and Ada search for Figgy's eccentric grandfather.

Caines, Jeannette. *Window Wishing.* Il. by Kevin Brooks. Harper, 1980. P.
> Two children visiting their Grandmother, Mag, find a vivacious woman who loves to window-shop.

Cameron, Eleanor. *A Room Made of Windows.* Il. by Trina Schart Hyman. Little, 1971. M, U.
> Mrs. Rhiannon Moore encourages Julie with her writing.

Carlson, Natalie Savage. *A Grandmother for the Orphelines.* Il. by David White. Harper, 1980. M.
> The French Orphelines search for the perfect grandmother and find a grandfather too.

Cawley, Winifred. *Gran at Coalgate.* Il. by Fermin Rocker. Holt, 1974. M, U.
> Dad disapproves of Gran's household and its modern influences: bobbed hair, short skirts, the moving pictures, and the Charleston.

Cleaver, Vera, and Bill Cleaver. *Queen of Hearts.* Lippincott, 1978. M, U.
> Granny Lincoln is seventy-nine when she has a mild stroke. Wilma is twelve when she comes to stay with her. They have a battle of wills.

Clifford, Eth. *The Rocking Chair Rebellion.* Houghton, 1978. M, U.
> Fourteen-year-old Opie Cross becomes involved in solving the problems of some of the inhabitants in a nursing home.

Cohen, Barbara. *Thank You, Jackie Robinson.* Il. by Richard Cuffari. Lothrop, 1974. M.
> Sam is a Brooklyn Dodger fan. His best friend is a sixty-year-old black man who shares his love.

Colman, Hila. *The Amazing Miss Laura.* Morrow, 1976. M.
> Josie becomes companion to the eccentric widow of a famous painter and learns to relate to her own crusty grandfather.

Corcoran, Barbara. *Hey, That's My Soul You're Stomping On.* Atheneum, 1978. M, U.
> Rachel is resentful that she must stay with her grandparents in a motel, but she becomes involved with them and their elderly neighbors.

Cornish, Sam. *Grandmother's Pictures.* Il. by Jeanne Johns. Bradbury, 1974. M.

Grandma's scrapbook gives a young boy a picture of the past.

Cummings, Betty Sue. *Let a River Be.* Atheneum, 1978. U.

Ella is a spunky seventy-six-year-old conservationist. Reetard is her ally in a fight to save Indian River.

de Paola, Tomie. *Nana Upstairs and Nana Downstairs.* Il. by author. Putnam, 1973. P.

A young boy and his relationship with two grandmas.

————. *Now One Foot, Now the Other.* Il. by author. Putnam, 1981. P.

A little boy helps his grandfather to recover after a stroke.

Distad, Audree. *The Dream Runner.* Harper, 1977. M, U.

Sam decides to go to the mountains and meets a retired teacher who befriends him.

Donnelly, Elfie. *Offbeat Friends.* Trans. from the German by Anthea Bell. Crown, 1982. M.

Mari, an Austrian school girl, befriends a seventy-eight-year-old "crazy" woman.

Donovan, John. *Remove Protective Coating a Little at a Time.* Harper, 1973. U.

Harry meets Amelia, a crusty, outspoken old woman in sneakers.

Fair, Sylvia. *The Bedspread.* Il. by author. Morrow, 1982. All ages.

Two "old, old" sisters remember different things about their childhoods while embroidering a bedspread.

Farber, Norma. *How Does It Feel To Be Old?* Il. by Trinia Schart Hyman. Dutton, 1979. All ages.

A sensitive picture essay tells the pros and cons of old age.

Fenton, Edward. *Duffy's Rocks.* Dutton, 1974. U.

Timothy's grandmother tries to protect him from the truth about his father.

————. *The Refugee Summer.* Delacorte, 1982. M, U.

Five children of different nationalities meet an aging, starving princess in Greece in 1922.

Forrai, Maria S. *A Look at Old Age.* Il. with photographs. Text by Rebecca Anders. Lerner, 1976. M.

A photographic survey of aging in America presented for young children.

Fox, Paula. *One-Eyed.* Bradbury, 1984. U.

Ned does chores for Mr. Siully and learns about old age and death.

Gauch, Patricia Lee. *Grandpa and Me.* Il. by Symeon Shimin. Coward, 1972. P.

Warm story of a boy and his grandfather sharing activities at the beach.

Godden, Rumer. *Mr. McFadden's Hallowe'en.* Viking, 1975. M.

Selina, "a solid child," and Haggis, her pony, reform a recluse.

Goffstein, M. B. *Fish For Supper.* Il. by author. Dial, 1976. All ages.

The story of Grandmother's day as she gets up and goes fishing in her rowboat.

————. *My Noah's Ark.* Il. by author. Harper, 1978. All ages.

A ninety-year-old woman looks back over her life through a toy her father made for her.

Goldman, Susan. *Grandma Is Somebody Special.* Il. by author. Whitman, 1976. P.

A child and her grandma share time together.

Gomi, Taro. *Coco Can't Wait.* Il. by author. Morrow, 1984. P.

Coco rides her scooter, Grandma her motorcycle, as they each try to visit the other.

Gonzalez, Gloria. *The Glad Man.* Knopf, 1975. M.

Melissa and her brother Troy bring trouble to an old man living in a dilapidated bus.

Grandparents' Houses: Poems about Grandparents. Selected by Corrine Streich. Il. by Lillian Hoban. Greenwillow, 1984. U.

A perfect combination of paintings and poems.

Greenfield, Eloise. *Grandmama's Joy.* Il. by Carole Byard. Collins, 1980. P.

A little girl reminds her unhappy grandmama of past joys.

Hentoff, Nat. *Does This School Have Capital Punishment?* Delacorte, 1981. U.
Sam interviews an elderly, zany trumpeteer for a school assignment.

Herman, Charlotte. *Our Snowman Had Olive Eyes.* Dutton, 1977. M, U.
Sheila shares a room with her grandmother, Bubbie.

Hest, Amy. *The Crack-of-Dawn Walkers.* Il. by Amy Schwartz. Macmillan, 1984. P.
It is a special treat for Sadie to walk through the fresh snow with her grandfather.

Hoover, H. M. *The Shepherd Moon.* Viking, 1984. U.
This science fiction novel shows Merry and her grandfather confronted by a visitor from a man-made moon.

Hurmence, Belinda. *Tough Tiffany.* Doubleday, 1980. M.
Granny is feisty and interesting as eleven-year-old Tiffany copes with her family's foibles.

Irwin, Hadley. *What about Grandma?* McElderry, 1982. U.
Sixteen-year-old Rhys and her mother find that Grandmother Wyn has her own ideas about managing her life.

Jansson, Tove. *The Summer Book.* Transl. from the Swedish by Thomas Teal. Pantheon, 1975. U.
Daily life with Sophia and her grandmother on an island off the coast of Sweden.

Johnston, Norma. *If You Love Me, Let Me Go.* Atheneum, 1978. U.
In a sequel to *The Swallow's Song* (Atheneum, 1978), sixteen-year-old Allison Standish must learn to cope with a senile grandmother.

Jones, Weyman. *Edge of Two Worlds.* Il. by J. C. Kocsis. Dial, 1968. U.
The only survivor of a Comanche massacre meets a Cherokee Indian in search of the origins of his people.

Kennedy, Richard. *Come Again in the Spring.* Il. by Marcia Sewall. Harper, 1976. M.
Old Hark tricks Death into giving him a longer life.

Kerr, M. E. *Gentlehands.* Harper, 1978. U.
Could Buddy's cultured, gentle grandfather really have run a Nazi concentration camp during World War II?

Kesselman, Wendy. *Emma.* Il. by Barbara Cooney. Doubleday, 1980. All ages.
A seventy-year-old woman discovers that painting pictures enlivens her lonely life.

Kirk, Barbara. *Grandpa, Me and Our House in the Tree.* Photographs by author. Macmillan, 1978. P.
Nico's grandfather has been sick. Can the two have the same fun as they have had in the past?

Klein, Leonore. *Old, Older, Oldest.* Il. by Leonard Kessler. Hastings, 1983. P.
Uses comparative ages in animals and humans to show young children the concept of aging.

Knotts, Howard. *Great-Grandfather, the Baby, and Me.* Il. by author. Atheneum, 1978. P.
A boy is helped by his great-grandfather to accept the arrival of a new baby sister.

Kojima, Naomi. *The Flying Grandmother.* Il. by author. Crowell, 1981. All ages.
A wordless picture book shows a little girl and her grandmother wearing wings and flying through adventures.

Konigsburg, E. L. "At the Home" in *Throwing Shadows.* Atheneum, 1979. M.
Phillip brings his tape recorder to an old folk's home and gets involved with the residents.

Lasky, Kathryn. *The Night Journey.* Il. by Trina Schart Hyman. Warne, 1981. M.
Rachel's great-grandmother, Nana Sashie, tells about her family's escape from Czarist Russia.

LeShan, Eda. *Grandparents: A Special Kind of Love.* Il. by Tricia Taggart. MacMillan, 1984. M.
A non-fiction book about grandparents.

Lobel, Arnold. *Uncle Elephant.* Il. by author. Harper, 1981. P.
"Why do you have so many wrinkles?" "Because I am old."

Lowry, Lois. *Anastasia Again!* Houghton, 1981. M.

A fourth-grade girl moves to the suburbs and makes friends with an older neighbor.

Lundgren, Max. *Matt's Grandfather.* Transl. from the Swedish by Ann Pyk. Il. by Fibben Hald. Putnam, 1972. P.

Matt visits his eighty-five-year-old grandfather in a nursing home.

MacLachlan, Patricia. *Through Grandpa's Eyes.* Il. by Deborah Ray. Harper, 1980. P.

A little boy learns to "see" through Grandpa's blind eyes.

Magorian, Michelle. *Good Night, Mr. Tom.* Harper, 1982. U.

A World War II evacuee learns about love when he goes to stay with a cantankerous older man.

Marzollo, Jean. *Halfway Down Paddy Lane.* Dial, 1981. M, U.

Kate slips through time and meets her great-grandfather as a young boy.

Mathis, Sharon Bell. *The Hundred Penny Box.* Il. by Leo and Diane Dillon. Viking, 1975. M, U.

Great-great-aunt Dew is 100 years old and a special person to Michael, who tries to protect her from knowing adults.

Miles, Miska. *Annie and the Old One.* Il. by Peter Parnall. Atlantic/Little, 1971. M.

A Navajo girl prepares for her grandmother's death.

Myers, Walter Dean. *Won't Know Till I Get There.* Viking, 1982. M.

Steve's family adopts a thirteen-year-old foster child and both boys end up working in an old age home.

Paulsen, Gary. *Tracker.* Bradbury, 1984. U.

John's grandfather is dying and John must go deer hunting alone this year.

Rylant, Cynthia. *Miss Maggie.* Il. by Thomas di Grazia. Dutton, 1983. All ages.

Nat befriends a frightening old woman.

Rylant, Cynthia. *When I Was Young in the Mountains.* Il. by Diane Goode. Dutton, 1982. All ages.

Lovely pictures illustrate a simple text describing meals, work, and play with grandmother and grandfather.

Schellie, Don. *Kidnapping Mr. Tubbs.* Four Winds, 1978. U.

Two teen-agers kidnap a nearly-100-year-old man from a nursing home and learn that "you can't go home again."

Shanks, Ann Zane. *Old Is What You Get: Dialogues on Aging by the Old and the Young.* Photographs by author. Viking, 1976. M, U.

Interviews with elderly people showing the diversity of attitudes toward aging.

Skolsky, Mindy. "Something Lovely" in *The Whistling Teakettle and Other Stories about Hannah.* Il. by Karen Ann Weinhaus. Harper, 1977. M.

Hannah's grandmother tells about her childhood in a Polish shtetl.

Skorpen, Liesel Moak. *Mandy's Grandmother.* Il. by Martha Alexander. Dial, 1975. P.

Mandy's grandmother comes to visit and they learn to enjoy each other.

Smith, Robert Kimmel. *The War with Grandpa.* Il. by Richard Lauter. Delacorte, 1984. M.

Peter is upset when his grandpa moves into his room and tries to get it back.

Sobol, Harriet Langsam. *Grandpa, a Young Man Grown Old.* Photographs by Patricia Agre. Coward, 1980. U.

A dialogue between a seventeen-year-old girl and her seventy-eight-year-old grandfather.

Spinelli, Jerry. *Who Put That Hair in My Toothbrush?* Little, 1984. M.

Megin makes an 89-year-old resident of a nursing home her honorary grandmother.

Stevens, Carla. *Anna, Grandpa, and the Big Storm.* Il. by Margot Tomes. Clarion, 1982. P.

A short story about a little girl and her grandfather being rescued from the elevated train in New York City during the blizzard of 1888.

Stevenson, James. *Could Be Worse!* Il. by author. Greenwillow, 1977. All ages.

Grandfather breaks his quiet routine to tell about a wild adventure.

Strete, Craig Kee. *When Grandfather Journeys into Winter.* Il. by Hal Frenck. Greenwillow, 1979. P.

Grandfather Tayhua has given his life to win a horse for his grandson, Little Thunder.

Taylor, Theodore. *The Cay.* Doubleday, 1969. M.

Philip, a young white boy, blinded in a shipwreck, is aided on a tropical island by Timothy, an elderly black man.

Thomas, Ianthe. *Hi, Mrs. Mallory!* Il. by Ann Toulmin-Rothe. Harper, 1979. P.

The friendship between a young black girl and an older white woman is described.

Tolan, Stephanie S. *Grandpa — and Me.* Scribner, 1978. U.

Kerry's grandpa has begun to change, and now he says and does strange things.

Turner, Ann. *A Hunter Comes Home.* Crown, 1980. U.

Fifteen-year-old Jonas returns from school to his Eskimo village and struggles to make peace with his grandfather.

Wersba, Barbara. *The Dream Watcher.* Atheneum, 1968. U.

Albert meets Mrs. Woodfin, who doesn't think he is strange at all.

Wilkinson, Brenda Scott. *Ludell and Willie.* Harper, 1977. U.

In this sequel to *Ludell* (Harper, 1975), Ludell worries about her grandmother, "Mama," and resents having to leave her friends to live with her mother after Mama's death.

Williams, Barbara. *Albert's Toothache.* Il. by Kay Chorao. Dutton, 1974. P.

Only Grandmother Turtle has time to listen and understand about Albert's "toothache."

———. *Kevin's Grandma.* Il. by Kay Chorao. Dutton, 1975. P.

A little boy describes the differences between his and his friend's grandma.

Williams, Jay. *The Magic Grandfather.* Il. by Gail Owens. Four Winds, 1979. M.

Sam's grandfather has a very special talent... for sorcery.

Wittman, Sally. *A Special Trade.* Il. by Karen Gundersheimer. Harper, 1978. P.

Bartholomew pushes Nelly in her carriage when she is small. When Nelly grows up, she pushes an elderly Bartholomew.

Wolf, Janet. *The Best Present Is Me.* Il. by author. Harper, 1984. P.

A little girl visits her grandparents and brings an outline drawing of herself as a present.

Yep, Lawrence. *Child of the Owl.* Harper, 1977. U.

Casey comes to live with her Grandmother Paw-Paw in San Francisco's Chinatown.

Zolotow, Charlotte. *My Grandson Lew.* Il. by William Pène Dubois. Harper, 1974. All ages.

Lewis and his mother share memories of Grandpa.

Oral History and Geneology

Caney, Steven. *Steven Caney's Kid's America.* Il. with photographs and drawings. Workman, 1978. pp. 26-37. M.

Gilfond, Henry. *Geneology: How to Find Your Roots.* Watts, 1978. M.

Hazen, Barbara Shook. *Last, First, Middle, and Nick: All about Names.* Il. by Sam Weissman. Prentice, 1979. M.

Henriod, Lorraine. *Ancestor Hunting.* Il. by Janet Potter D'Amato. Messner, 1979. M.

Hilton, Suzanne. *Who Do You Think You Are? Digging for Your Family Roots.* Westminster, 1976. M, U.

Scheier, Michael, and Julie Frankel. *Digging For My Roots.* Scholastic, 1977. M.

Showers, Paul. *Me and My Family Tree.* Crowell, 1978. P.

Weitzman, David. *My Backyard History Book.* Il. by James Robertson. Little, 1975. M.

Gone Fishin'

The art of fishing is sitting still for a long time until you don't catch anything.

This program can be used anytime throughout the year, but it might be particularly appropriate on three dates:

April first, our April Fool's Day, is celebrated as Poissons d'Avril (April fish) in France. The origin of the holiday goes back to the sixteenth century when Pope Gregory changed the calendar, making the beginning of the year January first instead of April first. Since news traveled slowly in those days, some people didn't know of the calendar change until months later. They were teased and called April Fish — or fools. Traditionally on this day, French children try to fasten paper fish onto unsuspecting friends and adults and are given chocolate fish as a treat.

May fifth is celebrated as Children's Day or Kodomo-no-Hi in Japan. Once, this was only celebrated as a boy's festival (Tonge-no Sekku) but now it has been expanded to include both sexes. Each family hangs a fish-shaped cloth or paper banner on a pole outside for each male child in the family. The fish represents the hardy carp, known for its bravery and strength. These fish swim upstream against rushing currents. The banners are symbols for these attributes.

The opening of fishing season in your area might also make an excellent time to introduce this program on fish. Each state or region will have its own season, so check with the Fish and Wildlife Department in your area.

Fish and fishing are featured in picture books and some novels, and nonfiction books for children and adults and are quite popular.

Although I personally don't think you should serve fish as a treat when you are reading about them, if you are able to get past the "fish are my friends" (à la Barbara Cohen's *The Carp in the Bathtub*) attitude there are many fish recipes you can make for your group. If you are friends with an avid fisherman, he or she might enjoy sharing thoughts on fishing and include a demonstration of fly-tying or even fish cleaning.

Prose Selections

Yankel Schlimazel is a fool. He can't seem to make a living. In this story he becomes a bit smarter.

Yankel the Fool

by SHAN ELLENTUCK

"If you can't work for anyone else—work for yourself," the old woman told him. And she gave him the little bit of money she had saved for her funeral, to set him up in business. "Buy fish at the river for two kopeks apiece," she advised him, "and sell them in the market place for three. What you don't sell we can eat!"

With the coins in the toe of his boot, Yankel went down to the river's edge, where the fishermen were drawing in their nets. There was one man there as fat as a wagon horse. "In a lean year a fat man is a good sign!" Yankel said, and to this man he went to do business.

"Excuse me, uncle," he said politely, just to start the conversation. "Are you in the fish business?"

The fisherman was a big joker. "No, my boy," he said, "I'm trying to catch bears."

Yankel's mouth dropped open. "Bears?" he cried. "What kind of bears?"

"Black bears, brown bears," said the man, "and maybe, if I have a bit of luck—maybe polar bears."

"I never heard of such a thing! Wait till I tell my grandmother. She'll never believe it!"

"Numskull!" laughed the man. "Idiot! Fool! Rattlebrain! Do you believe everything that comes out of anybody's mouth? Can't you see for yourself that I'm a fisherman?"

Yankel sat down on a rock and began to weep out loud. "It's true!" he sobbed, "I believe everything. I'm the biggest dolt in the world."

The fat fisherman looked slyly at Yankel. "I know a sure way to cure a fool," he said. "Why should you suffer? Do what I tell you and I promise, my boy, you'll be smarter in five minutes."

"Anything, uncle!" Yankel agreed joyfully. "Anything you say!"

83

"You know," said the man, "that fish is considered brain food. And what part of the fish is the best for this business? Why the head, of course! As a special favor I will sell you a fish head for only three kopeks." And with that he pulled a plump herring from his net and whacked off its head with one blow of his knife. "Here you are. Pay and eat — and a good appetite to you!"

You shouldn't think about what happened next. A raw fish head is no pleasure — not even for a hungry boy — but Yankel forced it down in two gulps.

"Do you feel anything?" asked the fisherman.

"Not in my head," said Yankel.

"Then lie down on the grass for a while. Your brain will begin to work by itself," the man said, and he went back to pulling on the net.

Yankel lay on the ground and stared up at the sky. Sure enough, his brain started working, and this is what was on his mind. One whole fish costs two kopeks. The fish head cost him three kopeks. For two kopeks he could have had a fish for the soup pot, a fish head for the brain, and a kopek left over. He jumped up and let out a yell. "You thief," he shouted. "You cheat! You fooled me!"

"You see," laughed the fisherman, "it works like a charm! Tell the truth — aren't you smarter already?"

The Mufferaw Catfish

by BERNARD BEDORE

Joe Mufferaw (Joseph Montferrand) was a lumberjack who lived in the Ottawa Valley during the last century; he became a legendary hero, even in his time, because of his great strength and prowess. This is one of the tall tales told about him.

I mind they used to tell about the time Joe Mufferaw was sitting on the river bank one day up near the mouth of the Bonnechere River. His Indian cook, Charlie Six-Hands, was fishing but had caught only a couple of rock bass and some sunfish.

Joe decided to fish so he hiked up to his camp at Snow Boom, which was about five miles away, and in a few minutes was back with a steel cable. He had a cant hook in his belt so he took the hook off this and knotted the cable on it. He had brought a hind-quarter of beef back with him so he baited his line with that and threw it about half a mile out in Chats Lake.

Joe then sat back and lit his pipe filled with shag tobacco. His pipe was made out of the top of a silo with a hollow young pine for the stem.

The smoke was so dense that soon the nearest forest ranger investigated for fire. When he saw Joe he sat down for a chat.

About an hour or so after, just as the ranger was about to leave, Joe's line twanged taut and he grabbed it just as it snapped from the rock he had tied it to.

Joe was big. Yes, siree. But that fish dragged him across the shore, and his heels ploughed a furrow in the sand until he hit a boom of logs snubbed to the bank. Joe hitched his leg over the boom chain and hung on but the fish took him, boom and all, and dragged him all over Chats Lake for two days and three nights.

Just before daylight of the third night some friends of Joe built a log fire on the shore of the lake.

The catfish saw the fire and thought it was the rising sun. He headed back for it full steam with his back fin out of the water like an ocean going sailboat, and old Joe trailing right behind him.

He hit land so hard he flipped Joe over his head, and when Joe landed he kind of snapped the whip with the steel cable and flipped the catfish inland.

Well sir, that fish hit hard and skidded deep until he dug a hole through the clay right up to where he hit the rock, and he bounced and landed a half a mile or more back from the river in a field. The furrow he dug is now the mouth of Dochart Creek.

I figured that was the biggest fish ever caught around here. Joe sold the hide to the British Navy to make whaleboats and the whiskers went for masts for ships sailing out of Nova Scotia.

The backbone was used to make a fence around a prison — that is, all except one section, and Joe kept that for a pocket comb.

The fins were sold for sails and the tail was used years later to make a new floor in an Air Force hangar at Uplands Airport in Ottawa.

The eyeballs were encased in glass, and Joe sold them to a maharajah, who used them as domes for the top of his new palace.

A local farmer got the ribs as rafters for a new barn, and Joe threw the teeth up in around Mount St. Patrick. The people there wakened one morning to find a new range of small hills.

He gave the flesh and the head to an Indian tribe up on Golden Lake and they made fishhead soup enough to last seven and one-half weeks. They ate off the carcass all winter and made a cave out of the skull.

Joe had the entrails buried by ten farmers and it took them five days to do the job. The next year the hay grew so high they had to cut it with crosscut saws and burn it for fuel. The dandelions were as big as sunflowers and clover was like basswood.

"Yes, siree, that was a big one."

Poetry Selections

A Fishy Square Dance

by EVE MERRIAM

Tuna turn,
flounder round,
cuttlefish up,
halibut hold;

clam and salmon
trout about,
terrapin,
shrimp dip in;

forward swordfish,
mackerel back,
dace to the left,
ide to the right;

gallop scallop,
mussel perch,
grunnion run,
bass on down;

finnan haddie
skate and fluke,
eel and sole,
shad and roe.

Ode to a Goldfish

by GYLES BRANDRETH

O
Wet
Pet!

The Hen and the Carp

by IAN SERRAILLIER

Once, in a roostery,
there lived a speckled hen, and
    whenever she laid an egg
    this hen
    ecstatically cried:
"O progeny miraculous, particular
    spectaculous,
    what a wonderful hen am I!"

    Down in a pond nearby
perchance a gross and broody
    carp
was basking, but her ears were
    sharp—
    she heard Dame Cackle cry:
"O progeny miraculous, particular
    spectaculous,
    what a wonderful hen am I!"

    "Ah, Cackle," bubbled she,
"for your single egg, O silly one,
I lay at least a million:
    suppose for each I cried:
'O progeny miraculous, particular
    spectaculous!'
    what a hullaballoo there'd be!"

A City Pet

by FRANK ASCH

Goldfish by the window,
Swimming in the moonglow,
If I lived in the jungle,
You'd be an elephant.

Goldfish by the window,
Swimming in the moonglow,
If I lived in the country,
You'd be a horse.

Goldfish by the window,
Swimming in the moonglow,
Maybe when we move to a bigger
    place,
You'll be a dog.

Fish Story

by RICHARD ARMOUR

Count this among my heartfelt
    wishes:
To hear a fish tale told by fishes
And stand among the fish who
    doubt
The honor of a fellow trout,
And watch the bulging of their
    eyes
To hear of imitation flies
And worms with rather droopy
    looks
Stuck through with hateful, horrid
    hooks,
And fishermen they fled all day
    from
(As big as this) and got away from.

Seven Fat Fishermen

ANON

Seven fat fishermen,
Sitting side by side,
Fished from a bridge,
By the banks of the Clyde.

The first caught a tiddler,
The second caught a crab,
The third caught a winkle,
The fourth caught a dab.

The fifth caught a tadpole,
The sixth caught an eel,
But the seventh, he caught
An old cartwheel.

My Fishes

by MARCHETTE CHUTE

My goldfish swim like bits of light,
Silver and red and gold and white.
They flick their tails for joy, and
    then
They swim around the bowl again.

Exhibit

Exhibit fishing equipment such as rods, lines, hooks, leaders, sinkers, floats, reels, creels, scalers, knives, lures, bait buckets, tackle box, and gaffers.

Do you have access to a portable aquarium?

Treats

Make chocolate fish cookies. Use your favorite rolled-cookie recipe or try this one using a cake mix.

Chocolate Fish Cookies

YOU NEED: 1/3 cup butter or margarine
½ cup other shortening, such as Crisco
1 egg
½ teaspoon vanilla
1 package (18.5 oz.) layer-cake mix, chocolate or vanilla
raisins or nuts for eyes
fish cookie cutter (instructions for making given below)

HOW TO: Mix butter, shortening, egg, and vanilla together. Add cake mix, blending in half the box at a time. Divide dough into four portions. Shape into balls and roll out on floured board to thickness of one-eighth inch. Cut with fish cookie cutter. Bake at 375° on ungreased pan for 6-8 minutes. Cool and frost with Marie's Chocolate Icing (p.90). Yield: 6-8 dozen cookies.

Fish Cookie Cutter

Design your own cardboard cookie cutter in the shape of a fish. Place the cardboard shape gently on the rolled-out dough and cut around the shape with a sharp knife dipped in flour.

Marie's Chocolate Icing

YOU NEED: 1 tablespoon butter
1 square (1 oz.) unsweetened chocolate
1½ tablespoons warm water
1 cup confectioner's sugar (sifted)

HOW TO: Melt butter and chocolate in double boiler. Remove from heat. Blend in hot water. Beat in confectioner's sugar. Spread on cookies by dropping icing onto center of cookie and spreading outward with a butter knife. Add raisins or nuts for eyes.

Fish Crackers

Pepperidge Farm produces tiny fish-shaped crackers, called Goldfish, in various flavors. Find them in the cookie and cracker section of the grocery store.

Bulletin Board

How Many Fish Can You Catch?

Use this quiz as a mix and match bulletin board. From *Riddles, Riddles, Riddles,* by Joseph Leeming

1. What is a struggling fish?
2. What is a cheating fish given to sharp practices?
3. What is a fish of precious metal?
4. What fish is man's best friend?
5. What fish is a royal fish?
6. What fish is a heavenly fish?
7. What fish is in the band?
8. What fish is an animal that is almost extinct?
9. What fish is an ugly old witch?
10. What fish is a household pet?
11. What fish do you find in a birdcage?
12. What fish is good with hot biscuits?
13. What fish is a sharp-pointed weapon that soldiers used in Robin Hood's time?
14. What fish is a member of a barbershop quartet?

15. What fish is a deep guttural sound?
16. What fish is used on certain boats?
17. What fish is very useful in hot weather?
18. What fish is used by a fencer?
19. What fish is seen at night?
20. What poor fish is always ailing?
21. What fish makes a good sandwich?
22. What fish is a very evil fish?
23. What fish is a very dark color?
24. What fish floats through the air?
25. What fish is a favorite with dairy farmers?
26. What fish is a rosy biter?
27. What fish represents a process used in refining metals?
28. What fish represents three letters used by stores delivering goods you buy?
29. What is a gloomy, down-in-the-mouth fish?
30. What fish warms the earth?

a. Angelfish
b. Balloon fish
c. Bass
d. Blackfish
e. Bluefish
f. Buffalo fish
g. Butterfish
h. Catfish
i. Cod (C.O.D.)
j. Cowfish
k. Devilfish
l. Dogfish
m. Drumfish
n. Fantail
o. Flounder
p. Goldfish
q. Grunt
r. Hagfish
s. Jellyfish
t. Kingfish
u. Perch
v. Pike
w. Red Snapper
x. Sailfish
y. Shark
z. Smelt
aa. Starfish
bb. Sunfish
cc. Swordfish
dd. Weakfish

ANSWERS:

1. o
2. y
3. p
4. l
5. t
6. a
7. m
8. f
9. r
10. h
11. u
12. g
13. v
14. c
15. q
16. x
17. n
18. cc
19. aa
20. dd
21. s
22. k
23. d
24. b
25. j
26. w
27. z
28. i
29. e
30. bb

Droodles

Roger Price invented Droodles in 1953, and both children and adults have enjoyed them ever since. Here are three of my favorites:

FISH FISHING

A number of Troublemakers have claimed this Droodle is farfetched. "How come no bait on the hook?" they say. Or "How could a fish tie a knot in a string?" Well, this fish isn't using bait because he's smart enough to realize that if he did he might catch himself. He's only interested in fishing—not catching. And if you look closely you'll see that the knot in the string was tied by the fish's grandmother as it is a *granny knot*. (I love to put in humorous lines like that last one so you can face the future with a smile. If you're not facing the future with a smile it shows you are too sophisticated. You should lead a simpler life and wear looser shoes.)

RICH SARDINE WITH PRIVATE CAN

The title of this section of the book was taken from this Droodle not because it is the most subtle, the easiest to draw or even the most typical. I chose it because it is the most *thought provoking*. If you are sensitive you will worry about it for at least twenty mintues because it poses certain questions: Why does this particular sardine have a private can? Did he strike oil in a Codfish? Did he win a jackpot prize on a television program such as "Name That Tuna"? And if he is so rich why has he no friends? Couldn't he at least hire a valet to squeeze a lemon over him several times a day? He must be depressed and lonely. Frankly, I think this sardine should join a Friendship Club.

FISH COMMITTING SUICIDE

This fish isn't really committing suicide. It's a publicity shot of a starlet in a new underwater teevee series "Subnanza" which eliminates people altogether. It stars Flipper and Sandra Crab in an honest, fishy heartwarming tale. Flipper, who is really in love with Sandra, has to get engaged to an ugly lady octopus who holds the mortgage on her shell. Naturally Miss Crab is heartbroken until her father (played by Roddy McLobster) saves the day by proving that the Octopus already has a husband (played by Squid Caesar). The finale is a hilarious scene in a Prawn Shop with Octopus trying to hock her eight engagement rings. A great program but don't tune it in unless you're sure your set doesn't leak.

DO-IT-YOURSELF DROODLE

Anyone can draw a Droodle. Why not draw these on your chalk board, or copy them and post them on your bulletin board? Ask your group to guess what the pictures represent, and then read them Roger Price's captions. You might also have a "do-it-yourself Droodle" activity. Ask your children to try creating their own Droodles in blank squares, and writing captions to accompany them. Post these creative Droodles for everyone to enjoy.

Activities

A good game for children is "Fishing for a Book." Using a fishing pole and string with a magnet for bait, fish for paper fish that have paper clips on their heads. Fish might have titles of fish books printed on them, or jokes and riddles about fish, or poems or facts about fish. Below are some examples to print on fish or use on a bulletin board.

Tongue Twisters

Frances Fowler's father fried five floundering flounder for Frances Fowler's father's father.

For fine fresh fish phone Phil. (Alvin Schwartz)

Sally's selfish selling shellfish
So Sally's shellfish seldom sell.

You can have—
fried fresh fish
Fish fried fresh
Fresh fish fried
Or, fish fresh fried. (Janet Rogers)

Jokes and Riddles

What kind of fish is good on toast?
  Jelly-fish.

What is the difference between a fisherman and a bad student?
  One baits his hook. The other hates his book.

How did Jonah feel when the big fish swallowed him?
  Down in the mouth.

Shopper: I don't like the way that codfish looks.
Storekeeper: If you want looks, go buy a goldfish.

Why should a fisherman always be wealthy?
  Because all his business is net profit.

What fish travels great distances?
  A goldfish. It travels around the globe.

What kind of fish makes a good piano tuner?
  A tuna fish.

What part of the fish is like the end of a book?
  The finis.

Why should fish be well educated?
  Because they travel in schools.

What has eight legs, lives at the bottom of the ocean, and says meow?
  An octapussy.

What do you call the king of Russian sardines?
  The czardine.

What does a deaf fish need?
  A herring aid.

Fish Facts

A flying hatchetfish can fly as far as ten feet.

A whale shark is the largest fish and can weigh up to fifteen tons.

The pygmy goby is the smallest fish, less than one-half inch long.

Ichthyologists are scientists who study fish.

Fish have no eyelids.

A female cod may lay nine million eggs during one spawning season.

In China, fish is a lucky sign. If you eat fish on New Year's Eve and leave the head and tail on the plate till New Year's Day, you will be wealthy and happy all year.

Crafts

GIANT FISH

Make a giant fish to fly from the ceiling of the classroom or library.

YOU NEED: brown wrapping paper
newspaper
poster paints
stapler
string

HOW TO: Draw a fish outline on wrapping paper, the bigger the better (three feet by two feet). Cut out two identical fish. Decorate fish with poster paint. Staple fish together leaving a wide opening to stuff with crumpled newspaper. Close opening with staples.

USE: Use string to hang fish from ceiling to create the illusion of fish swimming overhead.

A PAPER FISH

This fish can be used for a Poissons d'Avril celebration.

YOU NEED: tissue paper
scissors
glue
scotch tape

HOW TO: Let the children design their own fish and cut them free-hand from tissue paper. Explain that tissue paper must be handled with care but that it is light and will usually cling to clothes without falling off, or use scotch tape to stick the fish to people's backs.

Let the children try to stick their fish on each other, teachers, and administrators without their knowledge. (Be sure to advise your colleagues about this celebration beforehand.)

Games

Go Fish

This is one of the first card games children learn. If you have forgotten how to play, the children will probably remind you. Older children might like to learn to play in case they spend a day with a young child.

YOU NEED: a deck of cards
three to six players

OBJECT: To acquire the most sets of four cards.

HOW TO: Deal out five cards to each player. The remaining cards are laid face down in a pile.

Players arrange their cards in a fan. The first player (to the left of the dealer) asks each player in turn for a card's number. E.g., Hilary, do you have any fours? Players must give up their cards. If Hilary does not have a four, she says "Go Fish." The player then takes the first card from the pile. If the card is a four, the player may keep it. If not, it is the next player's turn. Player continues to ask for cards as long as he/she is successful. As soon as any player has all four cards of a suit, the player lays them down.

HINT: This can also be played with two decks of cards.

SARDINES

YOU NEED: a group of players

a house or building with lots of hiding places

HOW TO: All the players gather in one room. One player is IT and leaves the room and finds a hiding place. The remaining players give IT time to find the perfect place to hide. Count to fifty. Players disperse. As each player finds the hiding place, he or she quietly joins IT. Finally all the players are crammed, like sardines, into the secret hiding place. The last one to find the hiding place is the loser, and must be the next IT.

FISHING RACE

YOU NEED: drinking straws for each player

two fish cut out of paper

HOW TO: Divide players into two teams. The teams line up. The first person in line fastens the fish onto the straw by inhaling and passes it to the second player by exhaling as that player inhales. The fish are passed down the line and back. The first team to complete the pass wins. If a fish falls, the player who dropped it picks it up by inhaling.

Sources

Catalogue

Whale Gifts
Center for Environmental Education
624 9th Street N.W.
Washington, D.C. 20001

Jonah doll that turns into a fish

Jodi Bauernschmidt
P.O. Box 431
Hartford, Vermont 05047
or
Pierre Whimsicality
RD2 East Berry
Websterville Road
Berry, Vermont 05461

Three fish dolls that fit inside each other

Freemountain Toys, Inc.
The Vegimals
Bristol, Vermont 05443

Cloth or paper carp banners

Available seasonally (spring) from
Oriental import stores.

Satin fish that fit inside each other and satin sandwich

Bev Sokol
16825 S. Chapin
Lake Oswego, Oregon 97034

Fisherman and his wife finger puppets

Dorothy Tharp
213 S. 31st Avenue
Hattiesburg, Mississippi 39401

Books about Fish and Fishing:

Annixter, Paul. "Flounder, Flounder in the Sea" in *Full Forty Fathoms*. Phyllis R. Fenner, comp. Il. by Michael Eagle. Morrow, 1975. M, U.
Story about sunken treasure told from the side of the fish. Excellent read-aloud book.

Arnosky, Jim. *Freshwater Fish and Fishing*. Il. by author. Four Winds, 1982. M,U.
A short, attractive introduction to fishing.

Aronin, Ben. *The Secret of the Sabbath Fish*. Il. by Shay Rieger. Jewish Publication Soc., 1978. M.
The story of how gefilte fish was invented. Based on a Jewish folk tale.

Asch, Frank. *Just like Daddy*. Il. by author. Prentice, 1981. P.
A young bear imitates his daddy and ... his mommy on a fishing trip.

Bahrang, Samuel. *The Little Black Fish*. Il. by Farsheed Meskali. Carolrhoda, 1971. P.
Attractive woodcuts help tell the story of a fish that is swallowed by a pelican.

Beard, Henry, and Roy Mckie. *Fishing: An Angler's Dictionary*. Workman, 1983. M,U.
Funny definitions for situations involving fish and fishermen. E.g.: "Fishing trip: 'Journey undertaken by one or more anglers to a place where no one can remember when it has rained so much.' "

Benchley, Nathanial. *Kilroy and the Gull*. Il. by John Schoenherr. Harper. 1977. M.
A captured whale is befriended by Morris the seagull. OK, so Kilroy is not a fish, but it's a funny book.

Bulla, Clyde Robert. *Jonah and the Great Fish*. Il. by Helga Aichinger. Crowell, 1970. All ages.
Expressionistic graphics in an easy-to-read text tell the story of Jonah.

Cohen, Barbara. *The Carp in the Bathtub*. Il. by Joan Halpern. Lothrop, 1972. M.
Wonderful read-aloud story of two children who make friends with their mother's carp, which is destined to become gefilte fish.

Cole, Joanna. *A Fish Hatches*. Photographs by Jerome Wexler. Morrow, 1978. M.
Excellent photographs show the development of a trout embryo to full-grown fish.

Domanska, Janina. *If All the Seas Were One Sea*. Il. by author. Macmillan, 1971. All ages.
Folk rhyme illustrated with etchings.

Elkin, Benjamin. *Six Foolish Fisherman*. Il. by Katherine Evans. Children's, 1957. P.
The fishermen forget to count themselves in this tale based on folklore.

Gag, Wanda. "Doctor Know-it-all" in *Tales from Grimm*. Il. by author. Coward, 1936. All ages.
A peasant called Fish wins a fortune.

Gelman, Rita Golden, and Warner Friedman. *Uncle Hugh: A Fishing Story*. Il. by Eros Keith. Harcourt, 1978. M.
Tom catches "the biggest trout in the world." (Also in *Cricket*, September 1980.)

George, Jean Craighead. *Hook a Fish, Catch a Mountain*. Dutton, 1975. M,U.
Spinner and her cousin backpack into the Grand Tetons to catch a giant trout.

Goffstein, M. B. *Fish for Supper*. Il. by author. Dial, 1976. All ages.
A small-size book tells of a day of fishing for Grandma.

Gray, Catherine, and James Gray. *Tammy and the Gigantic Fish*. Il. by William Joyce. Harper, 1983. P.
Grandfather, father and Tammy go fishing and Tammy catches a fantasy fish.

Grimm Brothers. *The Fisherman and His Wife*. Trans. from the German by Randall Jarell. Il. by Margot Zemach. Farrar, 1980. All ages.
The classic story of greed. Compare the illustrator's interpretation with the Laimgruber version listed below.

———. *The Fisherman and His Wife*. Trans. from the German by Elizabeth Shub. Il. by Monika Laimgruber. Greenwillow, 1978. All ages.

Hall, Katy, and Lisa Eisenberg. *Fishy Riddles.* Il. by Simms Taback. Dial, 1983. P.
Easy to read riddles.

Hertz, Ole. *Tobias Catches Trout.* Trans. from the Danish by Tobi Tobias. Il. by author. Carolrhoda, 1984. P.
A boy from Greenland goes on a fishing trip with his family.

Houston, James. *Kiviok's Magic Journey: An Eskimo Legend.* Il. by author. McElderry, 1973. P.
The great trout, Kakah, teaches Eskimo Kiviok to breathe under water.

Hutton, Warwick. *Jonah and the Great Fish.* Il. by author. McElderry, 1983. All ages.
Glorious picture book version of the Bible story.

Kalan, Robert. *Blue Sea.* Il. by Donald Crews. Greenwillow, 1979. P.
Colorful fish swim in the sea.

Lane, Margaret. *The Fish: The Story of the Stickleback.* Il. by John Butler. Dial, 1982. M.
The life of the stickleback in picture-book form. Full-color paintings.

Lionni, Leo. *Fish Is Fish.* Il. by author. Pantheon, 1970. P.
A frog and a fish find out that "fish is fish and frog is frog."

————. *Swimmy.* Il. by author. Pantheon, 1963. P.
A fish who is different leads his friends to safety through an underwater world.

Long, Earlene. *Gone Fishing.* Il. by Richard Brown. Houghton, 1984. P.
Father and daughter spend a day fishing.

Mazollo, Jean. *Amy Goes Fishing.* Il. by Ann Schweninger. Dial, 1980. P.
A fishing trip with Amy and her father.

Olcott, Frances Jenkins. "The Most Significant Cook of All" in *It's Time for Story Hour,* by Elizabeth Hough Sechrist and Jannette Woolsey. Il. by Elsie Jane McCorkell. Macrae, 1964. M.
The cook thinks of a clever way to keep a sturgeon from swimming away.

Parnall, Peter. *The Great Fish.* Il. by author. Doubleday, 1973. M.
A Native American boy listens while his grandfather tells how the silver salmon saved his people from starvation.

Patent, Dorothy Hinshaw. *Fish and How They Reproduce.* Il. by Matthew Kalmenoff. Holiday, 1976. M.
Fish and their reproductive habits are discussed.

Potter, Beatrix. *The Tale of Mr. Jeremy Fisher.* Il. by author. Warne, 1906. All ages.
A frog spends a day fishing.

Schatell, Brian. *Midge and Fred.* Il. by author. Lippincott, 1983.
Midge's talented fish—he can balance objects on his head—is kidnapped.

Seuss, Dr. *McElligot's Pool.* Il. by author. Random, 1947. P.
A boy imagines some unusual fish while fishing in a pool.

Street, Julian. "The Goldfish" in *Told under the Magic Umbrella.* Association for Childhood Education International, comp. Il. by Elizabeth Orton Jones. Macmillan, 1962. P.
Seven-year-old Don makes friends with a goldfish that talks.

Thiele, Colin. *Blue Fin.* Il. by Roger Haldane. Harper, 1974. M,U.
Snook wants desperately to please his father aboard his fishing boat, but he seems only to cause trouble. A novel from Australia.

Thorne, Jenny. *My Uncle.* Il. by author. McElderry, 1982. All ages.
Uncle finally catches a fish in a sophisticated picture book.

Turnage, Sheila. *Trout the Magnificent.* Il. by Janet Stevens. Harcourt, 1984. M.
Trout wishes he could fly. When he does, it changes his personality.

Turner, Ann. *A Hunter Comes Home.* Crown, 1980. M,U.

An Eskimo boy, adjusting to two cultures, goes fishing with his grandfather.

Uchida, Yoshiko. "The Sea of Gold" in *The Sea of Gold.* Il. by Marianne Yamaguchi. Scribner, 1965. M.

Hikoichi is rewarded for befriending a fish. Excellent story to tell or read aloud.

Wahl, Jan. "Runaway Jonah" in *Runaway Jonah and Other Tales.* Il. by Uri Shulevitz. Macmillan, 1968. M.

The Bible story retold as a narrative.

Waterton, Betty. *A Salmon for Simon.* Il. by Ann Blades. McElderry, 1980. P.

A Canadian Indian finally gets a salmon but lets it go because it is so beautiful.

Weiner, Sandra. *I Want to Be a Fisherman.* Il. with photographs. Macmillan, 1977. P.

An eleven-year-old girl tells about her father who is a trap fisherman off the coast of Long Island.

Wolcott, Patty. *Tunafish Sandwiches.* Il. by Hans Zander. Addison-Wesley, 1975. P.

Big fish eat little fish and the giant fish end up in sandwiches. Good choice for multimedia storytelling.

Wyndham, Lee. "Foolish Emilyan and the Talking Fish" in *Russian Tales of Fabulous Beasts and Marvels.* Il. by Charles Mikolaycak. Parents', 1969. M,U.

A talking pike does Emilyan's work for him.

Yorinks, Arthur. *Louis the Fish.* Il. by Richard Egielski. Farrar, 1980. P.

Louis would rather be a fish than a butcher and turns into one.

Zim, Herbert S., and Hurst H. Shoemaker. *Fishes: A Guide to Fresh and Salt-Water Species.* Il. by James Gordon Irving. Golden, 1956. M.

An introduction to 278 species of fish.

Halloween: Monsters

"The gruesome ghoul,
The grisly ghoul,
Without the slightest noise
Waits patiently beside the school
To feast on girls and boys."

— JACK PRELUTSKY

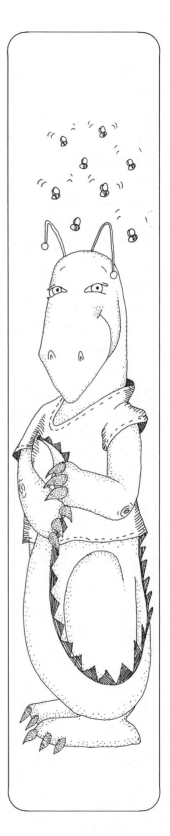

The most adaptable holiday of the entire year is Halloween. The fascination that children and adults have for spirits, ghouls, witches, and the like is so widespread that a group leader could celebrate Halloween every day of the year. I have chosen Monsters, a rather all-encompassing term for any frightening creature of the unknown, as the subject for this program.

103

The reading selection describes, in graphic and frightening detail, Beowulf's confrontation with Grendel, one of literature's classic monsters. Some adults might find this selection a bit too visual for their taste, but children will be properly respectful of one of the great descriptions in our literary tradition. The Robert Nye re-telling retains the spirit of the original while making the incident comprehensible to most middle- and upper-grade children. This edition of *Beowulf* has recently been reissued in paperback (Dell, 1982) and so should be easily available if suitable to your group.

Children seem to enjoy being frightened. Many of the current monster books show monsters as having the same fears (Natalie Babbit's *The Something*) and anxieties (Mercer Mayer's *There's a Nightmare in My Closet*) as the children reading about them. Many of the strictly fad monster books will probably slide out of print, so I have tried to include more literary collections of macabre happenings, ones that will remain in print.

If your own knowledge is inadequate, brush up on some of the monster terms by browsing through Daniel Cohen's *Everything You Need to Know about Monsters and Still Be Able to Get to Sleep*. Cohen writes short, lively chapters on vampires, werewolves, mummies, zombies, and assorted water and land monsters.

The booklist includes collections of frightening stories that appeal to monster lovers but ordinary ghosts lovers will find much that will appeal to them as well.

Prose Selection

Beowulf Against Grendel

A New Telling by ROBERT NYE

Beowulf's men were weary and soon slept. They lay stretched out on couches all round the hall. Their sea voyaging, followed by the march to Heorot and the many cups of mead Hrothgar had given them, made them sleep deep. Only Beowulf and Unferth stayed awake. They sat on either side of the empty throne, watching for Grendel's coming.

Unferth played with a silver trinket. He kept pouring the little chain through his fingers, its links making a tinkling sound. Sometimes he drew it so tight about his wrist that it hurt. He smiled to himself in the dark. He had stopped drinking. He was afraid, but his fear fascinated him. His bladder ached; he wanted to make water; but he did not dare go out in the night to do so. He twisted about on the hard uncomfortable step. He could feel the sweat trickling out of his hair.

Beowulf sat still.

It was a long night. It wore on slowly. The torches burned low. One of the Geats cried out in a bad dream. He woke, saw his leader's face, and turned back to sleep again. A torch sputtered and went out.

Beowulf could see well in half-light. He did not blink or shut his eyes. Once he cracked his knuckles. Otherwise he just watched, and waited.

There was no sign of Grendel.

Unferth began gnawing at his fingernails. They tasted of dirt and where he had been poking at his boil. Unferth hated the taste of himself, but he had to have it.

Beowulf still sat still.

Then, as dawn began to drain the dark, both men heard a sound. Beowulf heard it first. It was a sound like the breaking of ice underfoot. It came quick and was gone again. Unferth shook his head, wondering if he had imagined it. Then there was a hissing, gasping, panting noise outside the door, swiftly stifled, as though someone — or some Thing — was holding his breath in the dark, waiting to pounce.

Again there came that splintery sound.

Unferth's blood ran cold. He cowered into shadow. He felt his own water leaking down his leg, sore and warm and sticky.

Beowulf stood up. His voice rang through the raftered hall.

"Grendel," he cried, "Grendel, child of Cain, come down into Heorot. I am Beowulf, son of Ecgtheow. I am Beowulf, not afraid of you. I am Beowulf, come to kill you!"

The monster squealed with rage. His throat was full of the noise of crunching bones. He scrabbled at the door. He tore it down with his talons. He fell into hall Heorot!

The first thing Beowulf noticed was the smell. It hit him like a great wave of rotting matter: rank, malignant, bringing tears to his eyes and making him cough. It filled the hall like a poison gas. He retched at the stink of the beast.

It was because Grendel was so huge and black that the smell came before anything the eyes could make out. He was a foul fog, a choking murk of evil vapors, looming and slithering on the ivory floor. Then Beowulf saw coil after coil of slimy skin, mucid, spongy, dripping with the filth of the swamps, smeared thick with blood and scum, maggoty, putrid, and a pair of eyes glaring green, and slobbering lips, and huge claws reaching....

Before Beowulf could move, those claws snatched up one of the warriors stirring out of sleep.

Grendel tore his victim limb from limb, picking off arms and legs, lapping up the blood with a greedy tongue, taking big bites to crunch up bones and swallow gory mouthfuls of flesh. In a minute, all that was left of the man was a frayed mess of veins and entrails hanging from the monster's mouth.

Unferth was being sick. The green eyes flickered in his direction. He screamed and scratched at the wall for a hiding place, but there was none. Two torches went out as Grendel slithered past them.

The hall was left completely in darkness save for some inklings of dawn at the smashed door and where the windows were. The Geats jumped up in panic and fought with each other trying to find their swords and spears. Grendel made a new noise above the uproar. He gurgled bloodily with glee. The dark was his den, his home, his proper habit. He hated light. The hall shook to its foundations with his terrible laughter. He groped for Unferth.

But all at once the light had caught him. It had him by the claw. It was Beowulf!

The creature gave a dreadful squeal as Beowulf touched him. Ten strong fingers locked about his hairy wrist. To Grendel, it was as if the sun itself had caught him in its clutch. Made of wickedness as he was, the good in this man burned him. The mortal fingers were like ten red-hot nails driven into his skin. Grendel had never known strength like this. He roared and shook to be free, to crawl away, to escape into the ruins of the night. But Beowulf would not let him go.

Now Beowulf began to talk. His voice was quiet, and there was hullabaloo in the hall, what with the soldiers rushing about confusedly in the dark, and Unferth screaming, and the monster threshing about to get loose—yet Grendel heard every word like thunder in his brain. He did not know what was worse: Beowulf's grip or what Beowulf said.

Beowulf said: "Light holds you, Grendel. Light has you in its power. You, who have shunned the sun, meet me, once stung by bees that drank the sun. There's honey in my veins, Grendel, a liquid sunlight that can kill you quite. These fingers that you feel are ten great stars. Stars have no fear. I do not fear you, Grendel. I do not fear, therefore I do not fight. I only hold you, child of Cain. I only fix you fast in your own evil, so that you cannot turn it out on any other. It is your own evil, Grendel, that undoes you. You must die, creature of night, because the light has got you in a last embrace."

Grendel was in a fury. He bellowed and lashed. He wanted above all else to get away from this thing that was so contrary to himself. He tried every vicious trick he knew. But Beowulf stood firm, holding the monster in a grip so tight that it almost made his own big fingers crack and the bones poke out of the straining flesh. Hall Heorot rocked down to its stone roots with the rage of the demon's struggling.

Somewhere deep in Grendel's hellish heart a memory stirred. It grew and spread and flooded his whole being with despair. Something to do with light and another of these children of day—one who had flung herself between him and his food and by her love had thwarted him, so that he had felt powerless to approach and had slunk away, abashed by mystery. Grendel did not know the word "love" or the word "good." To him, they were part of the light he hated. There had been such light about that woman in the blue cloak. He had had to get away from it. But the light in the woman was as nothing to the light in this man Beowulf. And try as he would he could not get away.

Grendel grew angrier and angrier. He shook his arm about and dashed it against the wall. Beowulf, badly bruised, refused to relinquish his hold. When shaking did not work, and banging did not work, Grendel tried jerking his arm. But Beowulf wound his own legs round a pillar. He took the full force of the monster's pull—and still held on.

There was a fearful snapping of bones and tearing of sinews and muscles.

Then hot stinking blood fountained everywhere.

Beowulf had pulled Grendel's arm out of its socket!

Poetry Selections

Monsters Everywhere

by STEVEN KROLL

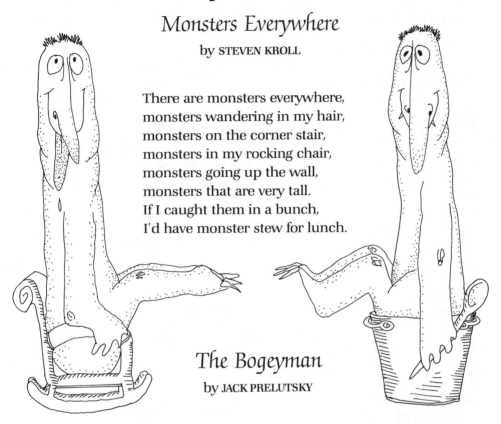

There are monsters everywhere,
monsters wandering in my hair,
monsters on the corner stair,
monsters in my rocking chair,
monsters going up the wall,
monsters that are very tall.
If I caught them in a bunch,
I'd have monster stew for lunch.

The Bogeyman

by JACK PRELUTSKY

In the desolate depths of a perilous
  place
the bogeyman lurks, with a snarl
  on his face.
Never dare, never dare to approach
  his dark lair
for he's waiting…just waiting…
  to get you.

He skulks in the shadows,
  relentless and wild
in his search for a tender,
  delectable child.
With his steely sharp claws and his
  slavering jaws
oh, he's waiting…just waiting…
  to get you.

Many have entered his dreary
  domain
but not even one has been heard
  from again.
They no doubt made a feast for the
  butchering beast
and he's waiting…just waiting…
  to get you.

In that sulphurous, sunless and
  sinister place
he'll crumple your bones in this
  bogey embrace.
Never never go near if you hold
  your life dear,
for oh!…what he'll do…when he
  gets you!

Midnight

by SEAN O'HUIGIN

There's scratching
on the front porch
there's a sniffing
'round the door
someone's whining
in the darkness
i can't stand it
anymore
i peek out through
the curtains
and in the night
i see
two shining evil
looking eyes
staring back
at me
the scratching's
getting louder
i can hear the beast
begin
to pant and huff
and push and shove
OH NO
it's gotten in

WOOF WOOF WOOF
pant pant pant

The Grebs...

by MIKE HARDING

When at night in bed I sleep
I hear the grebs around me creep,
I hear their whiskers scrape the
    floor,
I hear their fingers at the door.

I see their eyes shine in the dark,
I hear them squeal, I hear them
    bark.
"Oh, Grebs, if you'll just go away,
I'll be good tomorrow, all day!"

But voices say "Too late, too late!
We want you dead or alive!"
I tremble, shiver, shake and quiver
And beneath the bedclothes hide.

And feet and whiskers round me
    run
And closer, closer, closer come...
"Oh Grebs, if you'll just go away,
I'll be good tomorrow, all day!"

"Too late,
Too late,
We're here..."

110

Treats

These monstrous concoctions begin as a benign batter and end up overflowingly large, full of air, and delicious.

Cheese Popovers

YOU NEED: 1 cup milk
1 cup grated Cheddar cheese
2 eggs
1 cup sifted flour
¼ teaspoon salt

HOW TO: Preheat oven to 425°. Heat popover or muffin pans and grease. Place all ingredients in a blender and blend for twenty seconds. Pour batter into the heated pans, filling two-thirds full. Bake for about forty-five minutes, or until puffy and brown. Serve immediately, with butter and jam if you like.
Yield: 8-10 popovers.

HINT: Remember to use heated pans and don't open the oven door while the popovers are baking.

Creative Writing/Activities

Ask the children to explore the emotions of a monster of their own invention when confronted by an unfamiliar being: a person. How would a monster feel?

Monster Makeup

Face painting is a popular activity. Make sure you warn the children ahead of time so they can wear old clothes. Makeup smears. Makeup materials for special effects can be obtained at costume shops, theatrical supply companies, and at chain greeting card companies from August through October. Ask moms for old and discarded makeup as donations for your monster makeup kit.

Start with a clean face. Apply a light coat of hypoallergenic cream or cold cream to face. This is optional, but the cream protects sensitive faces and makes removal of makeup easier.

Have plenty of tissues and paper towels handy for easy clean-up.

A basic monster kit includes:

    light brown or white makeup

    blue makeup pencil

    red makeup pencil

    black eyebrow pencil

    brown eye shadow

    stage blood

Demonstrate a monster face on one child; then let them create on each other.

Caution children about using too much eye makeup.

Basic suggestions for monster faces:

    White makeup all over face.

    Draw lines downward next to nose and mouth.

    Use dark (blue or brown) color under cheekbones.

    Lines under eyes are effective, especially when black or brown lines are reinforced with red.

    Eyebrows that are extended and curve up are frightening.

Monster Jokes

How do you greet a four-headed monster?
Hello. Hello. Hello. Hello.

What do you call a charming, honest, sweet monster?
A failure.

What time is it when a monster knocks at the door?
Time to leave.

Why do monsters have a poor memory?
Everything goes in one ear and out the other.

What would a monster eat if it visited your home?
You.

How do monsters keep from dying?
They go into the living room.

Where do monsters pick up their mail?
At the dead letter office.

A Funny Monster Story

It was a dark, dark, night. Henry crept out of his house so that he wouldn't wake his parents. Henry's schoolmates had dared him to visit the graveyard at midnight, where it was said that monsters roamed. Since there was no moon shining, Henry used his flashlight to pick his way through the overgrown cemetery paths. Suddenly, in front of him, he saw a white coffin roll up on end and start toward him. How could he stop the coffin?

First he threw his flashlight at the coffin. The coffin kept coming toward him.

Next he threw his blue jacket at the coffin. The coffin kept coming toward him.

Finally he threw a full box of cough drops at the coffin.
The coffin stopped.

Books about Monsters:

Alexander, Martha. *Maybe a Monster.* Il. by author. Dial, 1968. P.
> A young boy makes a huge trap to capture a monster.

Aylesworth, Thomas G. *Movie Monsters.* Il. with photographs. Lippincott, 1975. M.
> Film monsters such as King Kong, Godzilla, and Dracula are described.

Babbit, Natalie. *The Something.* Il. by author. Farrar, 1970. P.
> A monster is afraid of the something (a little girl) in his nightmare.

———. *Kneeknock Rise.* Il. by author. Farrar, 1970. M.
> Egan discovers the monster that lives on Kneeknock Rise.

Bang, Molly. *The Goblins Giggle and Other Stories.* Il. by author. Scribners, 1973. M.
> Scary stories written with a lightness of spirit.

———. *Wiley and the Hairy Man.* Adapted from an American folktale. Macmillan, 1976, M.
> Wiley and his mother plot to rid the swamp of the Hairy Man.

Barkin, Carol, and Elizabeth James. *The Scary Halloween Costume Book.* Il. by Katherine Coville. Lothrop, 1983. M.
> Easy costumes for children to make for Dracula, orgre, mummy, werewolf, and other frightening monsters.

Baumann, Elwood D. *Monsters of North America.* Il. by Nicholas Kretisky. Watts, 1978. M.
> Firsthand accounts by people who have "seen" monsters.

Bendick, Jeanne. *The Mystery of the Loch Ness Monster.* McGraw, 1976. M.
> A nonfiction exploration of the origins of and investigations into the Scottish monster.

Bridwell, Norman. *How to Care for Your Monster.* Il. by author. Scholastic, 1970. M.
> A cartoon spoof on owning a monster. If your werewolf isn't feeling well, "it could be someone he ate...count your friends."

———. *Monster Jokes and Riddles.* Il. by author. Scholastic, 1972. M.
> Riddles and jokes about monsters.

Bulla, Clyde Robert. *My Friend the Monster.* Il. by Michele Chessare, Crowell, 1980. P.
> Prince Hal befriends a monster from beneath Black Rock Mountain.

Calhoun, Mary. *The Night the Monster Came.* Il. by Leslie Morrill. Morrow, 1982. P, M.
> Staying home alone, Andy imagines the monster Bigfoot is prowling outside.

Cameron, Ann. *Harry (The Monster).* Il. by Jeanette Winter. Pantheon, 1980. P.
> Harry discovers that the little people he is afraid of are more frightened of him.

Cameron, Eleanor. *The Terrible Churnadryne.* Il. by Beth and Joe Krush. Little, 1959. M.
> Tom and Jennifer track down the beast near Redwood Cove.

Campbell, Hope. *Peter's Angel: A Story about Monsters.* Il. by Lillian Obligado. Four Winds, 1976. M.
> Peter tries to get rid of the monster that has invaded his dreams and is following him to school.

Cohen, Daniel. *Everything You Need to Know about Monsters and Still Be Able to Get to Sleep.* Il. by Jack Stokes. Doubleday, 1981. M.
> A collection of "facts" about land and sea monsters in essay form.

———. *Monster Dinosaur.* Lippincott, 1983. M.
> An informal survey of facts about the Dinosaurs of long ago.

———. *Southern Fried Rat and Other Gruesome Tales.* Il. by Peggy Brier. Evans, 1983. M, U.
> Short horror tales from urban folklore. See also *The Headless Roommate* (Evans, 1980).

————. *Supermonsters.* Il. with photographs. Dodd, 1977. M.

The origins of classic monsters and reason for their popularity are discussed.

Coville, Bruce. *Sarah and the Dragon.* Il. by Beth Peck. M.

A huge dragon tries to keep Sarah as a guest.

Cox, Marcia Lynn. *Make-up Monsters.* Grosset, 1976. M.

Black-and-white photographs give step-by-step directions for monster make-up.

Delaney, A. *Monster Tracks?* Il. by author. Harper, 1981. P.

Could the footsteps in the snow be a monster?

Dickinson, Peter. *Emma Tupper's Diary.* Il. by David Omar White. Atlantic/Little, 1971. M.

Visiting her grandfather and her cousins in Scotland, Emma is involved in a plot to stage a reappearance of the monster of the Loch.

Dillon, Barbara. *The Beast in the Bed.* Il. by Chris Conover. Morrow, 1981. P.

A child's companion is a small green monster.

Elwood, Roger, and Howard Goldsmith. *Spine-chillers.* Doubleday, 1978. M, U.

Short stories by some of the classic terror writers: Algernon Black, Lafcadio Hearn, and Bram Stoker. Twenty-three stories for your frightening pleasure.

Engdahl, Sylvia. *Enchantress from the Stars.* Il. by Rodney Shackell. Atheneum, 1970. M, U.

Three civilizations, in various states of advancement, meet on the planet Andrecia. The Younglings are frightened by a monster of advanced technology.

Fisk, Nicholas. *Monster Maker.* Macmillan, 1980. M.

Matt is working in a science-fiction-film workshop and begins to think that the monsters he is creating...are alive.

Freedman, Sally. *Monster Birthday Party.* Il. by Diane Dawson. Whitman, 1983. P.

The real birthday party is illustrated in black and white, the monster party is brightly colored.

Galdone, Paul. *The Monster and the Tailor.* Il. by author. Clarion, 1982. P.

A tailor keeps sewing while a monster tries to frighten him.

Garden, Nancy. *Vampires.* Lippincott, 1973. M.

The how and why of vampires. Background material and stories. See also *Werewolves* (Lippincott, 1973).

Griffith, Helen V. *Alex Remembers.* Il. by Donald Carrick. Greenwillow, 1983. P.

A dog and a cat restlessly observe the night sky as they remember long-ago fears.

Hardendorff, Jeanne B. *Witches, Wit, and a Werewolf.* Il. by Laszlo Kubinyi. Lippincott, 1971. M, U.

Tales retold from various sources. Excellent for reading aloud or telling.

Haywood, Carolyn. *The King's Monster.* Il. by Victor Ambrus. Morrow, 1980. P.

Who will face the king's monster for the princess' hand in marriage?

Hoke, Helen, comp. *Demonic, Dangerous, and Deadly.* (Lodestar) Dutton, 1983. M.

One of Hoke's fine story collections. These will suit the taste of the horrorphile. See also *Thrillers, Chillers, Killers* (Elseirer/Nelson, 1978) and *Terrors, Terrors, Terrors* (Watts, 1979).

Hopkins, Lee Bennett, comp. *Monsters, Ghoulies and Creepy Creatures.* Il. by Vera Rosenberry. Whitman, 1977. M.

Poems and stories by Natalie Babbit, George Mendoza, John Gardner, and others.

Ish-Kishor. *The Master of Miracle: A New Novel of the Golem.* Il. by Arnold Lobel. Harper, 1971. M, U.

God creates a monster out of clay to help the Jews in this novelized legend.

Jonsen, George. *Favorite Tales of Monsters and Trolls.* Il. by John O'Brien. Random, 1977. M.

    Three troll stories: "Three Billy Goats Gruff," "The Trolls and the Pussycat," and "The Stone Cheese."

Kahn, Joan, comp. *Some Things Strange and Sinister.* Harper, 1973. M, U.

    The supernatural beings in these fourteen stories are mostly unseen.

Koelling, Caryl. *Mad Monsters Mix and Match.* Il. by Linda Griffith. (Intervisual Communications) Dell, 1977. P.

    Pages split into four sections to create mix-and-match stories.

Koide, Tan. *May We Sleep Here Tonight?* Il. by Yasuko Koide. Atheneum, 1983. P.

    Three gophers out camping take refuge in the house of a monster.

Krahn, Fernando. *April Fools.* Il. by author. Dutton, 1974. All ages.

    Two boys construct a monster in this wordless picture book.

Leach, Maria. *The Thing at the Foot of the Bed, and Other Scary Tales.* Il. by Kurt Werth. Collins, 1959. M.

    Short, easy-to-tell tales based on folklore traditions.

———. *Whistle in the Graveyard: Folktales to Chill Your Bones.* Il. by Ken Rinciari. Viking, 1974. M.

    Short, short scary stories based on folk material.

Lester, Helen. *The Wizard, the Fairy, and the Magic Children.* Il. by Lynn Munsinger. Houghton, 1983. P.

    Three competitive magicians band together to fight a monster.

Manning-Sanders, Ruth. *A Book of Monsters.* Il. by Robin Jacques. Dutton, 1975. M.

    Monster tales based on folktales from various countries. See also *A Book of Devils and Demons* (Methuen, 1970) and *A Book of Ghosts and Goblins* (Dutton, 1969).

Mayer, Mercer. *Little Monster's You-Can-Make-It Book.* Golden, 1978. M.

    Mazes, cut-out puppets, gliders, badges, masks, all with a monster theme.

———. *There's a Nightmare in My Closet.* Il. by author. Dial, 1968. P.

    A small boy introduces us to the monster in his closet.

McGovern, Ann. *Squeals & Squiggles & Ghostly Giggles.* Il. by Jeffrey Higginbottom. Four Winds, 1973. M.

    Short amusing collection of games, tricks, stories, and poems with a ghost theme.

McHarque, Georgess. *Meet the Werewolf.* Il. by Stephen Gammell. Lippincott, 1976. M.

    The origins, habits, myths, legends, and famous case histories of werewolves.

Meddaugh, Susan, *Too Many Monsters.* Houghton, 1982. P.

    Howard lives with ninety-nine other monsters, but he doesn't enjoy being nasty or mean.

Mendoza, George. *Gwot! Horribly Funny Hairticklers.* Il. by Steven Kellogg. Harper, 1967. P.

    Three monster stories: A snake grows bigger when its head is chopped off; an old woman eats a hairy toe; there is a hunt for the horrible Gumberoo.

Mooser, Stephen. *Monster Fun.* Il. by Dana Herkelrath. Messner, 1979. P.

    Directions for creating a chamber of horrors, giving a monster party, and applying monster makeup.

Pinkwater, Daniel. *I Was a Second Grade Werewolf.* Il. by author. Dutton, 1983. P, M.

    A little boy describes the day he became a werewolf and no one believed him.

Prelutsky, Jack. *Nightmares: Poems to Trouble Your Sleep.* Il. by Arnold Lobel. Greenwillow, 1976. M, U.

    Frightening poems describing various monsters. Excellent for reading aloud. See also *The Headless Horseman Rides Again Tonight* (Greenwillow, 1980).

Raskin, Joseph and Edith. *Strange Shadows: Spirit Tales of Early America.* Il. by William Sauts Bock. Lothrop, 1977. U.
Stories of communicating with spirits of the dead in early America.

Roach, Marilynne K. *Encounters with the Invisible World: Being Ten Tales of Ghosts, Witches, & the Devil Himself in New England.* Il. by author. Crowell, 1977. U.
Matter-of-fact tales based on legends.

Rockwell, Anne. *Thump, Thump, Thump!* Il. by author. Dutton, 1981. P.
The Thing wants its hairy toe back. Easy to read.

Ronan, Margaret. *The Dynamite Monster Hall of Fame.* (Dynamite) Scholastic, 1978. P, M.
Written in a popular style, this book examines various monsters and their movies.

Rosenbloom, Joseph. *Monster Madness: Riddles, Jokes, Fun.* Il. by Joyce Behr. Sterling, 1980. M.
Mostly old riddles and jokes that use a monster theme.

Sarnoff, Jane, and Reynold Ruffins. *The Monster Riddle Book.* Scribner, 1975. M.
Riddles with a monster theme — sophisticated drawings.

Schick, Alice. *Mary Shelley's Frankenstein.* Il. by Joel Schick. Delacorte, 1980. M.
A retelling of the classic tale with "comic strip" drawings.

Schwartz, Alvin. *In a Dark, Dark Room and Other Scary Stories.* Il. by Dirk Zimmer. Harper, 1984. P.
Short, easy-to-read folktales.

———. *Scary Stories to Tell in the Dark.* Il. by Stephen Gammell. Lippincott, 1981. M, U.
Short, short, easy-to-tell stories "collected from American folklore."

Simon, Seymour. *Space Monsters: From Movies, T.V. and Books.* Lippincott, 1977. M.
A quick and amusing look at familiar monsters.

Singer, Isaac Bashevis. *The Golem.* Il. by Uri Shulevitz. Farrar, 1982. M, U.
A clay giant from Jewish legend terrorizes the city of Prague.

Soule, Gardner. *Mystery Monsters of the Deep.* Watts, 1981. M.
Describes various unusual ocean creatures such as the great white shark and the sea wasp.

Steptoe, John. *My Daddy Is a Monster... Sometimes.* Il. by author. Lippincott, 1980. P.
Two children imagine their father as a monster when he is angry.

Stoker, Bram. *Dracula.* Tempo (Grosset), Doubleday, 1973. M, U.
"Welcome to my house! Enter freely and of your own will!" The original vampire novel.

Thorne, Ian. *Monster Tales of Native Americans.* Il. by Barbara Howell Furan. Crestwood House, 1978. M, U.
Read-Aloud stories are based on Indian folktales explaining nature phenomena.

Ungerer, Tomi. *The Beast of Monsieur Racine.* Il. by author. Farrar, 1971. All ages.
Monsieur Racine befriends a beast that is stealing the fruit in his garden. A satisfying surprise ending.

Viorst, Judith. *My Mama Says There Aren't Any Zombies, Ghosts, Vampires, Creatures, Demons, Monsters, Fiends, Goblins, or Things.* Il. by Kay Chorao. Atheneum, 1973. All ages.
Silly family incidents cause Nick to worry about his mom's denial that there are monsters.

Wallace, Daisy, comp. *Monster Poems.* Il. by Kay Chorao. Holiday, 1976. M.
Short collection of monster poems.

Willoughby, Elaine Macmann. *Boris and the Monsters.* Il. by Lynn Munsinger. Houghton, 1980. P.
Boris is afraid of night monsters, until he finds himself comforting his new watchdog.

Wise, William. *Monster Myths of Ancient Greece.* Il. by Jerry Pinkney. Putnam, 1981. M.

A short essay that introduces some of the important monsters of Greek mythology.

Wrightson, Patricia. *A Little Fear.* Atheneum, 1983. U.

Mrs. Tucker tries to live alone in Sunset House but is defeated by a Njimbin, a small acient gnome who acts "monstrous".

_____. *The Nargun and the Stars.* McElderry, 1974. M, U.

A rocklike monster seems to be coming closer.

Coloring Books:

Johnson, Fridolf. *Mythical Beasts Coloring Book.* (Dover, 180 Varick Street, New York, New York 10014)

Outline drawings with brief text.

Woskey, Leah. *Monster Gallery.* Il. by Mark Savee. Troubador (385 Fremont, San Francisco, California 94105), 1973.

Coloring book with outline drawings and short monster essays.

Jewish Humor

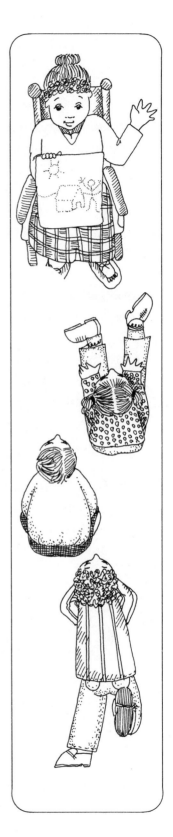

"To the storyteller yesterday is still here."
—ISAAC BASHEVIS SINGER. *Zlateh the Goat*

Jews celebrate sixteen different holidays and fast days each year. It's difficult to attempt a religious celebration of someone else's holidays. What if you do something in good faith but it turns out to be inauthentic or even offensive? Therefore, it may be easier for a non-Jewish group to have a secular celebration not keyed to any particular holiday. The following program presents the Jewish humorous folktale.

Through the centuries, Jews have dispersed all over the world. Despite their assimilation with other cultures, their folklore retains a special identity.

Some writers have expressed astonishment at the markedly intellectual and sophisticated character of so much of Jewish folklore. This is not so surprising when you consider the fact that Jewish tradition emphasizes a universal duty to study as a religious act. From this cherished tradition of learning comes ease of articulation, an emphasis on oral and thinking skills.

119

The rabbis who compiled the Talmud and the Misrash used familiar stories and legends to make their teachings more understandable to their students.

Material to choose for a Jewish folk humor program is vast. Written selections can be found that date from as early as the sixth century B.C.

Athough there are poetical and introspective stories as well as pious and moralistic ones, the most endearing aspect of Jewish folklore for me is its emphasis on wit and humor. Jewish jokes and funny stories exist in abundance, as do Jewish stand-up comedians.

The following program features a Jewish story collected by the Nobel Prize-winner Isaac Bashevis Singer. Singer has lived in the United States all of his adult life, but for the most part he still writes in Yiddish and then translates his work into English, often with the help of a translator. His adult novels often take place in the Jewish communitites of pre-World-War-I Europe. His children's stories, derived from traditional folk themes, are well worth presenting to young audiences.

I've also included a list of some useful Yiddish expressions that are often encountered in large metropolitan areas such as Chicago and New York.

Instead of a collection of poems to recite, I've chosen a few of the many Jewish jokes to use in your presentation.

Prose Selections

Shrewd Todie and Lyzer the Miser

by ISAAC BASHEVIS SINGER

In a village somewhere in the Ukraine there lived a poor man called Todie. Todie had a wife, Shaindel, and seven children, but he could never earn enough to feed them properly. He tried many trades and failed in all of them. It was said of Todie that if he decided to deal in candles the sun would never set. He was nicknamed Shrewd Todie because whenever he managed to make some money, it was always by trickery.

This winter was an especially cold one. The snowfall was heavy and Todie had no money to buy wood for the stove. His seven children stayed in bed all day to keep warm. When the frost burns outside, hunger is stronger than ever, but Shaindel's larder was empty. She reproached Todie bitterly, wailing, "If you can't feed your wife and children, I will go to the rabbi and get a divorce."

"And what will you do with it, eat it?" Todie retorted.

In the same village there lived a rich man called Lyzer. Because of his stinginess he was known as Lyzer the Miser. He permitted his wife to bake bread only once in four weeks because he had discovered that fresh bread is eaten up more quickly than stale.

Todie had more than once gone to Lyzer for a loan of a few gulden, but Lyzer had always replied: "I sleep better when the money lies in my strongbox rather than in your pocket."

Lyzer had a goat, but he never fed her. The goat had learned to visit the houses of the neighbors, who pitied her and gave her potato peelings. Sometimes, when there were not enough peelings, she would gnaw on the old straw of the thatched roofs. She also had a liking for tree bark. Nevertheless, each year the goat gave birth to a kid. Lyzer milked her but, miser that he was, did not drink the milk himself. Instead he sold it to others.

Todie decided that he would take revenge on Lyzer and at the same time make some much-needed money for himself.

One day, as Lyzer was sitting on a box eating borscht and dry bread (he used his chairs only on holidays so that the upholstery would not wear out), the door opened and Todie came in.

"Reb Lyzer," he said, "I would like to ask you a favor. My oldest daughter, Basha, is already fifteen and she's about to become engaged. A young man is coming from Janev to look her over. My cutlery is tin, and my wife is ashamed to ask the young man to eat soup with a tin spoon. Would you lend me one of your silver spoons? I give you my holy word that I will return it to you tomorrow."

Lyzer knew that Todie would not dare to break a holy oath and he lent him the spoon.

No young man came to see Basha that evening. As usual, the girl walked around barefoot and in rags, and the silver spoon lay hidden under Todie's shirt. In the early years of his marriage Todie had possessed a set of silver tableware himself. He had, however, long since sold it all, with the exception of three silver teaspoons that were used only on Passover.

The following day, as Lyzer, his feet bare (in order to save his shoes), sat on his box eating borscht and dry bread, Todie returned.

"Here is the spoon I borrowed yesterday," he said, placing it on the table together with one of his own teaspoons.

"What is the teaspoon for?" Lyzer asked.

And Todie said: "Your tablespoon gave birth to a teaspoon. It is her child. Since I am an honest man, I'm returning both mother and child to you."

Lyzer looked at Todie in astonishment. He had never heard of a silver spoon giving birth to another. Nevertheless, his greed overcame his doubt and he happily accepted both spoons. Such an unexpected piece of good fortune! He was overjoyed that he had loaned Todie the spoon.

A few days later, as Lyzer (without his coat, to save it) was again sitting on his box eating borscht with dry bread, the door opened and Todie appeared.

"The young man from Janev did not please Basha because he had donkey ears, but this evening another young man is coming to look her over. Shaindel is cooking soup for him, but she's ashamed to serve him with a tin spoon. Would you lend me—"

Even before Todie could finish the sentence, Lyzer interrupted. "You want to borrow a silver spoon? Take it with pleasure."

The following day Todie once more returned the spoon and with it one of his own silver teaspoons. He again explained that during the night the large spoon had given birth to a small one and in all good conscience he was bringing back the mother and newborn baby. As for the young man who had come to look Basha over, she hadn't liked him either, because his nose was so long that it reached to his chin. Needless to say that Lyzer the Miser was overjoyed.

Exactly the same thing happened a third time. Todie related that this time his daughter had rejected her suitor because he stammered. He also reported that Lyzer's silver spoon had again given birth to a baby spoon.

"Does it ever happen that a spoon has twins?" Lyzer inquired.

Todie thought it over for a moment. "Why not? I've even heard of a case where a spoon had triplets."

Almost a week passed by and Todie did not go to see Lyzer. But on Friday morning, as Lyzer (in his underdrawers to save his pants) sat on his box eating borscht and dry bread, Todie came in and said, "Good day to you, Reb Lyzer."

"A good morning and many more to you," Lyzer replied in his friendliest manner. "What good fortune brings you here? Did you perhaps come to borrow a silver spoon? If so, help yourself."

"Today I have a very special favor to ask. This evening a young man from the big city of Lublin is coming to look Basha over. He is the son of a rich man and I'm told he is clever and handsome as well. Not only do I need a silver spoon, but since he will remain with us over the Sabbath I need a pair of silver candlesticks, because mine are brass and my wife is ashamed to place them on the Sabbath table. Would you lend me your candlesticks? Immediately after the Sabbath, I will return them to you."

Silver candlesticks are of great value and Lyzer the Miser hesitated, but only for a moment.

Remembering his good fortune with the spoons, he said: "I have eight silver candlesticks in my house. Take them all. I know you will return them to me just as you say. And if it should happen that any of them give birth, I have no doubt that you will be as honest as you have been in the past."

"Certainly," Todie said. "Let's hope for the best."

The silver spoon, Todie hid beneath his shirt as usual. But taking the candlesticks, he went directly to a merchant, sold them for a considerable sum, and brought the money to Shaindel. When Shaindel saw so much money, she demanded to know where he had gotten such a treasure.

"When I went out, a cow flew over our roof and dropped a dozen silver eggs," Todie replied. "I sold them and here is the money."

"I have never heard of a cow flying over a roof and laying silver eggs," Shaindel said doubtingly.

"There is always a first time," Todie answered. "If you don't want the money, give it back to me."

"There'll be no talk about giving it back," Shaindel said. She knew that her husband was full of cunning and tricks — but when the children are hungry and the larder is empty, it is better not to ask too many questions. Shaindel went to the marketplace and bought meat, fish, white flour, and even some nuts and raisins for a pudding. And since a lot of money still remained, she bought shoes and clothes for the children.

It was a very gay Sabbath in Todie's house. The boys sang and the girls danced. When the children asked their father where he had gotten the money, he replied: "It is forbidden to mention money during the Sabbath."

Sunday, as Lyzer (barefoot and almost naked to save his clothes) sat on his box finishing up a dry crust of bread with borscht, Todie arrived and, handing him his silver spoon, said: "It's too bad. This time your spoon did not give birth to a baby."

"What about the candlesticks?" Lyzer inquired anxiously.

Todie sighed deeply. "The candlesticks died."

Lyzer got up from his box so hastily that he overturned his plate of borscht.

"You fool! How can candlesticks die?" he screamed.

"If spoons can give birth, candlesticks can die."

Lyzer raised a great hue and cry and had Todie called before the rabbi. When the rabbi heard both sides of the story, he burst out laughing. "It serves you right," he said to Lyzer. "If you hadn't chosen to believe that spoons give birth, now you would not be forced to believe that your candlesticks died."

"But it's all nonsense," Lyzer objected.

"Did you not expect the candlesticks to give birth to other candlesticks?" the rabbi said admonishingly. "If you accept nonsense when it brings you profit, you must also accept nonsense when it brings you loss." And he dismissed the case.

The following day, when Lyzer the Miser's wife brought him his borscht and dry bread, Lyzer said to her, "I will eat only the bread. Borscht is too expensive a food, even without sour cream."

The story of the silver spoons that gave birth and the candlesticks that died spread quickly through the town. All the people enjoyed Todie's victory and Lyzer the Miser's defeat. The shoemaker's and tailor's apprentices, as was their custom whenever there was an important happening, made up a song about it:

> Lyzer, put your grief aside.
> What if your candlesticks have died?
> You're the richest man on earth
> With silver spoons that can give birth
> And silver eggs as living proof
> Of flying cows above your roof.
> Don't sit there eating crusts of bread—
> To silver grandsons look ahead.

However, time passed and Lyzer's silver spoons never gave birth again.

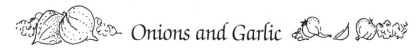 *Onions and Garlic*

David was always thinking of ways to get rich. He was also a very personable young man. At the cafe he talked to friends and strangers alike. It was while drinking coffee with a traveling salesman that he heard about the land across the sea.

"The people are wealthy, but their food is bland and boring. They've never even heard of onions."

"They don't cook with onions? And you say they have money?" asked David. Then he started musing. "If these people don't have onions, I'll have to introduce them to this delicious seasoning."

He sailed away the very next day to the land across the sea. The king of the place was hospitable but skeptical. However, he let David add onions to the food for the evening's banquet. "Delicious," cried all the guests. "Delectable," decreed the king. David was rewarded with two bags of solid gold pieces.

On his return he went back to the cafe to drink coffee with his friends. Abe was astonished at the story David had to tell. "If this king would give gold for a bag of onions, he would certainly give diamonds or emeralds for a bag of garlic. After all, it is certainly much tastier."

It took a long time for Abe to earn enough money for the voyage to the land across the sea. The trip was boring and he got seasick besides. Still he clutched the bag of garlic, and when he finally arrived, the king received him less skeptically than he had David.

The king ordered a state banquet, and Abe added garlic to the main-course dishes. Just as Abe predicted, the king was delighted to discover something new and even better than onions. "How can we possibly reward you for introducing us to garlic? Gold is certainly not good enough. We will give you some of our most precious possessions."

Abe left on the return voyage the next day, clutching a package given to him by the king. He imagined the fine house he would purchase with the diamonds he was sure he had been given.

Joyfully he opened the king's reward and found—a bag of onions.

Jokes

The rabbi was the most respected man in the Jewish town. It was to him that the people came for advice or to settle their disputes. No matter how foolish the rabbi's advice seemed to be, his word was the law. Jews observe the Sabbath from Friday at sundown to Saturday sundown.

Two disciples were bragging about the relative merits of their wonder-working rabbis. One said, "Once my rabbi was traveling on the road when suddenly the sky became overcast. It began to thunder and to lightning and a heavy rain fell—a real deluge. What does my rabbi do? He lifts up his eyes to heaven, spreads out his hands in prayer, and immediately a miracle happens! To the right, darkness and a downpour—to the left, darkness and a downpour. But in the middle a clear sky and the sun shining!"

"Call that a miracle?" sneered the other disciple. "Let me tell you what happened to my rabbi."

"Once he was riding in a wagon to a nearby village. It was on a Friday. He remained longer there than he had intended and, on his way back, he found that night was falling. What was to be done? He couldn't very well spend the Sabbath in the middle of the field, could he? So he lifted his eyes to Heaven, spread out his hands to the right and left, and immediately a miracle took place! To the right of him stretched the Sabbath, to the left of him stretched the Sabbath—but in the middle was Friday!"

Jewish jokes are so widespread that one can even make a collection of jokes about joke-telling. Here's a sample, and some other favorites.

A young man was sharing a train compartment with an older man. He watched as the old man mumbled to himself, smiled, and then put up his hand and was silent. After a few minutes he repeated the same pattern: a few mumblings, a chuckle or smiles, then raising his hand and silence. After a repetition of the same sequence over and over the young man said:

"Excuse me, sir. I can't help wondering if you need some help. Why are you laughing and then raising your hand?"

"Oh," said the man, "I am a bit bored while traveling so I would tell myself some jokes. That's why I was smiling."

"But why raise your hand?"

"Well, after I've started a joke I stop myself. After all, I've heard that joke before."

The author asked the composer how things were going.

"Fine," said the composer. "Twice as many people listen to my music as before."

"Really," said the author. "I didn't know you had gotten married."

"How did you sleep?" asked the innkeeper.

"Not well at all," replied the guest. "I found a dead bedbug in in my bed."

"And a tiny dead bug kept you awake all night?"

"Yes. All his cousins, uncles, aunts, and friends attended the funeral."

A student was living in a boarding house. The proprietor was a famous miser and served only the cheapest food. One night, when the student was served the usual thin watery soup, he bent his head close down to the soup.

"Whatever are you doing?" asked the proprietor.

"I'm listening to a noodle talking."

"Really? What is it saying?"

"I'm so lonely. I wish there was at least one other noodle in this soup to talk to."

All day Hershel had been walking through the countryside. At last he spied the light of an inn.

When the innkeeper saw Hershel's ragged, rumpled clothes he started to turn Hershel away.

"Please," begged Hershel. "I'd just like a bed for the night and a bit of dinner."

"A bed for the night you can have, but I'm afraid I can't serve you dinner. Everything is put away for the night."

"Don't say that," cried Hershel, his voice getting loud and raucous. "If you don't feed me dinner, I'll do what my father did."

Now the innkeeper was frightened. He roused his wife from her bed and together they fixed Hershel a fine feast. He was served herring and sour cream with fresh chopped onions, kasha, and brisket, and sweet tea in a glass.

"Ah," said Hershel, thanking his host. "Now I don't have to do what my father did."

"And what was that," the innkeeper asked, a little bolder now that his guest had been fed.

"Why, when my father did not eat dinner...he went to bed hungry."

You can find more Hershel stories in Novak and Waldok's *The Big Book of Jewish Humor* and Eric Kimmel's *Hershel of Ostropol*.

The summer weather was stifling hot. Mrs. Cohen needed a fan. She went to Hester Street and stood for hours in front of Kaplan's pushcart, handling each of his fans. Finally, she chose the cheapest one. It cost just one penny. Kaplan was disgruntled that Mrs. Cohen had taken so much of his time for a penny.

The next day Mrs. Cohen came back with a broken fan, demanding her money back.

"How did this fan break? Tell me how you used it," demanded Kaplan.

"Such a question. How do you think I used it! I held it in my hand and waved it back and forth in front of my face."

"Well, no wonder it broke. Mrs. Cohen, that's what you do with a fan that costs five cents. You spent only a penny. The way you use a penny fan is you hold it still and you wave your head."

Yiddish Expressions

Yiddish is a combination of Hebrew and German with a lot of Polish thrown in. It became the common language of the middle European Jews in America and the world. Many Yiddish words are in common usage in larger American cities such as New York, Chicago, and Los Angeles. These are some words difficult to live without.

Chutzpah: nerve, unmitigated gall

Goniff: thief

Kvetch: chronic complainer

Mazel: luck

Mazel tov: good luck

Meshuggener: crazy person

Nebbish: a nothing

Nudnik: a jerk

Oy: oh no! Use with *vey* (woe) as in *Ov vey.*

Shlemiel: bungler

Schlimazl: person with bad luck

Schnorrer: a beggar who uses his wits

Treats

Matzohs

For an easy introduction to Jewish food, buy a box of matzohs (unleavened crackers) from the grocery store and serve with butter.

Passover is a spring holiday that celebrates freedom: the Jews' exodus from Egypt. Each of the first two days of this eight-day observance is celebrated with a family dinner called a seder. The Passover story is read from a special book called a Haggadah, and food symbolizing the events in the story is eaten in a lavish feast.

Charosis

Charosis is served at the Passover seder as a symbol of the mortar and bricks that the Hebrews were forced to make during their long captivity in Egypt.

YOU NEED:
- 2 tart apples, peeled and chopped
- ½ cup chopped walnuts
- ¼ teaspoon cinnamon
- 1 teaspoon honey
- 1 tablespoon Passover wine

HOW TO: Mix ingredients together and serve on matzohs.
Makes enough for twelve people

Apples and Honey

Apples and honey are traditionally served for Rosh Hashanah (New Year) to insure a sweet new year. Dip apple slices into honey.

And of course, chicken soup! If you want matzoh balls, read the label on a package of matzoh meal.

Potato Latkes

Potato latkes are the traditional food served at Chanukah.

YOU NEED:
- 2 eggs
- 3 cups grated, drained potatoes
- 4 tablespoons grated onion
- 1 teaspoon salt
- ¼ teaspoon pepper
- 2 tablespoons cracker or matzoh meal
- ½ cup chicken fat or butter

HOW TO: Beat the eggs and add potatoes, onion, salt, pepper, and meal. Heat butter in frying pan and drop potato mixture by tablespoons into hot fat. Fry until brown on both sides.

Serve warm with applesauce or sour cream.

Bulletin Board

Under a headline like "Laughter is a universal language," post original jokes (or reproduce the jokes from this program) on the board.

Creative Writing/Activity

Ask the children to write a joke about a family or school tradition and present it orally.

Have a joke-telling contest. Children can tell jokes that they have heard at home or in the neighborhood or that they have read in a book. Joke tellers should be judged on clarity of telling, poise—and maybe laughter from the audience.

Books and Stories Containing Humor:

1. Jewish Humor: Picture Books

Aronin, Ben. *The Secret of the Sabbath Fish.* Il. by Shay Rieger. Jewish Publication Soc., 1978. All ages.
> How gefilte fish came to be. Sophisticated drawings in a picture-book format.

Chapman, Carol. *The Tale of Meshka the Kvetch.* Il. by Arnold Lobel. Dutton, 1980. All ages.
> Meshka learns not to complain.

Cohen, Barbara. *The Carp in the Bathtub.* Il. by Joan Halpern. Lothrop, 1972. M.
> Two children befriend a fish fated to be made into gefilte fish.

Goffstein, M. B. *Laughing Latkes.* Il. by author. Farrar, 1980. P.
> Why do latkes laugh? The answer is pure nonsense in a small picture book.

Hirsh, Marilyn. *Potato Pancakes All Around: A Hanukkah Tale.* Il. by author. Bonim, 1978. P.

> A peddler shows a family how to make potato pancakes from a crust of bread. A variant of "Nail" or "Stone Soup."

Kimmel, Eric A. *Hershel of Ostropol.* Il. by Arthur Friedman. Jewish Publication Soc., 1981. M.
> Five short, funny stories about the folk character Hershel.

Shulevitz, Uri. *The Treasure.* Il. by author. Farrar, 1978. M.
> Isaac finds a treasure in "his own backyard."

Suhl, Yuri. *Simon Boom Gives a Wedding.* Il. by Margot Zemach. Four Winds, 1972. All ages.
> Simon has to have the best of everything and ends up with nothing.

Zemach, Margot. *It Could Always Be Worse: A Yiddish Folk Tale.* Il. by author. Farrar, 1976. All ages.
> A family learns how to live in a small house. A glorious picture book.

2. Jewish Humor: Short Stories

Aleichem, Sholom. *Holiday Tales of Sholom Aleichem.* Trans. from the Yiddish by Aliza Shevrin. Il. by Thomas di Grazia. Scribner, 1979. U.
> Holiday themes from a famous Yiddish short story writer.

Brodie, Deborah, ed. *Stories My Grandfather Should Have Told Me.* Il. by Carmela Tal Baron. Bonim, 1977. M.
> Anthology of twelve stories about contemporary Jewish life.

Ellentuck, Shan. *Yankel the Fool.* Il. by author. Doubleday, 1973. M.
> Collection of stories about a foolish boy.

Howe, Irving, and Eliezer Greenberg. *Yiddish Stories Old and New.* Holiday, 1974. M.
> Stories by Sholom Aleichem, I. L.

Peretz, and Isaac Bashevis Singer.

Serwer, Blanche Luria. *Let's Steal the Moon: Jewish Tales, Ancient and Recent.* Il. by Trina Schart Hyman. Little, 1970. M.
> "Some people say that the Wise Men of Helm are fools. Don't you believe it. It's just that foolish things are always happening to them."

Singer, Isaac Bashevis. *Zlateh the Goat, and Other Stories.* Trans. from the Yiddish by Elizabeth Shub. Il. by Maurice Sendak. Harper, 1966. All ages.

———.*When Shlemiel Went to Warsaw & Other Stories.* Trans. from the Yiddish by the author and Elizabeth Shub. Il. by Margot Zemach. Farrar, 1968. All ages.
> A Nobel Prize winner shares folk stories. All are wonderful to read aloud.

3. Humorous Folklore from Other Countries

Chambers, Aidan. *Funny Folk: A Book of Comic Tales.* Il. by Trevor Stubley. Heinemann, 1976. M.
> Jokes and short folktales from Great Britain.

Emrich, Duncan. *The Nonsense Book of Rhymes, Tongue Twisters, Puzzles and Jokes from American Folklore.* Il. by Ib Ohlsson. Four Winds, 1970. M.
> This extensive collection of funny material is a good source book.

Ginsburg, Mirra. *The Lazies: Tales of the Peoples of Russia.* Il. by Marian Parry. Macmillan, 1973. M.
> Short, silly stories about lazy folks.

Gustafson, Anita. *Monster Rolling Skull and Other Native American Tales.* Il. by John Stadler. Crowell, 1980. M.
> Coyote trickster tales.

Schwartz, Alvin. *There is a Carrot in My Ear and Other Noodle Tales.* Il. by Karen Ann Weinhaus. Harper, 1982. P.
> Six easy-to-read folktales.

————. *Flapdoodle: Pure Nonsense from American Folklore.* Il. by John O'Brien. Lippincott, 1980. M.
> Another one of Schwartz's many fine folklore collections.

Van Woerkom, Dorothy O. *The Friends of Abu Ali: Three More Tales of the Middle East.* Il. by Harold Benson. Macmillan, 1978. P.
> Abu Ali gets in and out of trouble in this easy-to-read book. See also *Abu Ali* (Macmillan, 1976).

Wolkstein, Diane. *Lazy Stories.* Il. by James Marshall. Seabury, 1976. M.
> Stories from Japan, Mexico and Laos about lazy people.

4. Books of Jokes and Riddles

Beisner, Monika. *Monika Beisner's Book of Riddles.* Il. by author. Farrar, 1983. M.
> Clues to the answers to these riddles appear in the lovely illustrations.

Burns, Marilyn. *The Hink Pink Book or What Do You Call a Magician's Extra Bunny?* Il. by Martha Weston. Little, 1981. P, M.
> All the answers to these riddles have two rhyming words.

Clark, David Allen. *Jokes, Puns and Riddles.* Il. by Lionel Kalish. Doubleday, 1968. M.
> A big collection of old favorites.

Hoke, Helen. *Jokes, Giggles and Guffaws.* Il. by Haro. Watts, 1975. M.
> One of Hoke's excellent collections of standard jokes.

Keller, Charles. *Alexander the Grapefruit and Other Vegetable Jokes.* Il. by Gregory Filling. Prentice-Hall, 1982. P, M.
> One of Keller's funniest collections.

Schultz, Sam. *101 Knock-Knock Jokes.* Il. by Joan Hanson. Lerner, 1982. P, M.
> Enough knock-knocks to satisfy even you.

Stine, Jovial Bob. *How to Be Funny; An Extremely Silly Guidebook.* Il. by Carol Nicklaus. Dutton, 1978. M.
> Advice on being funny at parties, at school, and when you're in "big trouble!"

Vogel, Malvina G. *The Big Book of Jokes and Riddles.* Il. by Mel Mann. Playmore/ I. Waldman, 1978. M.
> Five hundred pages of mostly silly jokes.

National Nothing Day

"Nothing is absolutely the limit of nothingness —
it's the lowest you can go. If there were something that was left or less than nothing — then
nothing would be something (even though it's
just a very little bit of something)."

— E. B. WHITE. *Charlotte's Web*

National Nothing Day was originated by Harold Coffin, an American newspaperman. The purpose of the day is to give Americans one day when they can just sit, without celebrating, observing, or honoring anything.

A good time to observe this holiday is just after a period of frenzied activity. It can be a time for reflection and for just plain laziness. The official celebration takes place on January 16.

135

Years ago, when I worked for the New York Public Library, we had one month a year when there was no programming or exhibits on our bulletin boards or in the exhibit cases. In this way, we were trying to remind our patrons that a world without activity was a bit dull — but somehow restful too.

My theme for National Nothing Day is laziness, and both the prose selections and the poetry feature lazy characters. The recipe for peanut brittle is for people who are too tired to cook but want something good to eat.

The bibliography features no books. You can have your usual exhibit table completely bare. Or if you prefer, you could display wordless picture books, for a day of looking without reading.

Since there is no bibliography, I have included a bonus story. The story is by Richard Hughes, an adult writer who wrote a collection of nonsense stories for children. This one fits perfectly into the theme since it is titled "Nothing."

Prose Selections

Lazy Tok

by MERVYN SKIPPER

Tok was born lazy. When she was a baby everybody said what a good baby she was because she never cried, but really she was too lazy to cry. It was too much trouble. The older she grew the lazier she became, until she got so lazy that she was too tired to go and look for food for herself. One day she was sitting by the side of the river, too lazy to wonder where her next meal was coming from, when a nipah tree on the other side of the river spoke to her.

"Good evening, Tok," he said. "Would you like to know how to get your meals without having to work for them?"

Tok was too lazy to answer, but she nodded her head.

"Well, come over here and I'll tell you," said the nipah tree.

"Oh, I'm much too weary to come over there. Couldn't you come over here?" yawned Tok.

"Very well," said the nipah tree, and he bent over the river.

"Just tear off one of my branches," he said.

"Oh, what a nuisance," said Tok. "Couldn't you shake one down yourself?"

So the nipah tree shook himself, and down dropped one of his branches at Tok's feet.

"Good evening, Tok," said the nipah branch. "Would you like to be able to get your meals without having to work for them?"

Tok was too lazy to answer, but she nodded her head.

"Well," said the nipah branch, "all you've got to do is to make a basket out of me."

"Good gracious," said Tok. "What a bother. Couldn't you make yourself into a basket without my help?"

"Oh, very well," said the nipah branch, and he made himself into a nice, neat, wide, fat basket.

"Good evening, Tok," said the basket. "Would you like to be able to get your meals without having to work for them?"

137

Tok was too lazy to answer, but she nodded her head.

"Then pick me up," said the basket, "and carry me to the edge of the road and leave me there."

"Good gracious me," said Tok, "do you think I'm a slave? Couldn't you pick yourself up and go without bothering me?"

"Oh, very well," said the basket, and he picked himself up and went off and laid himself down by the side of the road.

He hadn't been waiting there long before a Chinaman came along.

"Shen mao tung shi!" said the Chinaman. "Here's a fine basket that somebody has dropped. It will just do for me to carry my goods home from market in."

So he picked up the basket and went off to market with it: He soon had it full of rice, potatoes, pumeloes, durians, dried shrimps, and other things too numerous to mention, and when it was full up he started off home with it.

After a while he felt hot and tired, so he put the basket down under a tree and went off to sleep. As soon as the basket saw that the China-man was fast asleep, up it jumped, and ran away back to Lazy Tok.

"Here I am," said the basket. "Here I am, full to the brim. You have only to empty me out, and you will have enough food to last you for a week."

"Dear, oh, dear!" said Lazy Tok. "What a bother. Couldn't you empty yourself out?"

"Oh, very well," said the basket cheerfully, and he emptied himself into Tok's lap.

Next week, when Tok had eaten all the food, the basket went off again and lay down on the grass by the side of the road. This time a Booloodoopy came along, and when he saw the basket he thought it would be fine to carry his goods home from market; so he picked it up and took it off to market. When it was full of pineapples and pu-meloes and all sorts of nice things too numerous to mention, he started off home with it, but he hadn't gone far before he felt tired and hot and sat down on the side of the road to have a nap. As soon as he had fallen asleep, up jumped the basket and ran home to Lazy Tok.

So every week the basket got itself carried to the market and came back full of fruit and rice and all sorts of other nice things too numerous to mention; and Lazy Tok sat on the riverbank and ate and ate and ate and got fatter and fatter and lazier and lazier, until she became so fat and so lazy that she simply couldn't feed herself.

"Here we are waiting to be eaten," said the fruit and the shrimps and the other nice things one day.

"Oh, bother," said Lazy Tok. "Couldn't you feed me yourself, without giving me so much trouble?"

"We'll try," said the fruit and the shrimps and the other nice things; so after that they used to drop into her mouth without giving her any unnecessary trouble.

So Lazy Tok grew fatter and FATTER and FATTER, and lazier and LAZIER and LAZIER; until one day the basket went off to lie down by the side of the road, just when the Chinaman who had picked it up the first time came along.

"Twee!" he said angrily. "There you are, you thieving scoundrel!" and he picked up the basket and took it to the market to show all his friends what had been robbing them. All his friends came round and looked at the basket and cried, "That is the rascal that has been robbing us!"

So they took the basket and filled it full of soldier ants, lizards, hot-footed scorpions, bees, wasps, leeches, and all sorts of other creeping, prickling, biting, stinging, tickling, and itchy things far too unpleasant to mention; after which they let the basket go.

Off ran the basket with his load of bugs and beetles and centipedes and gnats and ran straight home to Lazy Tok.

"What have you got for me today?" asked Lazy Tok.

"You'd better get up and look," said the basket.

"Oh, dear me, no!" said Tok. "I'm so tired, and I feel I couldn't stir a finger. Just empty yourself into my lap."

So the basket emptied the ants and beetles, and other things too horrible to mention, into Lazy Tok's lap.

Lazy Tok got up and ran and ran and ran, as she had never run in her life before. But the ants, beetles, and scorpions ran after her, and the leeches and lizards crawled after her, and the wasps and bees flew after her; and they stung her and bit her and pricked her; and the harder she ran the harder they bit her. As far as I know she may be running still, and she is thinner than ever.

Lazy Heinz

by THE BROTHERS GRIMM,
freely translated by WANDA GÁG

Heinz is so lazy he likes to do . . . nothing.

Heinz was a lazy fellow. He had nothing in all the world to do but drive his goat to pasture every day, and yet when he came home at night, he sighed and groaned.

"It is really a heavy task," he said, "and a toilsome business, yes! to take one's goat to pasture every day, year in, year out, from early spring, through the hot summer, way into the late autumn. And if one could only lie down and sleep while doing it! But no, one must keep his eyes open all the time to see that the creature won't chew up young trees or get into someone's garden, or perhaps run away altogether! With all that to do, how can a fellow possibly get any rest, or enjoy his life to the full?"

He sat down, gathered his thoughts together, and considered how he might best free his young shoulders from such a burden. For a long time all his thinking was in vain, but suddenly a thought flashed into his noodle.

"I know what I'll do!" he cried. "I'll marry Fat Katrina across the way. She has a goat of her own. When she takes her animal out to graze she may as well take mine, and then I won't have to torture myself with all these hardships anymore."

With that our lazy Heinz dragged himself to his feet. It took some time to bring his weary joints into action but at last he felt ready to walk. He ambled across the street to Fat Katrina's home and asked her parents if he might marry their good industrious daughter. Katrina's parents did not take much time to think this over. "Birds of a feather flock together," said they and gave their consent.

So Fat Katrina became Lazy Heinz's wife. Every day she went away to herd his goat and hers, but Heinz lay late abed to rest himself from his long, long sleep of the night before. When he got up he did nothing but sit around and was well content to have it so. Only now and then he would go out on the hillside with Katrina and help her a bit with the herding.

"I'm only doing this work," he would say to her, "because my sleep will taste better after it—one must stop resting now and then, lest one lose all taste for it."

But Fat Katrina was just as lazy as her husband Heinz, and it was not long before she, too, became weary of herding the goats.

"Dear Heinz," said she one day, "why should we sour our lives with labor, use up our youth, and tire ourselves out when it isn't even necessary? Those goats disturb our best sleep every morning with their

141

bleating—wouldn't it be better, Heinz, if we gave them to our neighbor and took one of his beehives in exchange? The beehive we could put in a sunny place behind the house, and pay no more attention to it after that. Bees don't have to be driven out and herded every day. They fly out alone, find their way home again all by themselves, and gather honey the whole day long without a bit of help from anybody. What do you think?"

Heinz sat up in bed.

"You've spoken like a sensible woman!" he said. "We will carry out your plan this very day. And do you know, Katrina, honey is very nourishing. Besides, it tastes better than goat's milk, and keeps better too—it never gets sour."

Their neighbor was willing enough to trade a beehive for two goats, and Lazy Heinz and Fat Katrina were more than pleased over the bargain.

The bees did their work well, flew in and out, back and forth, from dawn till dark every sunny day. They filled the hive with fine sweet honey, and in the autumn there was more than the bees could use themselves, so Heinz was able to take out a whole jarful of honey for himself and Katrina.

They put the honey jar on a shelf over the bed. But, as they were afraid it might be stolen by either mice or men, Katrina cut a stout hazel stick and kept it beside her bed. In this way she could chase away unwelcome guests without even getting up to do it.

Life was now very sweet for the lazy pair, and Heinz could never see any use in getting up before noon. "He who rises too early," he would say, "frets all his blessings away."

One day as he was thus busy preserving his blessings, lying snug among the feathers at noontime, he said to Fat Katrina (who was still in bed too, giving herself a much needed rest after her long night's sleep)—"Wife," he said, "women have a weakness for sweets, that we know. And I know that you are nibbling at that honey off and on. Before you eat it all up yourself, wouldn't it be better to trade it in for a goose and some goslings?"

"Well, yes," said Katrina, "but not before we have a child to herd them. Why should I worry myself with a flock of geese and use up my strength unnecessarily? Let the child do the work."

"Ho! Do you think our child will herd geese?" cried Heinz. "Nowadays children don't mind their parents anymore. They think they are wiser than their elders and do just as they please."

"Oh, no!" said Fat Katrina. "It will go hard with our child if he doesn't do as we say. A good stout stick—that's what I'll take, and I'll let him feel it too, if he doesn't mind us. See, Heinz?" she cried, picking up the hazel stick in her excitement. "See? This is the way I'll spank him!"

She raised the stick above her head, but unluckily in doing so, she hit the honey jar which stood above the bed. The jar fell down and broke, and the good sweet honey flowed over the floor.

"Well," said Heinz, as he leaned over the side of the bed and looked at it, "there lies our flock of geese now—and that's the end of that task; they won't have to be herded after all. But Katrina! Isn't it lucky that the jar didn't fall on my head? We can well be thankful that things turned out as they did."

His head was still hanging over the side of the bed as he spoke, and now he noticed a little pool of honey in one of the broken fragments. He reached out after it and said in deep contentment: "What's left of the honey, wife, we'll eat and enjoy. And then we'll lie back and rest ourselves so that we may recover from this frightful experience. What difference will it make if we get up a little later than usual? The day will still be long enough."

"Yes," said Fat Katrina, as her head sank back among the downy pillows, "there's always plenty of time to get anywhere, and haste will get us nowhere."

"Yes, it is better to take it easy," said Heinz, so they both went back to sleep once more.

Nothing

by RICHARD HUGHES

When the maid came in to do the dining-room in the morning, "Good gracious!" she said, "what a mess those children do leave the table in, to be sure!"

"What have they left on the table?" called the cook from the kitchen.

"Well, there's a drop of milk," said the maid.

"*That's* not much to make a fuss about," said the cook.

"There's also a dead Chinaman," said the maid.

"Never mind," said the cook; "it might be worse. Has he just died, or was he always dead?"

"I think," said the maid, "he was born dead, and was dead when he was a little boy, and finally grew up dead."

"What else is there?" asked the cook.

"There's a tooth, and I think it has dropped out of some passing shark."

"Dear, dear," said the cook, "children are *that* rampageous!"

"There is also," said maid, pulling up the blind and looking at the table more carefully, "unless I am much mistaken, a live Chinaman."

"Tut-tut!" said the cook; "what a fuss you do make! And was *he* always alive?"

"I don't know," said the maid. "And there's a Stocking Left Over From Before."

"Dearie me!" said the cook. "What else?"

"Nothing," said the maid.

"Well," said the cook, "don't you touch Nothing."

So the maid didn't touch Nothing: she cleared away the drop of milk, and the dead Chinaman, and the shark's tooth, and the live Chinaman, and the Stocking Left Over From Before, but Nothing she left in the middle of the table, and laid the breakfast round it.

Just then the seven children came down to breakfast.

"Why, what *is* that in the middle of the table?" said the youngest, and wanted to play with it.

"That's Nothing," said the eldest. "Leave it alone."

Then the father and mother came down to breakfast too.

"What is there for breakfast?" said the father.

"Amongst other things," said the mother, "there's Nothing. Would you like some?"

"No, thank you," said the father, "I prefer bacon."

So he had some bacon, and she had some bacon, and the children ate their eggs.

When breakfast was over, the mother sent for the cook.

"How often have I told you," she said, "to throw Nothing away?"

So the cook obediently went up to the table, and picked up Nothing and threw it out of the window.

But she never breathed a word to her mistress about the drop of milk, and the dead Chinaman, and the shark's tooth, and the live Chinaman, and the Stocking Left Over From Before; she hid them under her apron, and when the father and mother were gone she gave them back to the seven children, for she was a nice cook.

"Oh, thank you," sang the seven children; "what a nice cook you are!"

So she kissed them all, and then went back to the kitchen.

Poetry Selections

Tired Tim

by WALTER DE LA MARE

Poor Tired Tim! It's sad for him.
He lags the long bright morning
through,
Ever so tired of nothing to do;
He moons and mopes the livelong
day,
Nothing to think about, nothing to
say;
Up to bed with his candle to creep,
Too tired to yawn, too tired to sleep:
Poor tired Tim! It's sad for him.

Lazy Jane

by SHEL SILVERSTEIN

Lazy
lazy
lazy
lazy
lazy
lazy
Jane,
she
wants
a
drink
of
water
so
she
waits
and
waits
and
waits
and
waits
and
waits
for
it
to
rain.

Nada

by CHARLOTTE POMERANTZ

Nada is nothing.
Nothing at all.
Trip on a nada,
You never will fall.
Is the room empty?
Then nada is there.
Muchísima nada
Is everywhere.
So if you have nada,
Do not be sad.
Always remember
what you never had —
nada.

Souvenir

Blank books. Make them by stapling a few sheets of paper together with a colored paper cover, or try something fancier.

Treat

Enjoy a sweet that takes nothing of your time to make.

Peanut Butter Brittle

YOU NEED: 1 cup peanut butter
1 cup butterscotch chips
½ cup nuts (walnuts, pecans, or peanuts)

HOW TO: Combine ingredients in saucepan. Heat until just melted. Pour onto cookie sheet covered with foil. Refrigerate. Cut and enjoy.

Bulletin Board

Leave your board completely empty except for a tiny sign saying National Nothing Day.

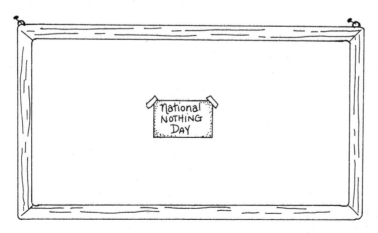

List of NO Books about Anything:

Give your children a chance to see what life would be like without books. If possible, drape the bookshelves with sheets covering the books and periodicals.

Shortest Ghost Story in the World

Two men met one day in the halls of a deserted castle.
"Do you believe in ghosts?" said one.
"Yes," said the other, and vanished into nothingness.

Joke

Mom: What are you looking for, David?
David: Nothing.
Mom: You'll find it in the jar where the cookies were.

Pigmania

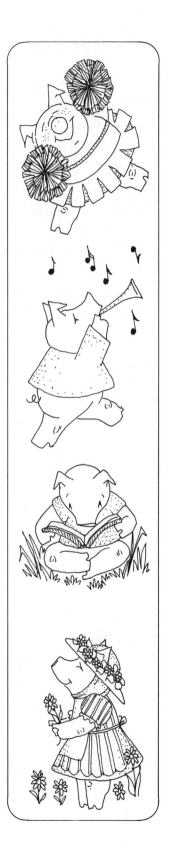

"The time has come," the Walrus said,
   "To talk of many things:
Of shoes — and ships — and sealing wax —
   Of cabbages — and kings —
And why the sea is boiling hot —
   And whether pigs have wings. "

— LEWIS CARROLL

I've tried to come up with an academic-sounding explanantion for the popularity of pigs in children's literature, but I can't. Let's just say that juvenile literature does seem to reflect the social and political climate. Some years will be dominated by books about minorities, women's rights, ecology. But books featuring pigs are published year in, year out.

I guess illustrators enjoy drawing pigs. Most of the pigs in children's books are not really pigs at all, of course, but human beings in disguise.

If you are presenting a pig program, you certainly will want to introduce your group to Jack Denton Scott's and Ozzie Sweet's *The Book of the Pig*. Any prejudices you may have had about the habits of pigs will be replaced by respect after you read this book. And certainly don't ignore the picture books if you are working with middle- or upper-graders. So many artists have illustrated *The Three Little Pigs* that it is a perfect book to show as an example of how the same story can change its mood with different art styles.

A pig celebration can be presented anytime during the year but especially on March first, which is National Pig Day. This day was created "to accord the pig its rightful, though generally unrecognized, place as one of man's most useful domesticated animals." Another excellent time to have a pig program is on a "pig" person's birthday. In the Oriental zodiac, those people born in the years 1935, 1947, 1959, 1971, 1983, and 1995 are born under the sign of the boar. People born in the year of the boar are gallant, honest, kind, and affectionate. I'm sure this is true, since I'm a pig person myself.

Prose Selections
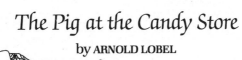
The Pig at the Candy Store
by ARNOLD LOBEL

All night long, the sleeping Pig dreamed of candy. He sprouted wings of spun sugar. He flew up through marshmallow clouds to a glowing marzipan moon. The stars that twinkled in the sky were chocolate kisses wrapped in shiny foil.

The Pig woke up with his mouth watering.

"Candy!" he cried. "I must have some this minute!"

The Pig ran to the candy dish. It was empty. The box of chocolate creams in the cupboard contained nothing but paper wrappers.

"I will go to the candy store," said the Pig, as he put on his clothes and rushed out of his house.

"On second thought," said the Pig, "I must remember that candy is bad for me. It makes me fatter than I already am. It gives me gas and heartburn."

Then the Pig remembered his sweet dreams. He decided that since he was halfway to the candy store, he might as well finish the journey.

"Just a few peppermints will not hurt me," he said.

As the Pig came near the store, his mouth began to water again. "Maybe I will buy a small bag of gumdrops as well," he said.

But the candy store was closed. A sign on the door said "On Vacation."

The Pig went back home.

"What wonderful willpower I have!" he cried happily. "I did not eat a single piece of candy!"

That night the Pig had a vegetable salad for supper. He drank a glass of cold, fresh milk. He felt thin and had neither gas nor heartburn.

A locked door is very likely to discourage temptation.

The Boy Who Took Care of the Pigs

retold by ANITA BRENNER

Juanito, the boy who took care of the pigs, was six years old. His father and mother were very poor. They all lived in a small house made of mud and stones. It had a straw roof. Inside, there was only one room and there was no floor. The ground was their floor. They cooked and they kept themselves warm with a fire that they made every day in the middle of the room. When they were sleepy they unrolled straw mats and put them down on the ground and covered themselves with old blankets and went to sleep on the mats. But sometimes they did not have enough wood for the fire and sometimes they did not have anything to cook. Juanito's father was sick. So the mother stayed to take care of him and Juanito got a job. His job was taking care of the pigs that belonged to a very rich man.

Every day Juanito took the pigs out in the woods and while they grunted and snuffled around looking for acorns, Juanito picked up all the good pieces of firewood that he could find. And in the evening he would say to the rich man, "Master, the pigs are asleep and the day is over. Will you give me permission to take this wood to my father so he can keep warm?"

People would see him every day gathering up wood and every evening carrying it on his back to his father and they would say, "Juanito is a very good boy. He deserves to have luck. If we wish hard enough and long enough, something nice must surely happen."

One day the rich man moved far away to his ranch and the pigs went too, so Juanito had to go and take care of them. He said, "I wonder how I can take wood to my father every night? It is so far, but I must do it somehow."

So every evening he asked for permission and he would walk and walk and walk until he got home with the firewood. It was dark. Then when he went back to the ranch it was still darker and cold, but Juanito was so happy that he could take wood to his father that he did not feel so cold.

152

Every day seemed just the same, but this day it was different. Juanito saw the pigs snuffling and grunting and digging into the ground with their feet and their snouts, and he saw them pulling things out of the ground that looked like nice, thick wood. He picked one piece up and it was very heavy. He said, "How wonderful. This will burn a long time."

The pieces were all the same size so he made a bundle easily, but when it was time to take the bundle home it seemed very heavy. Juanito was so happy to have such good wood that somehow he got the bundle home and he did not feel too tired.

He father said, "Listen, my son, where did you get this?"

The boy answered, "Dear father, the pigs dug it up out of the earth. I hope it will make you very warm."

The father said, "There is something very funny about these sticks. If the master sees them maybe he will want them. Maybe he will take your job away and go out in the woods with the pigs himself and gather up these sticks himself."

Juanito laughed. "Oh, Father, why should the master go out in the woods if he can hire me to do it for him?"

So every day Juanito came home with a bundle of these strange heavy sticks and his master did not notice how strange they were.

What could they be? Juanito did not know, but his father did. They were pure silver that some bandits had hidden away in the ground. Should he tell anybody? No, he was old and poor and sick. They would take it away from him. So he just kept it and he said, "When Juanito grows up he will know what to do with this."

Juanito took care of the pigs for ten years, and all this time the silver he was bringing home was piling up all around the inside of the house until it was like a wall around the room. "How nice," he said. "This extra wall certainly keeps the room much warmer."

But one day he came home with a very sad face and he said, "Dear Father, the master has sold all the pigs and I do not have a job anymore. What are we going to do?"

His father was a very very old man now and he just smiled and said, "You come with me."

153

They took one of the pieces to the place where the government makes money and there it was cut into round silver coins. They did this every day until they had a sack full of money and then they just stood and looked at it and laughed and said, "Ha, ha, now we are rich."

After a while the master came looking for Juanito to tell him that now he had some more pigs and to please come and take care of them. But he could not find the house because where it had been, there was now a very elegant pink house and it had roses growing all around it. He knocked at the door and said to the lady who answered, "Madam, can you tell me where to find Juanito, the pig boy?"

"Enter, enter sir. He is not a boy anymore. He has grown up, but he is still Juanito."

The master came in and he was astonished. They took him into the dining room and there was a big table with wonderful things to eat on it and many people sitting around it having a very good time eating all they wanted to. The master said, "What an elegant house! What rich furniture! What fine food! And what beautiful silver dishes! Did you get all this working for me?"

Juanito was sitting at the head of the table carving a ham and a turkey and six chickens for the people he had invited. They were all the poorest people in town.

He said, "Master, will you join us in a little bit of supper? Just what we have, of course—not so fine as you are accustomed to, but we would be happy to have you share our poor meal."

"Thank you, thank you, Juanito. I will be glad to have some of this wonderful supper, but please first answer my question. How could you get all this working for me?"

Juanito smiled and said, "Well, you see, I worked so long."

And everybody laughed and said, "Well, you see, we wished so hard."

The master wondered why they were laughing, but he never found out.

Poetry Selections

Flying Pigs

by WALTER R. BROOKS

Oh, the young pigs fly
About the sky
   And they zoom and dive and roll;
They yell and whoop
As they spin and loop
   Under the sky's bowl.

They sing and shout
As they whiz about,
   For there's elbowroom in the sky;
And it's lots more fun
Up there in the sun
   Than down in their stuffy sty.

The Pig

by OGDEN NASH

The pig, if I am not mistaken,
Supplies us sausage, ham, and
   bacon.
Let others say his heart is big —
I call it stupid of the pig.

Pig

by VALERIE WORTH

The pig is bigger
Than we had thought
And not so pink,
Fringed with white
Hairs that look
Gray, because while
They say a pig is clean,
It is not always; still,
We like this huge, cheerful
Rich, soft-bellied beast —
It wants to be comfortable,
And does not care much
How the thing is managed.

Pig

by WILLIAM JAY SMITH

Pigs are always awfully dirty;
   I do not think it bothers me.
If I were a pig, I would say: "My
   dears,
I do not intend to wash my ears
Once in the next eleven years,
   No matter how dirty they may
   be!"

Pigs are always awfully muddy;
   I do not think I really care.
If I were a pig, I would say: "My
   honeys,
While you stay as clean as the
   Easter bunnies,
I'll curl in the mud and read the
   funnies,
   And never, never comb my hair!"

Media Presentation

A PAPER-CUTTING STORY by ERIC HAWKESWORTH

Three Little Pigs

The three little pigs and their houses are cut from standard three-fold paper strips, but Mr. Wolf is developed by folding a paper square in a different fashion. After cutting, Mr. Wolf can be shown in two ways, full face and pro-file, depending on how the paper is unfolded, but when the pigs look for the wolf inside the paper, all they can find is a flowerbed design. When the sheet is re-folded, out pops Mr. Wolf again!

PREPARING THE PAPER FOLDS

The Three Little Pigs

Fold a sheet of newspaper measuring 12 inches by 24 inches into three equal parts by turning in each end of the strip. To obtain accurate folds, draw two pencil guidelines down the paper strip at 8-inch spacings and use these lines as the fold points. Press the creases in firmly, then make one more fold from right to left to form the center of the design. Mark out the half shape for the pigs, as shown. Note that a holding strip across the top is needed for displaying the figures. The pigs' feet are drawn across to the left-hand edge of the packet, and each figure is provided with a curly tail.

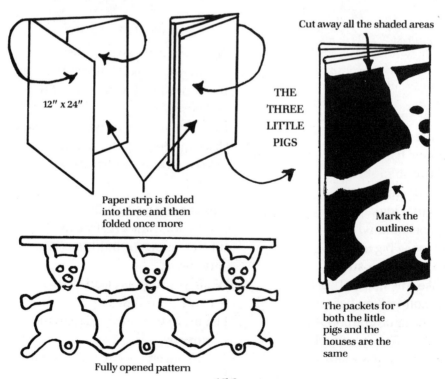

12" x 24"

Paper strip is folded into three and then folded once more

THE THREE LITTLE PIGS

Cut away all the shaded areas

Mark the outlines

The packets for both the little pigs and the houses are the same

Fully opened pattern

156

Three Pigs' Houses

These are marked on a folded paper strip, the same as for the previous figure. The sketch shows how the houses are joined together at the base of the walls and at the roof line. The two windows are simple rectangles, and the door is cut to the center-fold edge. No holding strip is needed with this figure.

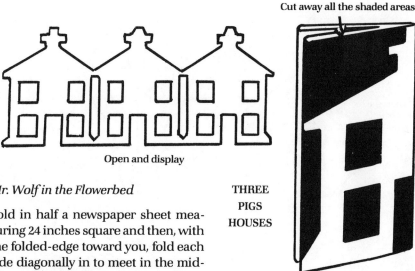

Open and display

Cut away all the shaded areas

THREE
PIGS
HOUSES

Mr. Wolf in the Flowerbed

Fold in half a newspaper sheet measuring 24 inches square and then, with the folded-edge toward you, fold each side diagonally in to meet in the middle, as shown. Make another fold from each side and then bring the folded edges together to produce the triangular-shaped packet for marking out. There are five small areas to cut out in this design, and they are penciled in the positions indicated on the sketch; these produce a design that is different in principle from the other figures because while the other shapes are formed by what is called relief cutting

—removing surplus paper *between* the characters so that the figures themselves stand out in bold relief—the flowerbed pattern is produced by a series of holes in a solid paper background. Place the three folded and marked papers on your table and you are ready to tell the story.

Preparing Mr. Wolf's head

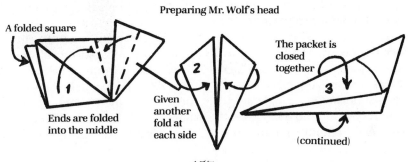

A folded square

Ends are folded into the middle

Given another fold at each side

The packet is closed together

(continued)

157

MR. WOLF IN THE FLOWERBED

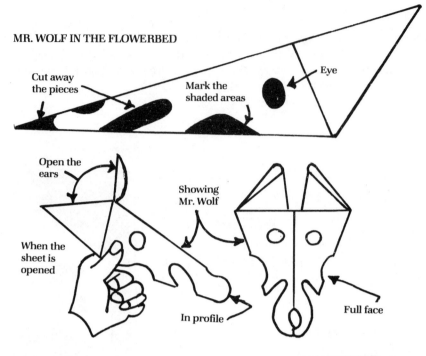

WHAT TO SAY AND DO

Presenting the story:
"Here is the tale of the three little pigs ...three fat little pigs that ate so much their mothers sent them away to look after themselves. You will see how chubby they looked after I've cut them out of this paper strip...ears, snout and feet...and we must not forget their little curly tails!"

You can unfold the first paper strip and let your audience see that it is just an ordinary newspaper piece, then refold the strip, ready to start cutting. Because the initial preparation of the papers is such an important part of the paper-cutting art, it adds greatly to a demonstration to let everyone see how at least one basic type of fold is put together during any single story presentation. Cut around the outlines and remove the snout, mouth, and

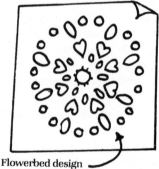

Flowerbed design

hollow section of the tail from the folded-edge crease. Open and display the figure, then make a start on the second paper fold.

"The story tells how the little pigs built three houses...one of straw, one of wood, and one of bricks...so our next illustration will be of these three houses. All the buildings had chimneys...and windows...and a door, which was essential to keep out Mr.

158

Wolf! This is how the row of houses looked when all the work was completed. But Mr. Wolf had been watching all the time from his lair amid the flowerbeds…just across the road!"

Children love to come on stage and hold the figures as they are produced, and by this point in the story you can have the pigs on display at one side of the platform and the strip of three houses on the other. Start cutting Mr. Wolf by snipping out the eye disc and removing the other sections as drawn. Bend back the two paper points and show Mr. Wolf in profile—the sketch shows how the figure is displayed by holding between the left-hand first finger and thumb.

"Mr. Wolf visited the first house and asked to come in…but when the first little pig refused, the wolf huffed and puffed…till the house of straw fell down! He went to the next house… and pressed his face up against the window…like this!"

Open the paper fold along its center crease and show Mr. Wolf full face. Tell how he blew the house of wood down when the second little pig refused to let him in. Next shake open the whole sheet and show the flower design.

"All three little pigs hurried to the house of bricks and looked out of their window…but Mr. Wolf had returned to the flowerbed and had disappeared into his secret lair!…he was nowhere to be seen!"

Refold the paper and produce Mr. Wolf in profile once more. Walk across to the row of houses that your assistant is holding and blow hard on the strip as you demonstrate how the wolf returned at night to try and blow down the house of bricks.

"But the house was too strong for Mr. Wolf…so he climbed onto the roof and slid down the chimney! The pigs were waiting…with a big kettle of boiling water! Mr. Wolf went yelping out of the house…just like a scalded cat!…and vanished for good in the flowerbed!"

Open the sheet and show the flowerbed design for a climax to the story.

159

Treat

Apple Pigs

For each pig:

YOU NEED: a large apple and a small apple

              7 toothpicks or cocktail sticks

              silver balls (cake decoration)

              lemon juice

HOW TO: Insert four toothpicks into the large apple as legs of pig. Cut the small apple in half. One piece will be the head. Using a toothpick, attach head, rounded side out, to body. Using second half of apple, cut a small piece for pig's snout, and attach to head with a toothpick. Use a toothpick to make eye- and snout-holes, and insert silver cake-decorating balls for eyes. Curls of apple skin can serve for ears. The apple stem can be the pig's tail.

When you have finished creating, admire your pig, and then eat it.

Bulletin Board

Use as a heading: If you could make a pig of yourself, what would you eat?

Leave blank space for children to put their names and things they like to eat.

Piggy Bank Poster and Coins Exhibit

YOU NEED: poster board
paints

HOW TO: Cut poster board and paint it to look like a Mexican piggy bank (something like Lynn's illustration below). Cut circles of poster board and paint them to look like coins. High up on the pig's back, cut a slit for the coins. Turn the poster over, and under the slit tape an envelope to catch the coins. Next, print the title of a book on each coin.

USE: Mount the pig poster on a bulletin board. As the leader talks about each book, she picks up the coin with the book title printed on it and drops it into the piggy bank.

HINT: Make enough book-title coins so that you will have a wide range of books to choose from for each group.

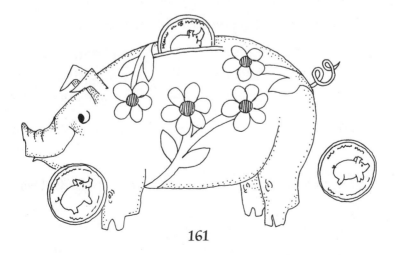

Creative Writing/Activities

The thought of a pig flying is ridiculous and incongruous, yet the image is a popular literary theme. Have the children write a paragraph describing how a real live pig might feel in actual flight.

Pig Jokes and Facts

What do you call a twenty-two-room, four-story mansion lived in by a pig?
   A pigsty.

What do you use on a sore arm?
   Oinkment.

How can you tell a pig from a giraffe?
   The pig is the one that doesn't look like a giraffe.

A pig is a baby hog.
A boar is a male hog.
A sow is a female hog.

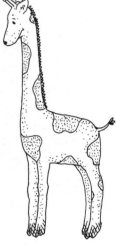

Pig Vocabulary

Use these in an introduction or on a bulletin board.

pigment	hog-wild	pigtail
"in a pig's eye"	hogwash	piggy bank
"pork barrel"	pig latin	male chauvinist pig

Did you know? Orthodox Jews and Moslems are forbidden to eat pork.

Pig Puns

What kind of cards do pigs send on February 14?
Valenswines.

What brand of jeans does the stylish pig wear?
Calvin Swines.

What kind of book is about a famous pig?
A biHOGraphy.

What would you call a beauty contest for pigs?
The Miss HAMerica contest.

Catalog of Pig Merchandise

Hog Wild
280 Friend Street
Boston, Massachusetts 02114
Catalog $1.00

Pig Mania (game)
Recycled Paper Products
3325 N. Lincoln Avenue
Chicago, Illinois 60657

Books about Pigs:

Andersen, Hans Christian. "The Swineherd" in *Hans Christian Andersen, the Complete Fairy Tales and Stories.* Trans. from the Danish by Erik Christian Haugaard. Doubleday, 1974. M, U.

The story of a flighty princess whose downfall is brought about by a prince disguised as a swineherd.

Bawden, Nina. *The Peppermint Pig.* Lippincott, 1975. M.

Johnnie, a runt pig, keeps a family entertained during a difficult time.

Blegvad, Lenore, ed. *This Little Pig-a-Wig.* Il. by Erik Blegvad. McElderry, 1978. P.

Pig nursery rhymes illustrated with small expressive sketches.

Bowman, Sarah, and Lucinda Vardey. *Pigs.* Macmillan, 1981. M, U.

Literary selections and paintings featuring the pig.

Boynton, Sandra. *Hester in the Wild.* Il. by author. Harper, 1979, P.

A spoof on camping with Hester the pig as the central character.

Brooks, Walter R. *Freddy Goes to Florida.* Il. by Kurt Wiese. Knopf, 1949. M.

The first in a series of books about the animals on Mr. Bean's farm.

Callen, Larry. *Pinch.* Il. by Marvin Friedman. Little, 1975. M.

Adventures with Pinch and Homer.

Carroll, Lewis. *The Pig-Tale.* Il. by Leonard B. Lubin. Little, 1975. M, U.

A wily frog tricks a plump pig into thinking he can jump.

Christelow, Eileen. *Mr. Murphy's Marvelous Invention.* Il. by author. Clarion, 1983. P.

Mr. Murphy's birthday surprise creates more problems than pleasure.

Copeland, Colene. *Priscilla.* Il. by Edith Harrison. Jordan Valley Heritage House (43502 Highway 26, Stayton, Oregon 97383), 1981. M.

First-person account of the life of a pet pig.

Dahl, Roald. "The Three Little Pigs" in *Roald Dahl's Revolting Rhymes.* Il. by Quentin Blake. Knopf, 1983. M, U.

The classic tale in a very modern guise.

De Jong, Meindert. *The House of Sixty Fathers.* Il. by Maurice Sendak. Harper, 1956. M.

Tien Pao and his pig are separated from his family during World War II.

Demong, Phyllis. *It's a Pig World Out There.* Il. by author. Avon, 1981. M, U.

A collection of pig poems.

Edmonds, Walter D. "Perfection of Orchard View" in *The Night Raider and Other Stories.* Little, 1980. U.

A wonderfully witty story about a gentleman farmer and his hired hand who have opposite views when it comes to pig-raising.

Galdone, Paul. *The Amazing Pig.* Il. by author. Clarion, 1981. P.

A peasant boy invents stories about his pig to win a king's daughter.

Geisert, Arthur. *Pa's Balloon and Other Pig Tales.* Il. by author. Houghton, 1984. P.

Three short stories about a family of pigs and their ballooning adventures. Short text and lots of pictures.

Getz, Arthur. *Humphrey, the Dancing Pig.* Il. by author. Dial, 1980. P.

A pig loses weight and is put to work chasing mice.

Golding, William. *Lord of the Flies.* Coward, 1955. U.

Golding shows the disintegration of society in a group of school children stranded on a desert island. See Chapter 8 for "the killing of the sow."

Goodall, John S. *The Adventures of Paddy Pork.* Il. by author. Harcourt, 1968. P.

A wordless picture book featuring a pig who runs away to the circus—half-size to full-size pages.

Grahame, Kenneth. "Bertie's Escapade" in *First Whisper of the Wind in the Willows.* Il. by Ernest H. Shepard. Metheun, 1949. P.

A bold pig sets off with his animal friends to sing Christmas carols to Mr. Stone.

Hoban, Lillian. *Mr. Pig and Family.* Il. by author. Harper, 1980. P.

I-Can-Read stories.

Hopf, Alice L. *Pigs Wild and Tame.* Holiday, 1979. M, U.

For those who want to know a bit about real live pigs.

Jeschke, Susan. *Perfect the Pig.* Il. by author. Holt, 1981. P, M.

A pig with wings finds happiness after being kidnapped by an unscrupulous street performer.

King-Smith, Dick. *Pigs Might Fly.* Il. by Mary Rayner. Viking, 1982. M.

The perfect read-aloud book. A charming pig learns to swim and ... fly. Warmth and humor.

Lavine, Sigmund A., and Vincent Scuro. *Wonders of Pigs.* Dodd, 1981. M.

Specific advice on selection, feeding, and housing; descriptions of ten specific American breeds; and an explanation of how every part of the pig except the squeal is used commercially.

Lobel, Arnold. "The Pig at the Candy Store" in *Fables.* Il. by author. Harper, 1980. P.

A short fable about a pig who didn't eat candy.

————. *Pigericks.* Il. by author. Harper, 1983. All ages.

Pig limericks.

————. *Small Pig.* Il. by author. Harper, 1969. P.

Small pig finds a mudhole that turns out to be wet cement.

————. *A Treeful of Pigs.* Il. by Anita Lobel. Greenwillow, 1979. P.

The farmer's wife teaches her husband that it takes two to take care of their pigs.

MacLachlan, Patricia. *Arthur, for the Very First Time.* Il. by Lloyd Bloom. Harper, 1980. M.

Arthur builds a pen for Bernadette's piglets, but she chooses to have them in a rainstorm.

Mark, Jan. "William's Version" in *Nothing to Be Afraid Of.* Harper, 1981. U.

William forces Granny to change the story of "The Three Little Pigs" to fit his cantankerous mood.

McPhail, David. *Pig Pig Goes to Camp.* Il. by author. Dutton, 1983. M.

A pig enjoys the adventure of summer camp (a large-size picture book).

————. *Pig Pig Grows Up.* Doubleday, 1980. P. Picture-book version of the trials and tribulations of piggy growing up.

————. *Pig Pig Rides.* Il. by author. Dutton, 1982. P.

Pig imagines his bicycle ride as a grand adventure.

Milne, A. A. "In Which a Search Is Organized," and "Piglet Nearly Meets the Heffalump Again," in *The House at Pooh Corner.* Il. by Ernest H. Shepard. Dutton, 1928. M.

Good dialogue if you want to use two voices to present this story of Piglet and Pooh looking for Small, the beetle.

————. "In Which Piglet Meets a Haffalump" in *Winnie-the-Pooh.* Il. by Ernest H. Shepard. Dutton, 1926. M.

Lots of silly action in this story about Piglet and Pooh and their trap to catch a Heffalump.

Orbach, Ruth. *Apple Pigs.* Il. by author. Collins, 1977. P.

A family's apple tree yields too many apples.

Orwell, George. *Animal Farm.* Harcourt, 1946. U.

"A devasting attack on the pigheaded, gluttonous, and avaricious rulers in an imaginary totalitarian state." Satire.

Oxenbury, Helen. *Pig Tale.* Il. by author. Morrow, 1973. P.

Two pigs find that riches bring them a loss of freedom.

Peck, Robert Newton. *A Day No Pigs Would Die.* Knopf, 1972. M.

Growing up Shaker in Vermont.

Peet, Bill. *Chester, the Worldly Pig.* Il. by author. Houghton, 1965. P.

A pig runs away to a circus but must perform with five tigers.

Potter, Beatrix. *The Tale of Pigling Bland.* Il. by author. Warne, 1913. P.

One of Potter's classic little books.

Rayner Mary. *Mr. and Mrs. Pig's Evening Out.* Il. by author. Atheneum, 1976. P.

Ten piglets outwit their wolf babysitter. See also *Garth Pig and the Ice Cream Lady* (Atheneum, 1977).

Ross, Tony. *The Three Pigs.* Il. by author. Pantheon, 1983. P.

In this contemporary version of a classic tale, the three pigs live in an urban setting.

Scott, Jade Denton. *The Book of the Pig.* Il. with photographs by Ozzie Sweet. Putnam, 1981. All ages.

A nonfiction book shows pigs as intelligent, clean, well-behaved, and sociable.

Sharmat, Mitchell. *The Seven Sloppy Days Of Phineas Pig.* Il. by Susan G. Truesdell. Harcourt, 1983. P.

Phineas is too neat and has to take dirty lessons from Cousin Humble.

Steig, William. *The Amazing Bone.* Il. by author. Farrar, 1976. P.

Pearl the pig is befriended by a talking bone.

Stevens, Carla. *Pig and the Blue Flag.* Il. by Rainey Bennett. Clarion, 1977. P.

Pig proves he can be a success in gym even though he's not an athlete. See also *Hooray for Pig!* (Clarion, 1974).

Stine, Jovial Bob. *The Pigs' Book of World Records.* Il. by Peter Lippman. Random, 1980. M, U.

A collection of riddles, jokes, and more for pigophiles.

The Story of the Three Little Pigs by Joseph Jacob. Il. by Lorinda Bryan Cauley. Putnam, 1980. P.

Realistic drawings with humor.

The Three Little Pigs. Il. by Leonard Leslie Brooke. Warne, 1905. P.

Traditional version of the classic tale.

Three Little Pigs. Il. by Rodney Peppé. Lothrop, 1979. P.

Bold colors, cartoons.

The Three Little Pigs. Il. by Erik Blegvad. Atheneum, 1980. P.

Small detailed drawings.

Van Leeuwen, Jean. *Amanda Pig and Her Big Brother Oliver.* Il. by Ann Schweninger. Dial, 1982. P.

Easy-to-read stories.

———. *Tales of Oliver Pig.* Il. by Arnold Lobel. Dial, 1979. P.

Easy-to-read stories about a pig family.

Van Loon, Dirk. *Small-Scale Pig Raising.* Garden Way, 1978. U.

How to buy, breed, and raise pigs.

Watson, Pauline. *Wriggles, the Little Wishing Pig.* Il. by Paul Galdone. Clarion, 1978. P.

Discontented with being a pig, Wriggles wishes he could look like other animals and does.

White, E. B. *Charlotte's Web.* Il. by Garth Williams. Harper, 1952. M.

Wilbur is the famous but humble pig who escapes being made into bacon.

Winthrop, Elizabeth. *Sloppy Kisses.* Il. by Anne Burgess. Macmillan, 1980. M.

Sometimes kisses are needed.

Wodehouse, P. G. *Pigs Have Wings.* Penguin, 1980. U.

The Empress of Blandings nearly lost her title as the fattest pig at the Shropshire Agricultural Show, but luck was with Lord Emsworth: she won again. A romp with Wodehouse.

Saint Patrick's Day

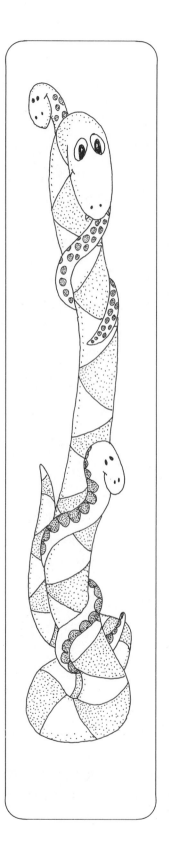

On Saint Patrick's day everyone is Irish.

One of the memorable legends concerning Saint Patrick is that he is responsible for drawing away all the snakes from Ireland.

Children's authors and poets have written some fine stories and poems about snakes, and so I would like to see Saint Patrick's Day set aside for a rousing snake program. The snake program features a charming Japanese story and some amusing snake poems, which I hope you will use. I certainly understand that snakes may not appeal to everyone, particularly as an alternative Saint Patrick's Day celebration, so I'm offering this program in two parts. Part I is the snake celebration. Part II is a much more traditional Saint Patrick's Day miniprogram.

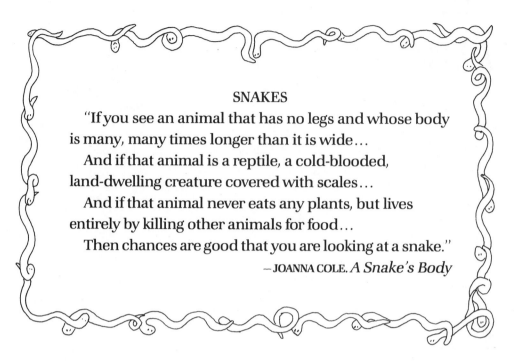

SNAKES

"If you see an animal that has no legs and whose body is many, many times longer than it is wide...

And if that animal is a reptile, a cold-blooded, land-dwelling creature covered with scales...

And if that animal never eats any plants, but lives entirely by killing other animals for food...

Then chances are good that you are looking at a snake."

—JOANNA COLE. *A Snake's Body*

Part I: Slithering Snakes

It's a fact: There are no snakes native to Ireland. Saint Patrick is said to have chased all the snakes away, and they have never come back.

Snakes do not have a good reputation. They are feared by many and have become a symbol of evil, although in some cases of wisdom. Snakes are cold-blooded animals that proliferate in tropical climates. The longest snakes are pythons that live in Asia and the anaconda of South America. These snakes can reach lengths of thirty feet. Other snakes are less than five inches long.

The most fascinating thing about a snake is the way it moves, since it has no legs. It slithers along the ground with its tongue darting in and out. Snakes molt several times a year, slipping out of their skins and leaving the old skin behind.

If possible, children should have a chance to visit with a snake. Those who have never touched snakes will be surprised to find that they are cool and dry to the touch. Actually, snakes will always be the same temperature as their environment. (Try the local zoo, pet shop, or science teacher for a live demonstration.)

Although snakes have teeth, they do not chew their food but grip it. A snake swallows animals and objects whole. It can live almost a year without eating, since it stores excess food as fat.

There are poisonous snakes, but in comparison to the many species of harmless snakes, these are rare. The United States has very few poisonous snakes, and they are easy to identify. Pit vipers and coral snakes are the two main types of poisonous snakes that live in the United States. Pit Vipers include water moccasins (also called cottonmouths), copperheads, and rattlesnakes. They all have a heat-sensitive pit below each eye, which helps them locate warm-blooded prey. Coral snakes are extremely poisonous and have rings of red, yellow, and black. The harmless scarlet king snake looks a lot like a coral snake, but has a red snout, while the poisonous snake has a black snout.

Books about snakes vary from Trinka Noble's humorous book *The Day Jimmy's Boa Ate the Wash* to the sophisticated *The Book of the Dun Cow* by Walter Wangerin. Make sure you exhibit some of the folktales that feature snakes, along with the picture books, novels, and nonfiction.

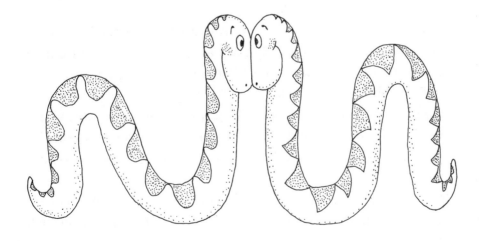

Prose Selections

Saint Patrick and the Snakes
by EILIS DILLON

When Saint Patrick first came to Ireland, the people were very much troubled by snakes, which tormented and frightened them. As the saint went through the country, these evil creatures retired before him and made their homes in the lovely lakes that are scattered throughout the country like clear blue jewels on a green robe. Only sometimes they dared to come out in remote places and destroy the hay and the young corn, and the newly planted gardens of the monasteries.

When the time was coming for Saint Patrick to die, he said to himself:

"What will become of my people when I am gone? The snakes have grown smaller, to be sure, but they are still there lurking in the deep lakes. Who knows but that in later times they may come out again and grow big and fat and powerful? Before I go, I will banish them for good."

So he went to a place near the borders of Cork and Kerry, where there was a huge lake. A farmer whose land ran down to the edge of the lake had complained to the saint that a snake came out at night and stole his sheep and cattle.

"If it's the last thing you do," said the farmer, "for the love of God do something with that snake. I'm afraid to close an eye at night for fear when I'd open it I'd see him before me."

"I will do it for the love of God," said Saint Patrick.

He went alone to the edge of the lake, and when he had prayed for a while he ordered the snake to come up out of the water, and go down to the sea and leave the country for ever. But the snake made no move.

"He feels safe from me in the water," said Saint Patrick. "Very well. I must change the water, not only of this lake but of every lake in Ireland."

170

That night, when the people were all asleep in bed, and the cattle were in the sheds and the sheep and goats penned up safely, the great saint went down to the lake again and prayed. The snake knew that he was there, but he thought that as long as he stayed perfectly still, no harm would come to him.

Then, very gradually, he felt that the cool water in which he lay was changing. It was no longer soft and comforting. It began to burn. It was not hot, but it stung and burned like fire. With a great shriek, the snake rose to the top of the water. He thrashed with his tail, and blew the terrible water in a long spout towards the quietly kneeling saint. Then he shot across the surface of the lake to the opposite bank. He did not pause to do any damage to the farms through which he had passed. His only thought was to get to the sea as quickly as possible and cool his aching body and put as long a distance as he could between himself and that dangerous quiet man who was more powerful than himself.

The same night, all over Ireland, shrieks and groans filled the air as the snakes hurried across country to the sea. Saint Patrick prayed until dawn, until the last sizzling tail had plopped below the water, until the last bloodcurdling wail was smothered in the waves of the sea. And from that day to this, not a single snake, big or small, is to be found in Ireland. For people and for animals, the water of the lakes is clear and good, but the snakes know that for them it burns like a hundred fires.

The Terrible Black Snake's Revenge
by YOSHOKO UCHIDA

High in a small mountain village, there once lived a man whose name was Badger. One day Badger had to go to the village on the other side of the mountains, and in order to do that, he had to travel through a deep and dark forest. The mountain forest was full of bears and wolves and snakes that hid in the tall grass, and Badger trembled as he thought about them.

"Be especially careful of the terrible Black Snake of the Mountains," the villagers warned, "for if he catches you, he will swallow you alive and we will never see you again."

"I know, I know," Badger answered weakly, and his knees wobbled at the very thought of this monstrous snake.

Before dawn the next morning, Badger set out so that he would be clear of the forest by nightfall. He walked briskly into the mountains, whistling to keep up his spirits. Soon he was tramping along the narrow path deep in the shadowy woods, trying hard not to think of the fearful snake. He walked and he walked and he walked, but no matter how far he went, he couldn't seem to get over the mountains. He looked up at the sky and saw the sun creeping higher and higher over his head. Soon it began to dip beyond the treetops and still Badger had not gotten out of the mountain forest. Before long, the dusky shadows of nightfall were all about him and poor Badger knew that he had lost his way.

"Of all the dreadful terrible places to be lost," he muttered, shuddering as he thought of what the night would bring. But it was useless to roam any longer. I must find a safe place to spend the night, he thought, and he looked about for a good hiding place.

At last he came upon a deep cave sheltered behind a mass of boulders. Ah, this will do nicely until morning, Badger thought, and he quickly crawled inside and tried to sleep.

172

As the night wore on, the wind shrieked and moaned, and the trees of the forest seemed to whisper and sigh like a gathering of sorrowful ghosts. An owl hooted dismally above his head, and somewhere in the distant hills a wolf was howling at the moon. Badger closed his eyes tight and tried not to hear the night sounds of the forest, but it was impossible for him to sleep.

About midnight he heard a strange sound. At first it was a faint rustle and then it came closer and closer and closer. Badger shrank into the corner of the cave scarcely daring to breathe. And then something appeared at the mouth of the cave and Badger saw a dark shadow moving inside. It was something long and black and slippery. It was the terrible Black Snake of the Mountains himself, and he slithered closer and closer and closer!

Badger tried to call for help. His mouth was open, but not a sound came out. Frantically, he looked about for a stone or a stick, for if he did not strike the snake first, he would surely be swallowed alive. As he fumbled about desperately, the snake suddenly stopped and spoke to him.

"Who are you and what are you doing in my cave?" he asked quite politely.

"M-m-m-my n-n-n-name —" Poor Badger was so terrified he could not speak. Finally, he simply stuttered. "B-b-b-badger!"

The snake hissed a snakelike laugh. "Ah, so you are a badger," he said. "For a moment I thought you were a human being. You have surely turned yourself into a very good imitation of a human being."

And the snake, believing that he was talking to another animal, relaxed and curled himself into a nice round coil.

"I have heard that you badgers are very clever at disguising yourselves," he said almost enviously. "Now I have seen for myself how well you do."

The snake talked on and on, for he did not have many friends, and furthermore they did not usually come to share his cave in the middle of the night. He told Badger of all the villagers he had swallowed and how delicious they had been.

"They are very frightened of me, I hear," he said boastfully. Then he turned to Badger and asked, "Tell me, is there anything at all that you are truly afraid of?"

Badger almost stammered, "You!" But of course he could never say that. "Well," he said thoughtfully, "I hear that gold is a very cursed thing and that it can very well ruin one. I suppose the thing I fear most is gold."

The snake nodded his big black head and then, because he believed he was talking to a friend, he said, "If you promise never to tell anyone, I will tell you what I fear the most."

"I promise," Badger replied. "Tell me what it is."

"Well," said the snake, writhing at the thought, "what frightens me most is hot melted tar. I could very well be trapped and killed with it." Then the snake stopped and looked straight into Badger's eyes. "If you tell anyone what I have just told you, I will find you no matter where you are and I will seek a fearful revenge. Do you understand?"

Once more Badger was too frightened to speak. He simply nodded his head and wished with all his heart that he were back home in his village.

At last the sun began to rise, and when a streak of light burst into the cave, the snake slithered off, muttering, "I must find another place of darkness until midnight."

Badger gave up all thought of doing any business in the village beyond the mountains. He somehow found his way out of the forest and ran back to his village like a mouse running from a cat. He sputtered out his story of spending the night in the dark cave with the terrible Black Snake of the Mountains. "And I have discovered what it is that the snake fears the most!" he burst out. "Now we can kill him and no one need ever be afraid of crossing the mountains again."

"Badger, you are a brave man!" the villagers cried. And that very night, Badger led them into the forest with a tub full of hot melted tar. They hid behind the boulders beside the cave and waited silently in the black-velvet forest night. About midnight they finally heard the

Black Snake moving over the leaves. The moment he entered his cave they leaped out, and with a great shout they poured in the hot melted tar.

"Never again will you swallow up our villagers!" they cried angrily.

The snake let out a great hissing sound, but he was very clever and very quick, and he somehow escaped the hot melted tar. He managed to slip out of the cave and disappeared into a deep mountain pool before any of the villagers could catch him.

"We have missed our chance," Badger said desolately. "We didn't kill the Black Snake after all." And they all returned to the village feeling anxious and disappointed.

But of all the villagers, Badger was more frightened than anyone else, for he remembered the snake's last words to him. Now he will surely come to find me and seek revenge, Badger thought miserably, and he wondered what terrible fate awaited him that night.

He bolted his door and pushed a great heavy charcoal brazier in front of it. He tried to sleep, but he was much too frightened for that, so he sat before the hearth and waited as the night grew cold and still. Then, at last, toward midnight, he heard a sound outside.

"He has found me already," Badger said with a shiver.

Now there was a rustling at the window, and soon the terrible Black Snake thrust his big black head inside.

"You traitor!" he hissed. "You not only lied to me, you broke your promise and you even tried to kill me. I have come to punish you with a basketful of the one thing you fear most!"

And with a great clatter and crash he threw in an enormous basket that was filled with gold coins.

"Now I have been avenged," the snake hissed and he quickly disappeared into the darkness.

Badger blinked hard and looked at all the gold that was strewn about his floor. Then, when he realized what had happened, he threw back his head and laughed until the tears rolled down his cheeks. He had not only fooled the Black Snake, he had become a wealthy man.

The snake soon discovered that he had been deceived and grew so angry and embarrassed that he disappeared completely from the mountains and never swallowed another human being again. The mountains and forest became safe once more, and Badger lived a good and long life with all the gold he received from the terrible Black Snake.

Poetry Selections

The Python
by JOHN GARDNER

One afternoon, while sitting in a
   tree,
God thought up the Python.
He cracked a grin and clapped his
   hands
And at once got down and made
   one.

When the Son came by, the Python
   hissed
When the Son only meant to touch
   him.
"He's a wonderful kind of snake,"
   said the Son,
"But if I was you, I'd watch him."

The Python from then on did
   nothing wrong
Till in Eden trouble came,
And Adam and Eve swore up and
   down
That the Python was to blame.

All Heaven had doubts, but the
   Python was cleared
By a full investigation;
Yet no one has trusted a Python
   since.
Beware of a bad reputation.

Boa Constrictor
by SHEL SILVERSTEIN

Oh, I'm being eaten
By a boa constrictor,
A boa constrictor,
A boa constrictor,
I'm being eaten by a boa
   constrictor,
And I don't like it—one bit.
Well, what do you know?
It's nibblin' my toe.
Oh, gee,
It's up to my knee.
Oh my,
It up to my thigh.
Oh, fiddle,
It's up to my middle.
Oh, heck,
It's up to my neck.
Oh, dread,
It's upmmmmmmmmmmffffffffff...

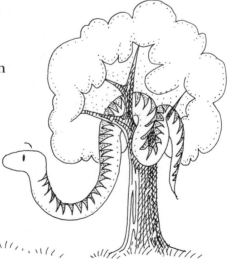

177

The Snake

by KARLA KUSKIN

A snake slipped through the thin
    green grass
A silver snake
I watched it pass
It moved like a ribbon
Silent as snow.
I think it smiled
As it passed my toe.

The Snake

by JACK PRELUTSKY

Don't ever make
the bad mistake
of stepping on
the sleeping snake

because
his jaws

might be awake.

Treat

Rope licorice.

178

Bulletin Board

Colored paper snakes each with a snake title lettered on it.

Creative Writing/Activity

A snake is a strange animal. Have your group write an original "why" story explaining how they think snakes came to be—were they invented? Did they just appear? Below is a list of "snake facts" that may provide some inspiration for this creative writing activity.

The longest snake ever measured was a Reticulated Python who was 32 feet, 9½ inches long (10 meters).

The heaviest snake ever weighed was an Anaconda who weighed 600 pounds (272 kilos).

Snakes keep growing all their lives. Each time that a snake gets too big for its skin it sheds it. A young snake may shed its skin seven times in one year.

Only about 400 of the 2700 species of snakes are poisonous. Less than 50 species are really dangerous to people.

If you travel in South Asia you may be entertained by a snake charmer and his cobra. Don't think that the snake is really dancing to the sound of a flute. A snake has no ears.

Books about Snakes:

Adams, Laurie, and Allison Coudert. *Alice and the Boa Constrictor*. Il. by Emily Arnold McCully. Houghton, 1983. M.

    Alice earns money to buy her own pet boa constrictor, Sir Lancelot.

Asch, Frank. *Pearl's Promise*. Il. by author. Delacort, 1984. M.

    Pearl, a white mouse, vows to free her brother Tony from the clutches of Prang, the snake.

Berson, Harold. *Joseph and the Snake*. Il. by author. Macmillan, 1979. P.

    A clever fox saves Joseph from being eaten by the snake whose life he has saved.

Boston, Lucy, M. *The Fossil Snake*. Il. by Peter Boston. McElderry, 1976. M.

    A fossil snake comes back to life as Ra.

Brenner, Barbara. *A Snake-lover's Diary*. Young Scott, 1970. M.

    A young boy collects snakes all summer and then lets them go in the fall so they can hibernate.

Carlson, Natalie Savage. *Marie Louise & Christophe*. Il. by Jose Aruego and Ariane Dewey. Scribner, 1974. P.

    A mongoose and a spotted green snake outwit their captors in a story of friendship.

Carter, Dorothy Sharp. "Snake the Postman" in *Greedy Mariani and Other Folktales of the Antilles*. Il. by Trina Schart Hyman. McElderry, 1974. M, U.

    Snake agrees to deliver Annancy's mail, but the arrangement doesn't work out well.

Cole, Joanna. *A Snake's Body*. Il. with photographs by Jerome Wexler. Morrow, 1981. All ages.

    Very clear, detailed photographs and text describe the internal and external organs of a snake.

Corbett, W.J. *The Song of Pentecost*. Il. by Martin Ursell. Dutton, 1983. M, U.

    Although Snake is scary, a group of mice join him to search for a new home.

Holman, Felice, and Nanine Valen. "The Vouivre; The Flying Serpent" in *The Drac: French Tales of Dragons and Demons*. Il. by Stephen Walker. Scribner, 1975. M, U.

    Once a year the Vouivre leaves her cave, giving those who dare a chance to steal from the flying serpent.

Israel, Abigial P. *A Boy and a Boa*. Il. by Kevin Brooks. Dial, 1981. M.

    Martin's pet boa constrictor gets loose in the library.

Jaquith, Pricilla. "Rattlesnake's World" in *Bo Rabbit He Smart for True: Folktales from the Gullah*. Il. by Ed Young. Collins, 1980. M.

    Bear outwits Rattlesnake in an illustrated folktale.

Kipling, Rudyard. *Jungle Book*. Il. by J. Lockwood Kipling and W.H. Drake. Macmillan (London), 1924. M.

    Mowgli, a human boy, is raised by a pack of wolves and advised and protected by a python, a bear, and a leopard.

Lang, Andrew, comp. "The Enchanted Snake" in *Green Fairy Book*, ed. by Brian Alderson. Il. by Antony Maitland. Viking, 1978. M.

    Magical story of transformation. Could be cut in the middle for an excellent read-aloud tale.

Leen, Nina. *Snakes*. Il. with photographs. Holt, 1978. P, M.

    The life cycle and behavior pattern of snakes in clear black-and-white photographs.

Noble, Trinka Hakes. *The Day Jimmy's Boa Ate the Wash*. Il. by Steven Kellogg. Dial, 1980. All ages.

    A zany class field trip features a boa constrictor and colorful humorous drawings.

Reinl, Edda. *The Little Snake*. Il. by author. Neugebauer Press, 1982. All ages.

    A little snake befriends a flower. Full-color drawings.

Roughsey, Dick. *The Rainbow Serpent.* Il. by author. Collins, 1980. All ages.

The Rainbow Serpent looks for his own tribe and shapes the mountains, rivers and hills of Australia. Winner of the Australian Picture Book of the Year Award.

Rounds, Glen. *Mr. Yowder and the Giant Bull Snake.* Il. by author. Holiday House, 1978. M.

Xenon Zebulon Yowder trains a huge snake to hunt buffalos with him in an American Western tall tale.

Simon, Hilda. *Snakes: The Facts and the Folklore.* Il. by author. Viking, 1973. M.

The role of snakes in myth is explored and then factual information is given.

Turpin, Lorna. *The Sultan's Snakes.* Il. by author. Greenwillow, 1980. All ages.

The sultan's snakes are hiding in the drawings. Find them.

Ungerer, Tom. *Crictor.* Il. by author. Harper, 1958. P.

Crictor, a boa constrictor, lives with Madame Bodot in a French village. He can spell, jump rope, and catch robbers.

Waber, Bernard. *The Snake: A Very Long Story.* Il. by author. Houghton, 1978. P.

A snake wriggles through time and place in a charming voyage.

Wangerin, Walter, Jr. *The Book of the Dun Cow.* Harper, 1978. U.

A sophisticated novel of Good versus Evil. The embodiment of Evil is the Wyrm who lives beneath the earth.

Wise, William. *Giant Snakes and Other Amazing Reptiles.* Il. by Joseph Sibal. Putnam, 1970.

Information about reptiles, including rattlesnakes, cobras, and sea snakes.

Part II:
Saint Patrick's Day

Saint Patrick's Day was originally observed as a church festival in Ireland. The holiday can be traced back as far as AD 493. In America Saint Patrick's Day was celebrated as early as 1737.

Saint Patrick's Day is an example of a holiday that Americans — of Irish backgrounds or not — have embraced as a people, and so most people are rather vague about what they are celebrating on March seventeenth and why. Probably one of the appeals of Saint Patrick's Day is that it comes just at the end of winter, heralding the green of spring. There are few official holidays in the winter, and most people are happy to put on a symbolic color and have a little fun.

My mother worked in an office on Fifth Avenue in New York City. The Saint Patrick's Day parade went right by her office building. Her coworkers could hardly wait for the parade to pass by because my mom would just walk into the parade and be a part of it for a block or two. The windows of the building would be jammed with people, all cheering for Alice Feller. The moral of the story is: Anyone can be Irish on Saint Patrick's Day.

"Murdoch's Rath" is one of my favorite Irish stories, filled with magic and little people. If you choose not to make an authentic Irish recipe to serve as a treat, just offer baked potatoes, cold or hot, with green-colored butter.

Prose Selection

Murdoch's Rath
by JULIANA HORATIA EWING

There was not a nicer boy in all Ireland than Pat, and clever at his trade, too, if only he'd had one.

But from his cradle he learned nothing (small blame to him, with no one to teach him) so when he came to years of discretion he earned his living by running messages for his neighbors; and Pat could always be trusted to make the best of a bad bargain and bring back all the change, for he was the soul of honesty and good nature.

It's no wonder then that he was beloved by everyone and got as much work as he could do; and if the pay had but fitted the work, he'd have been mighty comfortable; but as it was, what he got wouldn't have kept him in shoeleather, but for making both ends meet by wearing his shoes in his pocket, except when he was in town and obliged to look genteel for the credit of the place he came from.

Well, all was going on as peaceable as could be, till one market day, when business (or it might have been pleasure) detained him till the heel of the evening, and by nightfall, when he began to make the road short in good earnest, he was so flustered, rehearsing his messages to make sure he'd forgotten nothing, that he never bethought him to leave off his brogues but tramped on just as if shoeleather was made to be knocked to bits on the king's highway.

And this is what he was after saying:

"A dozen hanks of gray yarn for Mistress Murphy.

"Three gross of bright buttons for the tailor.

"Half an ounce of throat-drops for Father Andrew, and an ounce of snuff for his housekeeper," and so on.

For these were what he went to the town to fetch, and he was afraid lest one of the lot might have slipped his memory.

Now everybody knows there are two ways home from the town, and that's not meaning the right way and the wrong way, which my grandmother (rest her soul!) said there was to every place but one that it's not genteel to name. (There could only be a wrong way *there;* she said.) The two ways home from town were the highway and the way by Murdoch's Rath.*

Murdoch's Rath was a pleasant enough spot in the daytime, but not many persons cared to go by it when the sun was down. And in all the years Pat was going backwards and forwards, he never once came home except by the highroad till this unlucky evening, when, just at the place where the two roads part, he got, as one may say, into a sort of confusion.

"Halt!" says he to himself (for his uncle had been a soldier). "The left-hand turn is the right one," says he, and he was going down the highroad as straight as he could go, when suddenly he bethought himself. "And what am I doing?" he says. "This was my left hand going to town, and how in the name of fortune could it be my left going back, considering that I've turned round? It's well that I looked into it in time." And with that he went off as fast down the other road as he had started down this.

But how far he walked he never could tell, before all of a sudden the moon shone out as bright as day and Pat found himself in Murdoch's Rath.

And this was the smallest part of the wonder for the rath was full of fairies.

When Pat got in, they were dancing round and round till his feet tingled to look at them, being a good dancer himself. And as he sat on the side of the rath, and snapped his fingers to mark the time, the dancing stopped, and a little man comes up, in a black hat and a green coat, with white stockings and red shoes on his feet.

"Won't you take a turn with us, Pat?" says he, bowing till he nearly reached the ground. And, indeed, he had not far to go, for he was barely two feet high.

---

*Rath — a kind of moat-surrounded spot much favored by Irish fairies. The ditch is generally overgrown with furze-bushes.

"Don't say it twice, sir," says Pat. "It's myself will be proud to foot the floor wid ye"; and before you could look round, there was Pat in the circle dancing away for bare life.

At first his feet felt like feathers for lightness, and it seemed as if he could have gone on forever. But at last he grew tired, and would have liked to stop, but the fairies would not, and so they danced on and on. Pat tried to think of something *good* to say, that he might free himself from the spell, but all he could think of was:

"A dozen hanks of gray yarn for Mistress Murphy.

"Three gross of bright buttons for the tailor.

"Half an ounce of throat drops for Father Andrew, and an ounce of snuff for his housekeeper," and so on.

And it seemed to Pat that the moon was on the one side of the rath when they began to dance, and on the other side when they left off; but he could not be sure after all that going round. One thing was plain enough. He danced every bit of leather off the soles of his feet, and they were blistered so that he could hardly stand; but all the little folk did was to stand and hold their sides with laughing at him.

At last the one who spoke before stepped up to him, and—"Don't break your heart about it, Pat," says he, "I'll lend you my own shoes till the morning, for you seem to be a good-natured sort of a boy."

Well, Pat looked at the fairy man's shoes, that were the size of a baby's, and he looked at his own feet; but not wishing to be uncivil, "Thank ye kindly, sir," says he. "And if your honor'll be good enough to put them on for me, maybe you won't spoil the shape." For he thought to himself, "Small blame to me if the little gentleman can't get them to fit."

With that he sat down on the side of the rath, and the fairy man put on the shoes for him, and no sooner did they touch Pat's feet than they became altogether a convenient size, and fitted him like wax. And, more than that, when he stood up, he didn't feel his blisters at all.

"Bring 'em back to the rath at sunrise, Pat, my boy," says the little man.

And as Pat was climbing over the ditch, "Look round, Pat," says he. And when Pat looked round, there were jewels and pearls lying at the roots of the furze-bushes on the ditch, as thick as peas.

"Will you help yourself, or take what's given ye, Pat?" says the fairy man.

"Did I ever learn manners?" says Pat. "Would you have me help myself before company? I'll take what your honor please to give me, and be thankful."

The fairy man picked a lot of yellow furze-blossoms from the bushes, and filled Pat's pockets.

"Keep'em for love, Pat, me darlin'," says he.

Pat would have liked some of the jewels, but he put the furze-blossms by for love.

"Good evening to your honor," says he.

"And where are you going, Pat dear?" says the fairy man.

"I'm going home," says Pat. And if the fairy didn't know where that was, small blame to him.

"Just let me dust those shoes for ye, Pat," says the fairy man. And as Pat lifted up each foot he breathed on it and dusted it with the tail of his green coat.

"Home!" says he, and when he let go, Pat was at his own doorstep before he would look round, and his parcels safe and sound with him.

Next morning he was up with the sun and carried the fairy man's shoes back to the rath. As he came up, the little man looked over the ditch.

"The top of the morning to your honor," says Pat. "Here's your shoes."

"You're an honest boy, Pat," says the little gentleman. "It's inconvenienced I am without them, for I have but the one pair. Have you looked at the yellow flowers this morning?" he says.

"I have not sir," says Pat. "I'd be loath to deceive you. I came off as soon as I was up."

"Be sure to look when you get back, Pat," says the fairy man, "and good luck to ye!"

With which he disappeared, and Pat went home. He looked for the furze-blossoms, as the fairy man told him, and there's not a word of truth in this tale if they weren't all pure gold pieces.

Well, now Pat was so rich, he went to the shoemaker to order another pair of brogues, and being a kindly, gossiping boy, he soon told the shoemaker the whole story of the fairy man and the rath. And this so stirred up the shoemaker's greed that he resolved to go the next night himself, to see if he could not dance with the fairies, and have like luck.

He found his way to the rath all correct, and sure enough the fairies were dancing, and they asked him to join. He danced the soles off his brogues, as Pat did, and the fairy man lent him his shoes, and sent him home in a twinkling.

As he was going over the ditch, he looked round and saw the roots of the furze-bushes glowing with precious stones as if they had been glowworms.

"Will you help yourself, or take what's given ye?" said the fairy man.

"I'll help myself, if you please," said the cobbler, for he thought — "If I can't get more than Pat brought home, my fingers must all be thumbs."

So he drove his hand into the bushes, and if he didn't get plenty, it wasn't for want of grasping.

When he got up in the morning, he went straight to the jewels. But not a stone of the lot was more precious than roadside pebbles. "I ought not to look till I come from the rath," said he. "It's best to do like Pat all through."

But he made up his mind not to return the fairy man's shoes.

"Who knows the virtue that's in them?" he said. So he made a small pair of red leather shoes, as like them as could be, and he blacked the others upon his feet, that the fairies might not know them, and at sunrise he went to the rath.

The fairy man was looking over the ditch as before.

"Good morning to you," said he.

"The top of the morning to you, sir," said the cobbler. "Here's your shoes." And he handed him the pair that he had made, with a face as grave as a judge.

The fairy man looked at them, but he said nothing, though he did not put them on.

"Have you looked at the things you got last night?" says he.

"I'll not deceive you sir," says the cobbler. "I came off as soon as I was up. Not a peep I took at them."

"Be sure to look when you get back," says the fairy man. And just as the cobbler was getting over the ditch to go home, he says: "If my eyes don't deceive me," says he, "there's the least taste in life of dirt on your left shoe. Let me dust it with the tail of my coat."

"That means home in a twinkling," thought the cobbler, and he held up his foot.

The fairy man dusted it, and muttered something the cobbler did not hear. Then, "Sure," says he, "it's the dirty pastures that you've come through, for the other shoe's as bad."

So the cobbler held up his right foot, and the fairy man rubbed that with the tail of his green coat.

When all was done, the cobbler's feet seemed to tingle, and then to itch, and then to smart, and then to burn. And at last he began to dance, and he danced all round the rath (the fairy man laughing and holding his sides) and then round and round again. And he danced till he cried out with weariness and tried to shake the shoes off. But they stuck fast, and the fairies drove him over the ditch, and through the prickly furze-bushes, and he danced away. Where he danced to, I cannot tell you. Whether he ever got rid of the fairy shoes I do not know. The jewels never were more than wayside pebbles, and they were swept out when his cabin was cleaned, which was not too soon, you may be sure.

All this happened long ago; but there are those who say that the covetous cobbler dances still, between sunset and sunrise, round Murdoch's Rath.

Poetry Selections

The Pointed People

by RACHEL FIELD

I don't know who they are,
But when it's shadow time
In woods where the trees crowd
    close,
With bristly branches crossed,
From their secret hiding places
I have seen the Pointed People
Gliding through brush and
    bracken.
Maybe a peakèd cap
Pricking out through the leaves,
Or a tiny pointed ear
Up-cocked, all brown and furry,
From ferns and berry brambles,
Or a pointed hoof's sharp print
Deep in the tufted moss,
And once a pointed face
That peered between the cedars,
Blinking bright eyes at me
And shaking with silent laughter.

The Little Wee Man

An old Scottish ballad retold by IAN SERRAILLIER

As I was walking all alone
Between a river and a wall,
There I saw a little wee man —
I'd never seen a man so small.

His legs were barely a finger long,
His shoulders wide as fingers three;
Light and springing was his step,
And he stood lower than my knee.

He lifted a stone six feet high,
He lifted it up to his right knee,
Above his chest, above his head,
And flung it as far as I could see.

"O," said I, "how strong you are!
I wonder where your home can be."
"Down the green valley there;
O, will you come with me and see?"

So on we ran, and away we rode,
Until we came to his bonny hall;
The roof was made of beaten gold,
The floor was made of crystal all.

Pipers were playing, ladies
    dancing,
Four-and-twenty ladies fair;
Nimbly dancing, sweetly singing,
"Our little wee man's been too long
    from here."

Out went the lights, on came the
    mist.
Where were the ladies — where
    were they?
I looked and saw the wall and
    river...
But the little wee man was clean
    away.

189

Treat

Traditional Irish Soda Bread

YOU NEED: 4 cups unsifted all-purpose flour

2 tablespoons sugar

1 teaspoon baking soda

1 teaspoon salt

1 cup seedless raisins

1 to 1¼ cups buttermilk

2 tablespoons soft butter

HOW TO: Combine flour, sugar, soda, salt, and raisins in a mixing bowl. Stir well.

Make a well in the center of the mixture. Add buttermilk. Stir until lightly but thoroughly blended. Use only enough buttermilk to make a stiff dough.

Turn out onto a lightly floured board. Knead 5 times. Form into a ball.

Place on a lightly greased cookie sheet. Pat to an 8-inch circle, approximately 1½ inches thick.

With a floured knife make a large cross on top of the loaf to keep it from cracking during baking. Spread the top of the loaf with softened butter. Bake in a preheated 375°F oven forty to fifty minutes or until golden and the loaf sounds hollow when tapped. Serve bread hot with plenty of butter. Makes 1 loaf, 8 inches in diameter.

Bulletin Board

Saint Patrick's Day
is
Green

Have children list objects that are green, such as:

leaves	grass	leprechauns
peas	beans	chalkboards
cucumbers	green peppers	army uniforms
grapes	crocodiles	pistachio nuts
frogs	limes	traffic lights
mold	lettuce	moss
M & M's		

Activity

See the world in green.

YOU NEED: poster board
green cellophane
white glue

HOW TO: Cut a circle with a handle from poster board. Glue green cellophane to the frame to make a green spy glass. Use your green spyglass to look at a totally green world.

Irish Jokes

Pat: Why does cream cost so much more than milk?
Haggis: It's more expensive to train cows to sit on the small cartons.

The lazy farmer and his wife were lying in bed.
Husband: Go out, wife, and see if it's raining.
Wife: Nay. Call the dog in and see if he's wet.

Clancy: Did you know that heat makes things expand and cold
            makes them contract?
Shamus: What makes you say that?
Clancy: Days are long in the summer and short in the winter.

Flynn: Have you made your will?
Conan: Yes. Everything will be left to the doctor who saves my life.

Creative Writing

Think small. Write about a visit to the Wee Folk. How would you as
a "giant" have to adapt to their lifestyle?

192

Books for Saint Patrick's Day:

Balian, Lorna. *Leprechauns Never Lie.* Il. by author. Abingdon, 1980. P.

> Lazy Ninny Nanncy tries to trick a leprechaun into telling her where his gold is hidden.

Barth, Edna. *Shamrocks, Harps and Shillelaghs: The Story of the St. Patrick's Day Symbols.* Il. by Ursula Arndt. Clarion, 1977. M.

> Stories and legends surrounding Saint Patrick's Day.

Bunting, Eve. *Ghost of Summer.* Warne, 1977. M, U.

> Kevin spends a summer in northern Ireland where he discovers ruthless men searching for treasure and gets involved with a political fight to save his grandfather's church from demolition.

———. *St. Patrick's Day in the Morning.* Il. by Jan Brett. Clarion, 1980. P.

> Jamie decides he is old enough to march in the Saint Patrick's Day parade.

———. *The Haunting of Kildoran Abbey.* Warne, 1978. M, U.

> Eight children plan to steal from the rich to give to the poor during Ireland's 1945 potato famine.

Cummings, Betty Sue. *And Now Ameriky.* Atheneum, 1979. U.

> Brigid must leave Ireland for America, hopefully to earn passage money for her family.

de Paola, Tomie. *Fin M'Coul: the Giant of Knockmany Hill.* Holiday, 1981. P.

> Oonagh, Fin's wife, fools Cucullin the giant.

Evslin, Bernard. *The Green Hero: Early Adventures of Finn McCool.* Il. by Barbara Bascove. Four Winds, 1975. U.

> The Finn McCool legends are told as a continuous narrative.

Greene, Ellin, comp. "Wee Meg Barnileg and the Fairies" in *Midsummer Magic, a Garland of Stories, Charms, and Recipes.* Il. by Barbara Cooney. Lothrop, 1977. M.

> Meg is forced to live with the fairies to learn to be a well-bred child.

Haviland, Virginia. *Favorite Fairy Tales Told in Ireland.* Il. by Artur Marokvia. Little, 1961. M.

> Five popular tales retold for independent reading.

Jones, Diana Wynne. *Dogsbody.* Greenwillow, 1977. U.

> A fantasy in which the dogstar Sirius is befriended by an Irish girl living with hostile relatives.

Kennedy, Richard. *The Leprechaun's Story.* Il. by Marcia Sewall. Dutton, 1979. P.

> If you stare at the leprechaun you'll win his gold, but not if he tells "the saddest story that ever a man did hear."

Kessel, Joyce K. *St. Patrick's Day.* Il. by Cathy Gilchrist. Carolrhoda, 1982. P, M.

> Overview of Saint Patrick's Day for early readers.

Langford, Sondra Gordon. *Red Bird of Ireland.* McElderry, 1983. U.

> Aderyn tells of her life in nineteenth-century Ireland.

MacManus, Seumas, comp. *Hibernian Nights.* Il. by Paul Kennedy. Macmillan, 1963. U.

> A famous storyteller collected his favorite Irish tales to be read aloud.

Marzollo, Jean. *Halfway Down Paddy Lane.* Dial, 1981. U.

> In this time fantasy Kate finds herself back in the 1850's in a Connecticut milltown and must adjust to prejudices against Irish immigrants.

O'Faolain, Eileen. *Irish Sagas and Folk-tales.* Il. by Joan Kiddell-Monroe. Avenel, 1982. U.

Reprint of a 1949 collection of heroes, fairies, and leprechauns.

Shub, Elizabeth. *Seeing Is Believing.* Il. by Rachel Isadora. Greenwillow, 1979. P.

In this "Read-Alone Book" Tom is tricked by a wee man and so loses a leprechaun's gold.

Stoutenburg, Adrien. "The Giant Who Sucked His Thumb" in *Fee, Fi, Fo, Fum, Friendly and Funny Giants.* Il. by Rocco Negri. Viking, 1969. M.

Fingal's thumb warns him of danger but Oonaugh tricks Cucullin into submission.

Sutcliff, Rosemary. *The High Deeds of Finn MacCool.* Il. by Michael Charlton. Dutton, 1967. U.

The stories of the traditional Irish warrior hero collected by a master storyteller.

Wiggin, Kate Douglas, and Nora Archibald Smith, eds. "Hookedy-Crookedy" in *The Fairy Ring,* revised by Ethna Sheehan. Il. by Warren Chappell. Doubleday, 1967. M.

Jack works for a giant and makes friends with an enchanted mare and a bear. "The Bee, the Harp, the Mouse, and the Bum-Clock" and "The Long Leather Bag" are in the same collection.

Spring into Spring

Gardens are not made
By singing "Oh, how beautiful!" and
sitting in the shade.

— RUDYARD KIPLING

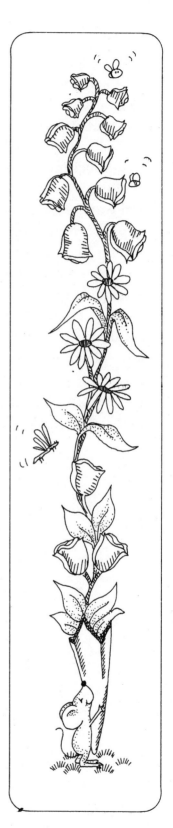

Spring arrives when the earth's axis begins to tilt toward the sun. Scientists and almanacs can give you the official date of this phenomenon (somewhere around March 20) but each of us has a private idea of when spring really comes to our town.

Perhaps spring comes to your house when you feel the windows need a good cleaning. Spring may mean a switch from heavy sweaters to T-shirts. The arrival of the first robin, the first day you feel the urge to toss a baseball, or lie on the grass — any of these might be your private signal that spring is finally, suddenly, here.

In some regions of the United States spring arrives with an explosion of color, and in other places with a lone bud on a tree. However it arrives, spring is a welcome sight, unless, of course, you sell snow shovels.

Although our family have always been complete failures at gardening—we own the tallest weeds in the neighborhood—reading and watching and thinking about growing things has always given us pleasure. Apparently other people really enjoy gardening because it is the fifth most popular spare-time activity in the United States.

Celebrate spring by growing a plant, reading about gardens, and singing the praises of spring.

Many of the books listed in the bibliography use the theme of growing things to parallel the growth of the characters in the story. Some books are fantasies or science fiction showing the plant world behaving in unnatural ways. The bibliography also includes non-fiction books that discuss gardening in a general way and relate growing things to folklore or seasonal activity.

Prose Selections

Spring is the time to get out the seed catalog and think about what to plant in your vegetable garden. Will you plant radishes? Peas? Corn? What about parsnips?

from "A Taste for Parsnips"

by ROGER B. SWAIN

Vegetable seed catalogs have replaced the penny candy store. The fireballs, the root-beer barrels, and the licorice whips aren't sold at the corner anymore. Now the sweets are sold by seed companies instead. There's "Candystick" and "Sweet Slice" and "Sugar Rock," but these aren't types of candy, they are varieties of sweet corn, cucumber, and muskmelon. Flipping through the pages of a seed catalog, one is reminded again and again of the confections that were once arrayed beneath a glass counter. "Cherry Sweet" pepper, "Honey Drip" muskmelon, "Small Sugar" pumpkin, "Sweetheart" carrot. The variety is as great as it was at the candy store, and it is no easier to make a selection now. How do you choose between "Supersweet," "Sweet 'n Early," and "Earlisweet" muskmelons, or between "Sugar Loaf," "Sugar King," and "Sugar Sweet" sweet corn? There is even "Sweet Spanish" onion, "Sugar Hat" chicory, "Sweet Meat" squash, and "Sugar Lump" tomato, "Short 'n Sweet," "Tiny Sweet," "Tendersweet" carrots. "Sweet Mama" squash is followed by "Sugar Baby" watermelon. There is no end to the sweet appellations.

Yet one vegetable is missing from this sweet assemblage — the parsnip. None of the catalogs are calling the parsnip *sweet* anything. What makes this so surprising is that the parsnip is unequivocally sweet. The long, conical, white roots are far sweeter than any carrot, cucumber, or chicory, especially after they have been subject to freezing weather....

In the light of the evidence that parships are delicious, nutritious, and prolific, one would expect them to be very popular. They aren't. Most seed catalogs offer only one variety, at most two or three, and most gardens have none at all. Ask someone why they aren't growing parsnips, and you are likely to provoke the following conversation:

"I don't like parsnips."
"What is it about parsnips that you don't like?"
"The taste. I don't like the taste of parsnips."
"Well, what is it about the taste that you don't like?"
(Pause.) "I just don't like them, that's all."
"Have you ever actually tasted parsnips?"
"Well, no."

There's something about unfamiliar food that makes people think they won't like the taste. It's virtually impossible to convince a child to taste something new, and it's not much easier to persuade an adult. In both cases, the name that is given to the food is very important. Try giving tapioca the varietal name "Fish-Eyes and Glue" and see if anyone will try it.

This brings us back to the proliferation of sweet names in seed catalogs. One almost suspects a conspiracy aimed at persuading children (and adults) to eat vegetables. Consider the edible podded pea for example. Names like "Little Sweetie" and "Sugar Snap" seem designed specifically to make this strange vegetable seem good to eat. Is "Super Sweetpod" aimed at admirers of Superheroes? If "Dwarf Gray Sugar" proves unappetizing, then there is always "Mammoth Melting Sugar."

I suspect that incorporating *sweet* or *sugar* into a name of a vegetable goes a long way toward assuring its popularity. Parsnips languish under such names as "Offenham" and "Hollow Crown." Why not revive some of the sweet names for parsnips? I say revive, because seventy-five years ago seed catalogs contained a lot of them. In the *List of American Varieties of Vegetables for the Years 1901* and 1902, a compendium of every name found in seed catalogs, the following names were used for "Hollow Crown" parsnips: "Improved Sugar," "Large Improved Sugar," "Large Sugar," "Long Sugar," "Long White Sugar," "Sugar Cup," and simply "Sugar." Resurrect some of these names and parsnips may once again become a staple garden crop.

An old southern proverb says "Fine words butter no parsnips." They don't, but sweet ones will help people to take the first bite.

Persephone

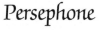

retold by INGRI AND EDGAR PARIN d'AULAIRE

Persephone grew up on Olympus and her gay laughter rang through the brilliant halls. She was the daughter of Demeter, goddess of the harvest, and her mother loved her so dearly she could not bear to have her out of her sight. When Demeter sat on her golden throne, her daughter was always on her lap; when she went down to earth to look after her trees and fields, she took Persephone. Wherever Persephone danced on her light feet, flowers sprang up. She was so lovely and full of grace that even Hades, who saw so little, noticed her and fell in love with her. He wanted her for his queen, but he knew that her mother would never consent to part with her, so he decided to carry her off.

One day as Persephone ran about in the meadow gathering flowers, she strayed away from her mother and the attending nymphs. Suddenly, the ground split open and up from the yawning crevice came a dark chariot drawn by black horses. At the reins stood grim Hades. He seized the terrified girl, turned his horses, and plunged back into the ground. A herd of pigs rooting in the meadow tumbled into the cleft, and Persephone's cries for help died out as the ground closed again as suddenly as it had opened. Up in the field, a little swineherd stood and wept over the pigs he had lost, while Demeter rushed wildly about in the meadow, looking in vain for her daughter, who had vanished without leaving a trace.

With the frightened girl in his arms, Hades raced his snorting horses down away from the sunlit world. Down and down they sped on the dark path to his dismal underground palace. He led weeping Persephone in, seated her beside him on a throne of black marble, and decked her with gold and precious stones. But the jewels brought her no joy. She wanted no cold stones. She longed for warm sunshine and flowers and her golden-tressed mother.

Dead souls crowded out from cracks and crevices to look at their new queen, while ever more souls came across the Styx, and Persephone watched them drink from a spring under dark poplars. It was the spring of Lethe, and those who drank from its waters forgot who they were and what they had done on earth. Rhadaman- thus, a judge of the dead, dealt out punishment to the souls of great sinners. They were sentenced to suffer forever under the whips of the avenging Erinyes. Heroes were led to the Elysian fields, where they lived happily forever in never-failing light.

Around the palace of Hades there was a garden where whispering poplars and weeping willows grew. They had no flowers and bore no fruit and no birds sang in their branches. There was only one tree in the whole realm of Hades that bore fruit. That was a little pomegranate tree. The gardener of the underworld offered the tempt- ing pomegranates to the queen, but Persephone refused to touch the food of the dead.

Wordlessly she walked through the garden at silent Hades' side, and slowly her heart turned to ice.

Above, on earth, Demeter ran about searching for her lost daughter, and all nature grieved with her. Flowers wilted, trees lost their leaves, and the fields grew barren and cold. In vain did the plow cut through the icy ground; nothing could sprout and nothing could grow while the goddess of the harvest wept. People and animals starved and the gods begged Demeter again to bless the earth. But she refused to let anything grow until she had found her daughter.

Bent with grief, Demeter turned into a gray old woman. She returned to the meadow where Persephone had vanished and asked the sun if he had seen what had happened, but he said no, dark clouds had hidden his face that day. She wandered around the meadow and after a while she met a youth whose name was Triptolemus. He told her that his brother, a swineherd, had seen his pigs disappear into the ground and had heard the frightened screams of a girl.

Demeter now understood that Hades had kidnaped her daughter, and her grief turned to anger. She called to Zeus and said that she would never again make the earth green if he did not command Hades to return Persephone. Zeus could not let the world perish and he sent Hermes down to Hades, bidding him to let Persephone go. Even Hades had to obey the orders of Zeus, and sadly he said farewell to his queen.

Joyfully Persephone leaped to her feet, but as she was leaving with Hermes, a hooting laugh came from the garden. There stood the gardener of Hades, grinning. He pointed to a pomegranate from which a few of the kernels were missing. Persephone, lost in thought, had eaten the seeds, he said.

Then dark Hades smiled. He watched Hermes lead Persephone up to the bright world above. He knew that she must return to him, for she had tasted the food of the dead.

When Persephone again appeared on earth, Demeter sprang to her feet with a cry of joy and rushed to greet her daughter. No longer was she a sad old woman, but a radiant goddess. Again she blessed her fields and the flowers bloomed anew and the grain ripened.

"Dear child," she said, "never again shall we be parted. Together we shall make all nature bloom." But joy soon was changed to sadness, for Persephone had to admit that she had tasted the food of the dead and must return to Hades. However, Zeus decided that mother and daughter should not be parted forever. He ruled that Persephone had to return to Hades and spend one month in the underworld for each seed she had eaten.

Every year, when Persephone left her, Demeter grieved, nothing grew, and there was winter on earth. But as soon as her daughter's light footsteps were heard, the whole earth burst into bloom. Spring had come. As long as mother and daughter were together, the earth was warm and bore fruit.

Demeter was a kind goddess. She did not want mankind to starve during the cold months of winter when Persephone was away. She lent her chariot laden with grain to Triptolemus, the youth who had helped her to find her lost daughter. She told him to scatter her golden grain over the world and teach men how to sow it in spring and reap it in fall and store it away for the long months when again the earth was barren and cold.

Poetry Selections

Spring

by KARLA KUSKIN

I'm shouting
I'm singing
I'm swinging through trees
I'm winging sky-high
With the buzzing black bees.
I'm the sun
I'm the moon
I'm the dew on the rose.
I'm a rabbit
Whose habit
Is twitching his nose.
I'm lively
I'm lovely
I'm kicking my heels.
I'm crying "Come dance"
To the freshwater eels.
I'm racing through meadows
Without any coat
I'm a gamboling lamb
I'm a light leaping goat
I'm a bud
I'm a bloom
I'm a dove on the wing.
I'm running on rooftops
And welcoming spring!

A Commercial for Spring

by EVE MERRIAM

Tired of slush and snow and sleet?
Then try this dandy calendar treat!

You'll like the longer, king-size
days;
You, too, will sing this season's
praise.

It's the scientific sunshine pill
(Without that bitter winter chill).

It's naturally warmer, it's toasted
through,
Exclusively mild for you and *you*.

It comes in the handy three-month
pack:
March, April, May — or your money
back.

So ask for S-P-R-I-N-
G, you'll never regret it;
Remember the name, it's headed
for fame:
Be the first on your block to get it!

203

The Parsnip

by OGDEN NASH

The parsnip, children, I repeat,
Is simply an anemic beet.
Some people call the parsnip
    edible;
Myself, I find this claim incredible.

A Flash of Lightning

by KAZUE MIZUMURA

A flash of lightning sparks.
Forsythia:
Spring opening here today!

Tulips open one by one;
Each is bringing you
A cupful of spring.

Fueled

by MARCIE HANS

Fueled
by a million
man-made
wings of fire —
the rocket tore a tunnel
through the sky —
and everybody cheered.
Fueled
only by a thought from God —
the seedling
urged its way
through thicknesses of black —
and as it pierced
the heavy ceiling of the soil —
and launched itself
up into outer space —
no
one
even
clapped.

Spring Is

by BOBBI KATZ

Spring is when
        the morning sputters like
bacon
        and
        your
        sneakers
        run
        down
        the
        stairs
so fast you can hardly keep up with
    them,
and
spring is when
    your scrambled eggs
    jump
    off
    the
    plate
and turn into a million daffodils
trembling in the sunshine.

Treat

Sugared Parsnips

YOU NEED: 1½ pounds parsnips
salt
pepper
¼ cup butter
flour
sugar
vegetable oil

HOW TO: Peel parsnips and slice lengthwise. Boil until tender but still firm. Drain. Sprinkle with salt, pepper, and nutmeg. Dip in melted butter. Coat lightly with flour, sprinkle lightly with sugar. Brown the parsnips in hot oil, turning them as they brown.

Bulletin Board

"Spring into Books." Flower cutouts with book titles printed along the flower stems.

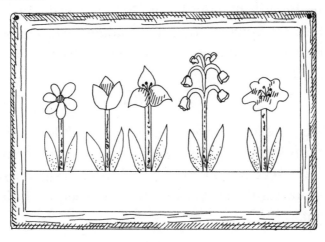

Creative Writing

Ask your group what symbolizes spring for them: the return of the robins, the birth of a lamb, warmer weather, spring games, or the appearance of spring flowers? Have them write about their private symbol of spring — as a narrative or a poem.

Activities

Chalanda Marz

Chalanda Marz is a Swiss celebration to welcome spring. It is held on March first in the Engadine region, which includes the famous spa and ski resort Saint Moritz, in Switzerland.

Children wear cowbells suspended on a leather thong around their waists or necks. They go from house to house in small groups singing folksongs and ringing their bells to welcome or wake the spring. The house owners give them candy or, usually, some money to spend on a spring outing.

The appealing aspect of this holiday for American children is making noise. To adapt this folkfest, use bells (I have Christmas bells purchased on sale after Christmas), and have the children tie them to their belts or belt loops. Pots and pans or any large type of noisemaker works.

A picture book featuring this holiday as its theme is *A Bell for Ursli* by Selina Chönz (Il. by Alois Carigiet, rev. ed. Walck, 1953). You may be able to find it on some library shelves.

Souvenir

Vegetable seeds can be given out to inspire children to grow their own plants. Individual seed packets have now become prohibitively expensive. Buy seed in bulk from your garden shop or a seed wholesaler. Pass out sandwich bags with some seed and directions on how to plant.

Sprout Some Sprouts

YOU NEED:
1 empty quart jar
piece of cheesecloth or nylon net to cover jar opening
rubber band
2 tablespoons alfalfa seeds (available from a health-food store)

HOW TO:
Put seeds into jar. Put 1 cup water into jar. Fasten net across the top with a rubber band. Swish water around. Store in a dark place overnight.

The next day pour off the water through the netting. For the next five days, pour water into jar twice a day. Swish water around and pour it off and leave jar by a window.

Your sprouts are now ready to eat or store with a lid. Use your sprouts in a sandwich or a salad.

Grow a Bean Drawing

Barbara Swanson of the Kern County Library in California gave each of the children in her group a dried bean. It was glued to the bottom of a piece of drawing paper. The children painted fantasy plants sprouting from the bean.

Books about Spring and Growing Things:

Anno, Mitsumasa. *The King's Flower.* Il. by author. Collins, 1979. P.

"The biggest and best flower in all the world is bound to take longer to grow than an ordinary flower."

Atwood, Ann. *Haiku: The Mood of Earth.* Il. with photographs by the author. Scribner, 1971. P.

Full-color photographs complement Haiku verses about nature.

Bodecker, N. M. *Carrot Holes and Frisbee Trees.* Il. by Nina Winters. McElderry, 1983. M.

William and Pippin Plumtree grow carrots as big as third graders.

Brown, Marc. *Your First Garden Book.* Il. by author. Atlantic/Little, 1981. P, M.

Attractive introduction to gardening. Includes directions for growing plants and vegetables indoors and outdoors.

Buck, Pearl. *The Good Earth.* John Day, 1965. U.

Nobel Prize-winning book about a Chinese peasant's love for the land.

Burnett, Frances H. *The Secret Garden.* Il. by Tasha Tudor. Lippincott, 1962. M.

A walled garden works its magic on Mary and Colin.

Cleaver, Vera and Bill. *Where the Lilies Bloom.* Il. by Jim Spanfeller. Lippincott, 1970. M, U.

Mary Coll studies a book that belonged to her mother and learns which barks, herbs, and leaves will earn money.

────. *Hazel Rye.* Lippincott, 1983. M.

An eleven-year-old girl learns from her twelve-year-old employee the value of growing things.

Cole, Brock. *The Winter Wren.* Il. by author. Farrar, 1984. All ages.

Lovely paintings show Simon on his quest for spring.

Dahl, Roald. *James and the Giant Peach.* Il. by Nancy Ekholm Burkert. Knopf, 1961. M.

Adventures inside a giant peach pit.

de Paola, Tomie. *The Legend of the Blue-bonnet: An Old Tale of Texas.* Il. by author. Putnam, 1983. All ages.

The reappearance of the Texas bluebonnets every spring is explained in a legend.

Dillon, Barbara. *The Teddy Bear Tree.* Il. by David Rose. Morrow, 1982. M.

A little girl plants the eye of an old teddy bear and a tree that blooms with teddy bears sprouts.

Domanska, Janina. *The Turnip.* Il. by author. Macmillan, 1969. P.

A rhythmic folktale in which Grandma and Grandpa grow a giant turnip.

Druon, Maurice. *Tistou of the Green Thumbs.* Trans. from the French by Humphrey Hare. Il. by Jacqueline Duhèmel. Scribner, 1958. M.

A boy brings flowers to the world, brightens hospitals, and stops wars with his magical green thumb.

Forrester, Victoria. *The Touch Said Hello.* Il. by author. Atheneum, 1982. P.

Spring comes to a tree in a tone poem illustrated with soft grays and whites.

George, Jean Craighead. *The Wild, Wild Cookbook.* Il. by Walter Kessell. Crowell, 1982. M, U.

Recipes from nature: maple syrup, dandelion salad.

Godden, Rumer. *An Episode of Sparrows.* Viking, 1955. M, U.

Lovejoy Moon dreams of cultivating flowers in a run-down section of London.

Greene, Bette. *Philip Hall Likes Me, I Reckon Maybe.* Il. by Charles Lilly. Dial, 1974. M.

Eleven-year-old Beth thinks that Philip Hall likes her, but their on-again-off-again relationship sometimes makes her wonder.

Heller, Ruth. *The Reason for a Flower.* Il. by author. Grosset, 1983. M.

Colorful illustrations show seeds growing into flowers, fruit, and vegetables.

Holman, Felice. *The Escape of the Giant Hogstalk.* Il. by Ben Schecter. Scribner, 1974. M.

A plant escapes from the Royal Botanical Garden in a funny escapade.

Hunt, Irene. *The Lottery Rose.* Scribner, 1976. M.

Georgie Burn's greatest treasure is a rosebush he won at a grocery store. The problem is that he wants to plant it in Mrs. Harper's garden.

Ichikawa, Satomi. comp. *Sun through Small Leaves: Poems of Spring.* Il. by comp. Collins, 1980. P.

Short poems celebrating spring illustrated with gentle drawings.

Jaspersohn, William. *How the Forest Grew.* Il. by Chuck Eckart. Greenwillow, 1980. P.

Evolution of a cleared field to a dense forest.

Jobb, Jamie. *My Garden Companion: A Complete Guide for the Beginner.* Il. by Martha Weston. Sierra Club, 1977. M.

The gardening book for people who know nothing about gardening.

Krasilovsky, Phyllis. *The First Tulips in Holland.* Il. by S. D. Schindler. Doubleday, 1982. All ages.

Large-size picture book fictionally traces the spread of the spring flower.

Kraus, Robert. *Leo the Late Bloomer.* Il. by Jose Aruego. Windmill, 1971. P.

In this story, a tiger who can't read, write, draw, or even talk is the bloomer.

Krauss, Ruth. *The Carrot Seed.* Il. by Crockett Johnson. Harper, 1945. P.

A little boy plants a carrot seed that grows into a giant carrot "just as the little boy had known it would."

Le Tord, Bijou. *Rabbit Seeds.* Il. by author. Four Winds, 1984. P.

A rabbit gardener plants a garden, and the reader watches as it grows from seed to produce.

Lobel, Arnold. "The Garden" in *Frog and Toad Together.* Il. by author. Harper, 1972. P.

Toad admires Frog's garden and tries to grow one too.

———. *The Rose in My Garden.* Il. by Anita Lobel. Greenwillow, 1984. All ages.

Cumulative house-that-Jack-built story that takes place in a flower garden.

Luckhardt, Mildred Corell. *Spring World, Awake.* Il. by Ralph McDonald. Abingdon, 1970. M, U.

A collection of stories and poems featuring a spring theme.

Muntean, Michaela. *Alligator's Garden.* Il. by Nicole Rubel. Dial, 1984. P.

Alligator works the soil, plants some seeds and waits for the flowers to grow. A puzzle is included.

Murphy, Louise. *My Garden: A Journal for Gardening Around the Year.* Il. by Lisa C. Ernst. Scribner, 1980. M.

Stories, recipes, garden experiments, and facts in a book for browsing.

Nikly, Michelle. *The Emperor's Plum Tree.* Il. by author, Trans. from the French by Elizabeth Shub. Greenwillow, 1982. M.

An emperor will go to any lengths to maintain the perfection of his garden.

Norton, Andre. *Lavender-Green Magic.* Il. by Judith Gwyn Brown. Crowell, 1974. M.

Rare herbs play a major part in a fantasy that reaches from the present back to colonial times. Directions for plant crafts are included in an appendix.

O'Brien, Robert C. *Z for Zachariah.* Atheneum, 1975. U.

Ann Burden may be the only person left in the entire world. She must grow her own crops and learn to save the seeds for the next season's planting.

Sarton, May. *A Walk through the Woods.* Il. by Kazue Mizumura. Harper, 1976. P.

A gentle poem chronicles a walk in this picture book.

Selsam, Millicent E. *Eat the Fruit, Plant the Seed.* Il. with photographs by Jerome Wexler. Morrow, 1980. M.

Clear simple directions for planting edible fruit.

_____. *Tree Flowers.* Il. by Carol Lerner. Morrow, 1984. M, U.

Describes 12 common flowering trees with text and illustration.

Skelsey, Alice, and Gloria Huckaby. *Growing Up Green: Children and Parents Gardening Together.* Workman, 1973. M.

Easy-to-follow directions for working with indoor and outdoor plants.

Springstubb, Tricia. *Give and Take.* Atlantic/Little, 1981. U.

Crow's first garden is the background for the story of two friends.

_____. *Which Way to the Nearest Wilderness.* Atlantic/Little, 1984. M, U.

Eunice grows a garden to prepare herself for living in the wilderness *à la* Thoreau at Walden.

Swain, Roger B. *Earthly Pleasures: Tales from a Biologist's Garden.* Il. by Laszlo Kubinyi. Scribner, 1981. U.

Charming essays explore the nature of living things.

Wescott, Nadine Bernard. *The Giant Vegetable Garden.* Atlantic/Little, 1981. All ages.

The townspeople of Peapack work hard to produce giant vegetables to win the prize at the fair.

Wyndham, John. *Day of the Triffids.* Doubleday, 1951. U.

A futuristic novel tells of plants that seem to be trying to conquer the world. A science-fiction classic.

Tantalizing Television

"Television is the whole world in a box that has knobs and buttons on it. You push the button for the part of the world you want to see.

Most of it you don't want to see, but about once a week there's something worth watching."
—JEAN CARRIS. *Witch Cat*

Turn on a switch and a living moving picture comes right into your living room or bedroom on your television set. It's a miracle that we now take for granted. Survey your students and you will discover that most families spend a considerable amount of time watching television. In fact, you may be surprised at the total number of television sets that your students have in their homes.

211

Whether you approve or disapprove of the television habit, the medium gives us lots of topics for a group discussion:

Cartoons, soap operas: What stereotypes do they teach?

Commercials: Does television advertising put unfair pressure on children to buy certain products?

News: Do the media make the news or report it?

Political campaigns: Can television market a candidate as it does a product?

Television in general: What are the advantages and disadvantages of the medium?

It is interesting that although television is an integral part of our society, juvenile fiction offers few books involving the medium. Be sure to share Florence Parry Heide's *The Problem with Pulcifer* with your group as well as selections included here. It will make you laugh as well as make you think. Pulcifer refuses to watch television and instead is satisfied to read books. Naturally, his family is worried. Special classes and psychologists seem to be the answer to Pulcifer's problem.

Two booklists are included. One lists books that use television as a theme. The other contains a short selection of books I personally would like to see made into television specials. These are meant to inspire your group into thinking about which books or stories they think would work well in the television medium. Of course, when you're choosing a book to be made into a movie you'll have to do a lot of reading.

Celebrate television with books any time of the year!

Prose Selections

Absolute Zero is a very funny book about a wacky family that lives with a lovable, but not very clever dog. His name, Zero, gives you a hint of his intelligence. In this portion of the book, Zero is about to be in a television commercial. The problem is: How do you get Zero to cooperate?

Zero and the Commercial

by HELEN CRESSWELL

Zero's hour was now at hand. Jack exulted in the certainty. His dog was now, at last, to have his day.

His ears will never droop again, he thought. I shall let him watch the commercial every time it comes up. He can take a just pride in his own achievements just like everybody else.

Making the commercial (which turned out to be only the first of many) was an achievement anyone could have taken a just pride in. Rosie, using her new equipment to take photographs of the BURIED BONES people trying to get Zero to act the way they wanted, realized that she could easily win a Competition with these pictures too.

Jack was given an outline script to study and asked to train Zero up to playing his part as much as he could. He had only two days to do this, because BURIED BONES were in such a rush to launch their campaign.

The idea was that Jack and Zero were to be filmed walking along together in an idyllic setting, while an unseen voice said, "Zero goes for a walk every day. He just loves it." Then Zero, without Jack seeming to notice, was to stop suddenly, and sniff hard. He was then to start digging furiously and turn up a packet of BURIED BONES dog biscuits. Jack, meanwhile, was to saunter off into the far distance, oblivious of the fact that he was no longer accompanied, while the voice said, "Zero likes walks, all right—but he likes BURIED BONES better. Ask any dog."

213

None of this was easy. The walking part was straightforward enough, but when Zero was supposed to stop dead in his tracks and sniff, complications set in. For one thing, Zero had been made nervous lately by the house being always full of noisy strangers and stayed glued to Jack even more than usual. He did not want to stand there by himself sniffing while Jack walked off and left him alone with a lot of eccentric people with cameras. He did not even seem to want to sniff if Jack stayed with him. He just edged up and sat on Jack's feet and looked dolefully around.

"I don't think he's a very good actor," Jack told the film people apologetically. "I don't think he's going to be able to act sniffing."

It was then suggested that a technique similar to the one Jack had employed for training Zero to Fetch and Beg should be used. This entailed everyone present getting down on all fours and sniffing and snuffing around, while Jack urged, "Sniff, Zero! Good old boy. Sniff!"

Zero was completely thrown by this incomprehensible behavior and went and hutched right up next to Jack and squeaked a little and kept wetting his lips.

The whole morning was spent like this. After lunch the director asked,

"Is there anything that really excites that dog? Does he ever get eager?"

"He does in the woods, sometimes," Jack told him. "He gets eager when he sees squirrels."

The unit trekked on foot, carrying all their equipment, to the woods. There, indeed, Zero did become excited. He seemed to forget what he was there for, and bounded off and started barking nonstop at the squirrels, as he always did. Jack was pleased.

"He *can* get excited, you see," he told them.

"The only trouble is," said the director wearily, "that he's looking up in the air. I can't see any way he's going to turn up BURIED BONES in the air."

Someone had brought along two large mutton bones.

214

"If we can cover them up with soil and get him sniffing after them, we'll be halfway there," said the director.

Unfortunately this did not work. It was hard to tell *why* Zero did not want to sniff these bones out. He must just not have been very hungry, or he might have been overexcited by the squirrels. Whatever the reason, he did not sniff.

The film unit all sat down and had a think.

"We've got to think this thing through," the director told them. "We must have that dog. We could get a trained Alsatian to make this film in ten minutes flat. But we must have that dog."

He sat a long time thoughtfully watching Zero as he made his futile lunges after squirrels running a full thirty feet above him.

"What we've been doing," he finally announced, "has been all wrong."

No one contradicted what seemed a self-evident truth.

"I'm going to turn the whole idea upside down on its head."

A respectful silence ensued.

"I am deliberately trying to keep my voice calm and controlled," he went on, "because I have just come up with the most stupefying and sensational idea that I believe has ever been used in advertising. And I am dazed and shattered by the pure and immaculate simplicity of it."

They all sat and waited. In the distance Zero barked on a high, monotonous note.

"What would your reaction be," went on the director, "if I told you that we are going to film the truth?"

He held up a hand.

"No. Don't answer right away. Take your time. Think about it. Just take in the sheer enormity of the concept. We are going to make a true commercial."

Jack took a quick look around. Everyone present was looking very concentrated and wise, and he made an effort to assume a similar expression himself.

215

"That dog," went on the director discerningly, "is not clever. He's a numbskull. He's a great, clumsy, stupid, lovable numbskull. You get the key word? *Lovable.* Now there is nothing lovable about being clever. Even if we did spend six months getting that dog to sniff and turn up BURIED BONES, nobody would love him for it. He'd just be another ordinary, smart dog on a commercial. No. What we do, we ditch the whole script, and we capitalize on his assets."

This is what happened. The BURIED BONES people went away and came back the following day with not one, but two film units. Then the second unit filmed the first one trying to get Zero to sniff. Everyone went down on their hands and knees again and sniffed and snuffed, and Zero just looked hopeless and was the only one *not* sniffing.

The director had written a new commentary. This time, the voice said:

"We wanted to show Zero digging up a packet of BURIED BONES. But Zero is never going to play Hamlet. He can't act. We can't even get him to understand what we want him to do. Sniff! Come on, boy, sniff! You see? Hopeless. But there's one thing Zero doesn't have to act. He really *does* like BURIED BONES. Here Zero — good boy!"

At this point Zero never quite managed to capture the look of keen interest one might have expected. He had by this time had enough of filming, and it was beginning to show. He crunched the BURIED BONES biscuit all right, but only in a resigned, world-weary kind of way. He definitely looked as if he were doing it for the fifth time in an hour.

To Jack's surprise, however, the director seemed enchanted by Zero's performance.

"My God!" he exclaimed after the final take. "Just look at him (meaning Zero). I've never seen anything so understated in my life. He just threw the whole thing away. Olivier could take lessons from him when it comes to understatement. The whole thing is brilliant."

He turned out to be right about this. After the first showing of the BURIED BONES commercial the lines of Borderland TV were jammed all night with calls from people who wanted to give Zero a home. He had apparently given the impression of being orphaned and sad, and half of England, it seemed, wanted to make him happy.

After the third or fourth showing the telephone inquiries were mainly about where one could get a dog exactly like Zero. Everywhere little children were sobbing themselves to sleep because they wanted one so badly, and their parents were trying to get hold of one for Christmas. They would pay anything, they said.

Breeders began to ring up, begging for details of Zero's parentage. They came and examined him and tried to work out the various strains that had come together to produce him. There was a fortune awaiting the man who could breed Zeros. No one seemed very hopeful about this.

"My guess," said one of them gloomily, "is that it's taken centuries of unbridled crossbreeding to produce that. This is the biggest single blow ever struck at the Kennel Club. It could even be mortal. No one wants our dogs anymore."

BURIED BONES had posters made of Zero at his most bewildered looking, and gave one away for every ten packets of their product bought. People with five children thus had to purchase fifty packets at one go, and the sight of people trundling through supermarkets with trolleys piled high with BURIED BONES became a familiar one.

Due to popular demand a Zero Fan Club was founded, called "Zero Worshipers," and people got their photographs autographed with a large paw mark and badges saying, "I am a Zero Worshiper" or Absolute Zero" or "Zero is the Most."

None of this had any real effect on Zero. If anything, he became more dislocated than ever because of the habit people now had of suddenly diving on him in the street or in shops, and shouting, and causing crowds to form. These were friendly crowds but could not have seemed so to him. Jack tried to fend them off by denying

Zero's identity, but no one ever believed him. Sometimes Zero would be patted for half an hour on end. It was lucky, as Mr. Bagthorpe pointed out, that whatever Zero's other shortcomings, he was not the sort that bit.

"If he was," he said, "then this country would be clean out of tetanus shots."

Television in the Snow
by MARGRET RETTICH

By afternoon Mama had had enough. Early in the morning she had gone to the city. With lots of other people she had crowded into the department stores, all Christmas-decorated, and had bought presents. Later, in the bus, her shopping bag had torn, and by the time she got home her arms were nearly paralyzed from carrying all the packages. At noon she had frozen her fingers washing the windows. Then, after she got the Christmas cookies into the oven, someone telephoned, and all the cookies were burned. Then, while she was washing the dishes, she dropped the lid to the coffee-pot, so now she couldn't use the pot anymore. She'd had enough; she wanted to rest awhile.

Just about that time the children's program began on the television. Mama heard the TV babbling and screaming and Melanie and Peter laughing loudly with delight.

"Please go outside for a while. You haven't had any fresh air today," Mama cried. Melanie and Peter were cross, but she wouldn't listen to their arguments. She shoved them both out the door, turned off the television, and lay down.

Peter and Melanie stood out in the courtyard. It was cold and wet, for it had snowed a few days before. The janitor had shoveled the snow into huge piles, which were now gray and dirty. His shovel was still there. Angrily Peter took the handle and rammed holes in the snow, one after the other.

"Oh, I'm mad!" he screamed.

"But I'm even madder," cried Melanie and kicked the snow pile.

"What makes you so angry?" asked the janitor.

"Mama turned off the television and sent us outside, just because she wants to rest," cried Peter and Melanie.

"If you always yell like that, I can understand why," said the janitor. "And so you're making television for yourselves?" He gestured toward the holes.

"What do you mean?" asked Peter and Melanie.

"Well, if you want to, you can look way down in the holes and see a different program in each. Naturally it isn't as clear as on an ordinary set, but if you try, you can see it."

"I don't believe that," said Peter.

The janitor bent way over a hole in the snow. "Well, in this one here...there's a cowboy movie on — fantastic! The horses are galloping so fast it's scary.... There! I thought the little fat one would fall off. He's just about broken his neck!"

Melanie sat beside him. "But I don't see anything at all!"

The janitor stood up and pushed Melanie so that her nose almost went into the hole. "Just look in! It's way down and pretty small, but you can make it out."

"Is that so?" asked Peter.

"I don't know," said Melanie. "I think so."

"But Melanie," said the janitor. "You see how the cowboys are dismounting and making a campfire. And there — on the hill to the left — an Indian has just appeared."

"I see him, I see him!" screamed Melanie.

"Let me look now," cried Peter and shoved Melanie to one side.

"Come here," said the janitor. He dragged Peter by the collar to another hole. "You get the next channel. Lean close to it and pay attention. It will take awhile before you can make anything out, just like the other television. Now, is the picture there yet?"

"Not yet," said Peter, disappointed.

"Make an effort. You aren't any less intelligent than Melanie. As far as I know, there is a cartoon on now about a duck who can't swim. She keeps on trying, but she goes under like a stone."

"Can you see it?" asked Melanie.

"Yes," answered Peter. "The duck is so dumb that she can't get her wings to work right and keeps falling on her beak. Lucky she can walk at least!"

"Please, please let me see the duck," cried Melanie.

But Peter wouldn't let her. Then Melanie squatted in front of another snow hole and said, "Then you can't look either and see how our car broke down on vacation and how everyone was so shaken up and I had to drive."

"So what!" cried Peter. "I have a hole with the moon landing. And who gets to set foot on the moon first? Me! I'm the one!"

"I don't care," replied Melanie, for she was watching a wonderful film in which she played the leading role.

Peter and Melanie kept poking new holes in the snow with the shovel handle and sticking their heads in. Above them Mama opened the window and called down, "Peter, Melanie, get up at once. You are soaked through! Come up before you catch cold!"

They had to put on warm slippers, and Mama said, "If you want, you can watch television now." But they didn't want to anymore. Instead, they looked out the window.

Down below stood the janitor. He bent over one of the holes, looked for a long time, then shook his head, and walked away.

"What do you suppose he saw?" asked Melanie.

Poetry Selections

The Day the T.V. Broke

by GERALD JONAS

It was awful. First,
the silence. I thought I'd die.
This is the worst,
I said to myself, but I
was wrong. Soon the house began
   to speak.
(There are boards in the halls
that creak
when no foot falls.
The wind strains
at the door, as if in pursuit
of someone inside, and when it
   rains,
the drainpipe croaks. Nothing is
   mute.)
That night, there came a noise
   from the shelves
like mice creeping.
It was the books, reading
   themselves
out loud to keep me from sleeping.
I can tell you I was glad to see
the repairman arrive.
Say what you will about a T.V. —
at least it isn't alive.

TeeVee

by EVE MERRIAM

In the house
of Mr. and Mrs. Spouse
he and she
would watch teevee
and never a word
between them spoken
until the day
the set was broken.

Then "How do you do?"
said he to she,
"I don't believe
that we've met yet.
Spouse is my name.
What's yours?" he asked.

"Why, mine's the same!"
said she to he,
"Do you suppose that we could
   be—?"

But the set came suddenly right
   about,
and so they never did find out.

221

Tube Time

by EVE MERRIAM

I turned on the TV
and what did I see?

I saw a can of cat food talking,
a tube of toothpaste walking.

> Peanuts, popcorn,
> cotton flannel.
> Jump up, jump up,
> switch the channel.

I turned to Station B
and what did I see?

I saw a shampoo bottle crying,
a pile of laundry flying.

> Peanuts, popcorn,
> cotton flannel.
> Jump up, jump up,
> switch the channel.

I turned to station D
and what did I see?

I saw two spray cans warring,
a cup of coffee snoring.

> Peanuts, popcorn,
> cotton flannel.
> Jump up, jump up,
> switch the channel.

I turned to station E
and what did I see?

I saw dancing fingers dialing,
an upset stomach smiling.

> Peanuts, popcorn,
> cotton flannel.
> Jump up, jump up,
> turn off the set.

Treat

Gorp for the T.V. (television-viewing snack)

YOU NEED: a handful each of:

raisins	dried dates, chopped
granola	spanish peanuts
dry coconut flakes	chocolate chips
sunflower seeds	raw cashew nuts

HOW TO: Mix together and munch.

HINT: Addictive.

Bulletin Board

Producing a television series — or even a 45-second commercial — is a fascinating project. It is difficult to imagine that the people, animals, and settings appearing on the television screen represent only a small portion of the people power that goes into television production.

List these terms on poster-board TV screens with the definitions listed below.

Match the terms with the definitions:

EXECUTIVE PRODUCER: Responsible for executive decision to initiate series, for hiring, and budget.

PRODUCER: Responsible for gathering the people, content, and materials for the entire series.

DIRECTOR: Responsible for coordination of activities of all people involved in production. Makes artistic selection of images and sound.

CAMERA OPERATORS: People who operate the cameras in the studio.

TALENT: The person or people who perform in front of the cameras.

FLOOR PERSON: Gives signals to talent telling her when and in which direction to move or look and how much time remains in the program. The communication link between the director and the talent.

AUDIO ENGINEER: Responsible for the audio portion of the program including music at the open and close of the program and the microphones and sound levels for the talent.

BOOM OPERATOR: Operates overhead microphone in studio.

VIDEO ENGINEER: Responsible for the technical quality of the television images.

LIGHTING TECHNICIAN: Responsible for studio lighting.

SWITCHER: Switches and mixes images on Director's command.

VIDEO TAPE OPERATOR: Operates and maintains video tape machine. Controls electronic side of editing.

CHAIN ENGINEER: Responsible for feeding film clips and slides onto video tape.

GRAPHIC DESIGNERS: Create the visuals including title slides.

SET DESIGNER: Responsible for designing the set.

Creative Writing/Activity

Have your students write a commercial for a book or author for television and perform it for the class. If you have access to a video tape machine, tape the commercials.

Exhibit books that have been made into television specials. *School Library Journal* lists these under media-tie-ins.

Exhibit books you wish they would make into TV specials.

Books about Television:

1. Tantalizing Television

Blume, Judy. *Tales of a Fourth Grade Nothing.* Il. by Roy Doty. Dutton, 1972. M.
The perfect boy for the Toddle-Bike commercial seems to be Fudge…until the filming begins.

Brown, Marc, and Laurene Krasny Brown. *The Bionic Bunny Show.* Il. by Marc Brown. Atlantic/Little, 1984. M.
Wilbur Bunny is an actor on a TV series in production. A delightful picture book.

Buchwald, Art. *Irving's Delight.* Il. by Reynold Ruffins. McKay, 1975. M.
A famous French detective is called in to rescue a beloved TV cat in this spoof on cat commercials.

Burns, Marilyn. "The TV Picture" in *I Am Not A Short Adult!* Il. by Martha Weston. Little, 1977. M.
This section raises questions about advertising on television, commercial and public stations, and feelings about television.

Byars, Betsy. *The TV Kid.* Il. by Richard Cuffari. Viking, 1976. M.
Lennie imagines himself a TV hero until he has to live through a real-life terrifying incident in an abandoned summer cottage.

Carris, Joan. *Witch-Cat.* Il. by Beth Peck. Lippincott, 1984. M.
A magic witch-cat sent to help a young girl discovers her powers as a witch and learns about the twentieth century by watching television.

Cleary, Beverly. *Ramona Quimby, Age 8.* Il. by Alan Tiegreen. Morrow, 1981. M.
Ramona gives her book report in the form of a TV commercial.

_____. *Ramona and Her Father.* Il. by Alan Tiegreen. Morrow, 1977. M.
Ramona hopes to earn a million dollars doing television commercials when her father is unemployed.

Collier, James Lincoln. *Rich and Famous: The Further Adventures of George Stable.* Four Winds, 1975. U.

A sequel to *The Teddy Bear Habit* (Dell, 1970). George sings and plays the guitar on a TV pilot amid sponsors, agents, and some relatives he dislikes.

Corbett, Scott. *What Makes TV Work?* Il. by Len Darwin. Little, 1965. All ages.
A beginner's book describing technical terms used in TV production.

Fields, Alice. *Television.* Il. by E. Smart. Watts, 1980. M.
An introduction to the television industry.

Gerson, Corinne. *Son for A Day.* Il. by Velma Ilsley. Atheneum, 1980. M.
Danny makes friends with divorced fathers and their sons at the zoo. When he makes friends with Ms. Andersen, his story gets on television.

Heide, Florence Parry. *The Problem with Pulcifer.* Il. by Judy Glasser. Lippincott, 1982. M, U.
Pulcifer's parents are very worried because their son refuses to watch television.

Klever, Anita. *Women in Television.* Westminster, 1975. U.
Interviews with women who work in a broad range of jobs in the television industry.

Levy, Elizabeth. *Something Queer Is Going On.* Il. by Mordicai Gerstein. Delacorte, 1973. M.
Jill's basset hound is used in a TV commercial.

McPhail, David. *Fix-It.* Il. by author. Dutton, 1984. All ages.
Emma, a small bear, is upset when the TV doesn't work, but then she discovers books. Wonderful.

Miles, Betty. *The Secret Life of the Underwear Champ.* Il. by Dan Jones. Knopf, 1981. M.
Larry is thrilled to be doing a television commercial until he finds out he has to appear in underwear.

Polk, Lee, and Eda Le Shan. *The Incredible Television Machine.* Il. by Roy Doty. Macmillan, 1977. M.

> A sprightly examination of the world of television.

Rettich, Margret. "Television in the snow" in *The Silver Touch and Other Family Christmas Stories.* Il. by Rolf Rettich. Transl. from the German by Elizabeth D. Crawford. Morrow, 1978. M.

> Two children discover that they can see television programs in holes they create in the snow. Good read-aloud.

Rodgers, Mary. *A Billion for Boris.* Harper, 1974. M.

> An old television set shows programs a day in advance.

Rosen, Winifred. *Ralph Proves the Pudding: "The Proof of the Pudding is in the Eating."*

Il. by Lionel Kalish. Doubleday, 1972. M.

> Ralph films a TV commercial even though he thinks the dessert "tastes like shoes."

Shyer, Marlene Farta. *Adorable Sunday.* Scribner, 1983. M, U.

> The story of Sunday's career as a performer in television commercials.

Weber, Judith Eichler. *Lights, Camera, Cats!* Il. by Pat Grant Porter. Lothrop, 1978. M.

> "Wanted, female cat to play opposite Clarence the Cat in a television commercial advertising Kitty Cat Food."

Wildsmith, Brian. *Daisy.* Il. by author. Pantheon, 1984. P.

> Daisy, an inquisitive cow, becomes a television performer.

2. My List of Books for TV Specials. Read Them and Find Out Why.

Branscum, Robbie. *Spud Tackett and the Angel of Doom.* Viking, 1983. M, U.

Cleary, Beverly. *Ralph S. Mouse.* Il. by Paul O. Zelinsky. Morrow, 1982. M.

Cresswell, Helen. All the books in the Bagthorpe series: *Ordinary Jack* (1977), *Absolute Zero* (1978), *Bagthorpes Unlimited* (1978), *Bagthorpes vs. the World* (1979), all published by Macmillan. M, U.

Cummings, Betty Sue. *Turtle.* Il. by Susan Lodge. Atheneum, 1981. M, U.

Fenton, Edward. *The Refugee Summer.* Delacorte, 1982. M, U.

Fritz, Jean. *Homesick, My Own Story.* Il. by Margot Tomes. Putnam, 1982. M.

Glenn, Mel. *Class Dismissed!* Photographs by Michael J. Bernstein. Clarion, 1982. U.

Hammer, Charles. *Me, the Beef, and the Bun.* Farrar, 1984. U.

Horwitz, Elinor Lander. *When the Sky*

Is Like Lace. Il. by Barbara Cooney. Lippincott, 1975. P.

Jones, Diana Wynne. *Dogsbody.* Greenwillow, 1977. U.

King-Smith, Dick. *Pigs Might Fly.* Il. by Mary Rayner. Viking, 1982. M.

Lasky, Kathryn. *Beyond the Divide.* Macmillan, 1983. M, U.

Lester, Julius. *This Strange New Feeling.* Dial, 1982. U.

Margorian, Michelle. *Good Night, Mr. Tom.* Harper, 1982. M, U.

McKinley, Robin. *The Blue Sword.* Greenwillow, 1982. U.

Noble, Trinka Hakes. *The Day Jimmy's Boa Ate the Wash.* Il. by Steven Kellogg. Dial, 1980. P.

Salassi, Otto R. *And Nobody Knew They Were There.* Greenwillow, 1984. M.

Spier, Peter. *People.* Il. by author. Doubleday, 1979. All ages.

Terrific Turtles

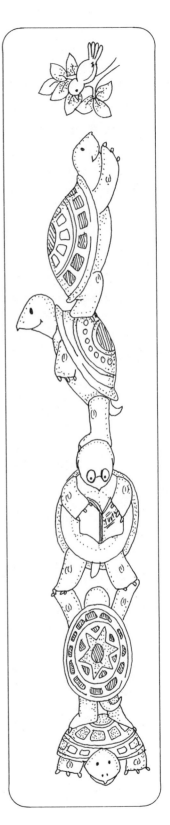

"That's how come I got a dime-store turtle. Thirty-nine cents—that's all my friend Turtle cost me. A sign over him said, 'Lives fifty years.' Just what I needed, for I figured I had about fifty years to go.

I didn't expect to get to love him. Who could love a turtle? That was over fifteen years ago, and now I'm not so certain about not loving a turtle. Turtle got into my heart, he did."

— BETTY SUE CUMMINGS. *Turtle*

Turtles have been the subject of various folktales and legends as well as of more modern stories.

If you read the selections in the booklist, you will discover that authors have used the various attributes of the turtle as a "peg" for stories. The turtle's slowness has been featured in "The Tortoise and the Hare" and in Dorothy Van Woerkom's easy reader *Harry and Shellburt*. The fact that turtles have no teeth is the theme for Barbara Williams' *Albert's Toothache*. Turtles' ability to put their heads in and out of their shells is puzzled about in Frank Asch's *Turtle Tale*. Turtles as pets are given fictional treatment in Johanna Hurwitz's *Superduper Teddy*, Judy Blume's *Tales of a Fourth Grade Nothing*, and Betty Sue Cummings' *Turtle*.

Teachers or librarians can use these short books about a familiar creature to show the writer's craft. Young writers might consider the longevity of the turtle. What would it be like to live over 100 years in a zoo? Jack Prelutsky, the children's poet, was driving by a tavern that had posted a sign Turtle Races Tonight. He immediately took out his writer's notebook and thought about a poem that would have people waiting for years while turtles finished their race. Could your children think about what it would be like to do everything in slow motion?

Turtles International (P.O. Box 96, Westchester, Il. 60153) is an organization that helps handicapped children through its club and "turtle creepstakes."

Celebrate a turtle day to liven up your week any day time seems to be going slowly.

Prose Selections

The Tortoises' Picnic

ANONYMOUS

There were once three tortoises — a father, a mother, and a baby. And one fine spring day they decided that they would like to go for a picnic. They picked the place they would go to, a nice wood at some distance off, and they began to get their stuff together. They got tins of salmon and tins of tongue, and sandwiches, and orange squash, and everything they could think of. In about three months they were ready, and they set out, carrying their baskets.

They walked and walked and walked, and time went on, and after about eighteen months they sat down and had a rest. But they knew just where they wanted to go and they were about halfway to it, so they set out again. And in three years they reached the picnic place. They unpacked their baskets and spread out the cloth and arranged the food on it and it looked lovely.

Then Mother Tortoise began to look into the picnic baskets. She turned them all upside down, and shook them, but they were all empty and at last she said, "We've forgotten the tin-opener!" They looked at each other, and at last Father and Mother Tortoise said, "Baby, you'll have to go back for it."

"What!" said the baby. "Me! Go back all that long way!"

"Nothing for it," said Father Tortoise, "we can't start without a tin-opener. We'll wait for you."

"Well, do you swear, do you promise faithfully that you won't touch a thing till I come back?" said the baby.

"Yes, we promise faithfully," they said and Baby plodded away, and after a while he was lost to sight amongst the bushes.

And Father and Mother Tortoise waited. They waited and waited and waited and a whole year went by, and they began to get rather hungry. But they'd promised, so they waited. And another year went by, and another, and they got really hungry. "Don't you think we could have just one sandwich each?" asked Mother Tortoise. "He'd never know the difference."

"No," said Father Tortoise, "we promised. We must wait till Baby comes back."

So they waited and another year passed, and another, and they got ravenous. "It's six years now," said Mother Tortoise. "He ought to be back by now."

"Yes, I suppose he ought," said Father Tortoise. "Let's just have one sandwich while we're waiting."

They picked up the sandwiches, but just as they were going to eat them, a little voice said, "Aha! I knew you'd cheat," and Baby Tortoise popped his head out of a bush. "It's a good thing I didn't start at all for that tin-opener!" he said.

How the Turtle Saved His Own Life
retold by ELLEN C. BABBITT

A king once had a lake made in the courtyard for the young princes to play in. They swam about in it, and sailed their boats and rafts on it. One day the king told them he had asked the men to put some fishes into the lake.

Off the boys ran to see the fishes. Now, along with the fishes, there was a turtle. The boys were delighted with the fishes, but they had never seen a turtle, and they were afraid of it, thinking it was a demon. They ran back to their father, crying, "There is a demon on the bank of the lake."

The king ordered his men to catch the demon, and to bring it to the palace. When the turtle was brought in, the boys cried and ran away.

The king was very fond of his sons, so he ordered the men who had brought the turtle to kill it.

"How shall we kill it?" they asked.

"Pound it to powder," said some one. "Bake it in hot coals," said another.

So one plan after another was spoken of. Then an old man who had always been afraid of the water said: "Throw the thing into the lake where it flows out over the rocks into the river. Then it will surely be killed."

When the turtle heard what the old man said, he thrust out his head and asked: "Friend, what have I done that you should do such a dreadful thing as that to me? The other plans were bad enough, but to throw me into the lake! Don't speak of such a cruel thing!"

When the king heard what the turtle said, he told his men to take the turtle at once and throw it into the lake.

The turtle laughed to himself as he slid away down the river to his old home. "Good!" he said. "those people do not know how safe I am in the water!"

Tortoise, Hare, and the Sweet Potatoes
retold by ASHLEY BRYAN

Listen, brothers and sisters, to this story of how Tortoise outwitted Hare.

Hare was a born trickster. He was always dreaming up new riddles and tricks to try on others. He'd spring an impossible riddle, wait a little, then rattle off the answer. Riddles and tricks, Hare never tired of either.

Tortoise on the other hand was much too busy keeping her little pond clean to worry about tricking anyone. Animals came from field and forest, far and near, to drink in the pond where she lived.

Tortoise believed in the proverb, "Give the passing traveller water and you will drink news yourself." So, although she rarely left her pool, her visitors kept her well informed. She knew more than most and was seldom fooled.

It happened one season then that the news Tortoise heard again and again was disgracefully bad. Someone was stealing, stealing food from all the fields around. Now most creatures were willing to give when another was hungry. But stealing was taboo.

Everyone asked, "Who would do what's taboo?" And no one knew. But Tortoise had a few well-founded ideas.

One day Hare came by Tortoise's pond. He drank his fill, then was ready for mischief. "Aha! Now to muddy the pond and have a little fun," he thought. He had never cared for the proverb, "Do not fill up the well after having drunk. Where would you drink tomorrow?"

Tortoise was on her guard, however, and all Hare could do was sit beside her and ask riddles. Tortoise answered every one.

"I know one you can't answer," said Hare. "Tell me the thing that you can beat without leaving a scar?"

"I live by it and I drink it," said Tortoise. "Water."

So Hare gave up trying to catch Tortoise with riddles. But he was not through.

After a while he said, "Now old Tortoise, let's go and till a field together."

"Me! Till the land? I can just manage to scratch out my little garden patch. How could I hoe a whole field with my short legs?"

"Short legs? Your legs are beautiful. Just the right length for hoeing."

"Do say! But how could I hold a hoe?"

"No problem at all. I'll tie you to it. I'd love to do that for you."

There was truth in that statement, Tortoise decided. Hare knew how to trick people, all right. But she wasn't taken in. She said aloud, "I don't think I'll try, thanks."

So they sat in silence. And after a while Hare said, "I'm hungry, Sis. Aren't you?"

"A little, but I don't have a leaf left in my garden."

"Well, poor thing, let me help you. I came upon a wide field of good things on my way here. Come on! Let's help ourselves to some of Wild Boar's sweet potatoes."

"Ooo, ooo! What are you saying? You know better than that, Mr. Hare. No pilfering!"

So they sat on in silence, Hare not willing to give up.

And after a while Tortoise became really hungry. Besides she had a few worthwhile ideas.

"Where did you say that field of sweet potatoes was?" she asked.

"It's not far, just past the bush."

"Well now," said Tortoise, seeming to overcome her scruples, "I guess Wild Boar won't miss a few."

Off they went together. And when they came to Wild Boar's field it was no job at all to root out the sweet potatoes. Soon Hare's sack was filled.

Hare with a great show of strength steadied the bag on Tortoise's back, and they headed for the bush to cook the potatoes. When they found a good quiet spot, they gathered dry grass and made a crackling fire in which the sweet potatoes were soon roasted.

"Mmm-yum," said Tortoise as she bit into one.

"Wait a minute," said Hare. "Did you hear that?"

"Mmm-yum," said Tortoise, her mouth full of sweet potato.

"Stop munching and mumbling!" said Hare. "What if we're caught?"

"Mmm-um-yum," said Tortoise, reaching for another sweet potato.

"Wow-wow," said Hare, "do you want to be beaten and bitten by Wild Boar? Put down that potato! We've got to scout around first and make sure that Boar's not after us."

Hare forced Tortoise to stop eating, and they went off in opposite directions to scout the field.

Tortoise who had a good notion of what was afoot and was ready, waddled a few reluctant steps; Hare bounded out of sight. As soon as he was gone, Tortoise turned back, took another sweet potato, and crawled into the empty sack.

"Mmm-yum," she said. She was about to crawl out for another when suddenly a rain of roasted sweet potatoes fell around her. Hare was back, very quietly, very quickly.

"Good," said Tortoise, biting into another sweet potato, "saves me the trouble."

Old trickster Hare filled his sack in a hurry.

"Mistress Tortoise," he shouted then. "Get going! Take off! Run for your life! Wild Boar and his big, fat wife are coming."

He threw the bag over his back. "Save yourself! Fly!" he cried, but inside he thought: "Best trick in ages. Now to put some miles between me and Slowpoke." He took off, running and laughing as hard as he could.

Tortoise made herself comfortable in the sack. She ate one sweet potato after another. "Too bad Hare is missing the feast," she thought. "But maybe he prefers running to eating."

Hare ran as fast and as far as he could. By the time he stopped to rest, Tortoise had eaten all of the finest and fattest sweet potatoes. In fact, there was only one very small sweet potato left.

"Aha, good," said Hare as he put his hand into the sack. "Too bad Tortoise is miles away."

"Sweet potatoes," Hare sang, "Sweet, sw-eeeet potatoes!" Tortoise put the last sweet potato into Hare's outstretched hand.

When Hare saw the size of it, he cried, "Ha! What a miserable one this is. I didn't run my head off for that!" And he flung it into the bushes.

Hare put his hand back into the sack. This time he felt a big one, a nice firm, juicy one.

"Oho!" he chortled, "here's a beauty. What a prize!"

Imagine Hare's surprise when he saw what he had in his hand.

"Mistress Tortoise!" he cried as he dropped her to the ground.

Hare shook out the sack. Tears of unbelief welled up in his eyes when he saw it was empty. "My potatoes, the sweet ones I rooted up . . . oh no, oh no! You didn't eat mine, too? Sister Tortoise, how could you be so unfair?"

But Mistress Tortoise didn't stand around for the lecture. She took to her toes and scuttled away to her pond as fast as she could go.

Hungry Hare lay on the ground and screeched, "Woe, woe, that wily Mistress Tortoise ate all my sweet potatoes. Wa, Waa. How awful of her. When I think that I carried her all the while, I could cry!"

And that's just what he did.

Poetry Selections

House Moving

by PATRICIA HUBBELL

Look! A house is being moved!
  Hoist!
  Jack!
  Line!
  Truck!

  Shout!
  Yell!
  Stop!
  Stuck!

  Cable!
  Kick!
  Jerk!
  Bump!

  Lift!
  Slide!
  Crash!
  Dump!
This crew could learn simplicity from turtles.

The Turtle

by OGDEN NASH

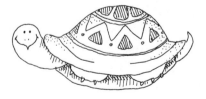

The turtle lives 'twixt plated decks
Which practically conceal its sex.
I think it clever of the turtle
In such a fix to be so fertile.

235

Turtle

by JAMES S. TIPPETT

I have not heard a turtle talk,
Or even make a sound;
But I have watched a turtle walk—
  Trick-track
  Trick-track—
Slowly on the ground.

I have not felt a turtle bite,
Or seen it snap its jaws;
But I have followed trick-track trails
Of a turtle's claws.

And I have seen a turtle pull
Its head and legs, and tail as well,
Quickly into safety
Inside its hard clean shell.

Turtle

by VALERIE WORTH

The turtle
Does little
but sleep
On a stone,
Alone
In his glass
Bowl.

Is he bored
By it all?
Does he hope
Something
Will happen,
After a hundred
Naps?

Or is it enough
To wake
Quietly,
Shawled
In the shade
Of his
Shell?

Creative Writing/Activity

Have the children write a skit for one or more turtle characters. Turtles can be given personality through dialogue. Skit can be performed with finger puppets.

Have the children make a turtle finger puppet using green construction paper (see picture). Puppets can be decorated with poster paint, felt-tip pens, or crayons. Cut out finger holes. To use the puppet, put first two fingers through the holes, up to the second knuckle. Fingers become the turtle's legs.

Turtle Facts

People who study turtles are called Herpetologists.

Turtles live a long time. A turtle from the Galapagos Islands captured by Captain Cook lived 190 years.

The Wyandot Indians have a legend that tells that the earth is resting on a turtle's back. When there is an earthquake it is the turtle moving a foot.

In Thailand you can buy a turtle from a street merchant. Write the name of a person that you have quarreled with on the turtle's back. Release the turtle in the river and as the turtle swims away your quarrel will be forgotten.

In Uxmal, Mexico you can visit a temple built by the Mayans dedicated to the turtle.

Bulletin Board

Display decorated finger puppets made by children.

For a turtle newsletter contact: The California Turtle and Tortoise Club, P. O. Box 90252, Los Angeles, California 90045 OR The New York Turtle and Tortoise Society, c/o Anderson, 21 St. Paul's Court, Brooklyn, New York 11226.

Treat
Lynn's Turtle Salad

YOU NEED: 1 leaf of lettuce. I like to use butter or red leaf.
½ cling peach (body)
½ regular-sized marshmallow (head)
2 raisins (eyes)
1 small carrot cut into four small sticks two inches long (legs) and one sliver about one inch long for the tail

HOW TO: Arrange ingredients to represent a turtle on a lettuce leaf.

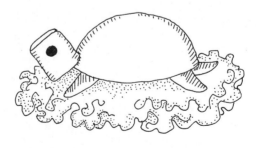

Books about Turtles:

Asch, Frank. *Turtle Tale.* Il. by author. Dial, 1978. All ages.

In a brightly colored picture book, a turtle discovers when to leave his head out of his shell and when to pull it in.

Blume, Judy. *Tales of a Fourth Grade Nothing.* Il. by Roy Doty. Dutton, 1972. M.

Peter's pet turtle, Dribble, is the cause of much anxiety when brother Fudge is nearby.

Christian, Mary Blount. *Devin & Goliath.* Il. by Normand Chartier. Addison-Wesley, 1974. P.

Devin tries to make a pet of a turtle but eventually returns him to his natural habitat.

Courlander, Harold. "Terrapin's Pot of Sense" in *Terrapin's Pot of Sense.* Il. by Elton Fax. Holt, 1957. M,U.

This folktale explains why Terrapin's shell is cracked and why he has little sense.

Cummings, Betty Sue. *Turtle.* Il. by Susan Lodge. Atheneum, 1981. M,U.

Turtle goes off on an adventure but misses his friend the old woman. The old woman misses the turtle. An excellent read-aloud.

Dobrin, Arnold. *Taro and the Sea Turtles: A Tale of Japan.* Coward, 1966. P.

Two turtles repay Taro's kindness by rescuing him from the sea.

Duff, Maggie. *Dancing Turtle.* Il. by Maria Horvath. Macmillan, 1981. P.

Turtle loves to sing and dance and saves herself with her artistic talents.

Freeman, Don. *The Chalk Box Story.* Lippincot, 1976. P.

The chalk from a chalk box draws a story of a boy on a desert island and the turtle who rescues him.

Freschet, Berniece. *Turtle Pond.* Il. by Donald Carrick. Scribner, 1971. P.

Eleven baby turtles try to travel toward water despite the creatures who threaten them.

Galdone, Paul. *The Turtle and the Monkey.* Clarion, 1983. P.

Turtle outsmarts Monkey in a colorful picture book.

Hoban, Lillian. *Stick-in-the-mud Turtle.* Greenwillow, 1977. P.

Fred's turtle family are envious of their new neighbors until they realize that their life is simpler and pleasanter. Read-Alone.

Holling, Holling Clancy. *Minn of the Mississippi.* Il. by author. Houghton, 1951. M.

A snapping turtle travels the length of the Mississippi.

Hurwitz, Johanna. "A Superduper Pet" in *Superduper Teddy.* Il. by Susan Jeschke. Morrow, 1980. M.

Teddy's family finds a pet that is clean, doesn't eat much, doesn't shed, and makes no noise: a turtle.

Macgregor, Ellen. *Theodore Turtle.* Il. by Paul Galdone. McGraw, 1955. P.

The story of a forgetful turtle.

Marshall, James. *Yummers!* Il. by author. Houghton, 1972. All ages.

Eugene, a turtle, goes for a walk with Emily Pig and tempts her to eat too much.

Plante, Patricia, and David Bergman. "The Turtle and the Two Ducks" in *The Turtle and the Two Ducks: Animal Fables retold from La Fontaine.* Il. by Anne Rockwell. Crowell, 1981. P.

Two ducks take a turtle for a flying trip. This short fable also appears in the Jataka stories.

Robertson, Keith. *Tales of Myrtle the Turtle.* Il. by Peter Parnall. Viking, 1974. M.

Myrtle's adventures take place in and around Princeton University.

Scott, Jack Denton. *Loggerhead Turtle: Survivor from the Sea.* Photographs by Ozzie Sweet. Putnam, 1974. M.

A photographic essay exploring the attributes of a sea turtle.

Selsam, Millicent E. *Let's Get Turtles.* Il. by Arnold Lobel. Harper, 1965. P.

A science I-Can-Read book. Two boys decide to get turtles and learn how to care for them.

Sharmat, Marjorie Weinman. *Edgemont.* Il. by Cyndy Szekeres. Coward, 1976. M.

A 101-year-old turtle leaves his home for adventure and meets Blanche, aged 99.

Van Woerkom, Dorothy O. *Harry and Shellburt.* Il. by Erick Ingraham. Macmillan, 1977. P.

The hare-and-the-tortoise story with a new twist in an easy-to-read format.

Waters, John F. *Green Turtle Mysteries.* Il. by Mamoru Funai. Crowell, 1972. M.

Describes, in a short text, the habits of the green turtle.

Williams, Barbara. *Albert's Toothache.* Il. by Kay Chorao. Dutton, 1974. P.

Although it is impossible for a turtle to have a toothache, Albert complains of one. Grandma is the one who finds the cure.

Thanksgiving:
Thank You, America

"America is a tune. It must be sung together."
— GERALD STANLEY LEE. *Crowds* Bk V, iii, 12.

Thanksgiving: I like it because it is a totally American holiday. Other cultures and countries have harvest festivals, but this one is ours. It's certainly a feast holiday since central to the holiday is the traditional harvest dinner, but because it does not have its origins in a religion, everyone in your class can celebrate it wholeheartedly.

Pilgrims and turkeys are usually the focal point of Thanksgiving programs, but this program emphasizes the giving of thanks. The theme is Thank you, America, and the booklist features books about child immigrants to the United States.

241

Between 1880 and 1920, twenty-three million people immigrated to the United States. America is still admitting immigrants. The 1965 immigration law admits 270,000 people a year. With the present influx of immigrants we need to show today's children their own heritage and to encourage multiracial understanding.

Traditionally, newcomers to this country have tried to conform to the customs of the majority. Formerly, we described this assimilation as the "great melting pot." In practice, however, different ethnic groups have retained many of their old customs.

Juvenile literature dealing with children of different ethnic backgrounds tends to show families retaining their own customs but learning to accept the strangeness of America. Dorothy Canfield Fisher's "Thanksgiving Day" was written in the 1940's, when prayer was permitted in the schools. Many European refugees came to live in the United States to escape the Nazi regime, just as Southeast Asians have immigrated in the 1980's. The newspaper story below (edited for length) appeared in 1981. Instead of reciting a prayer like the girl in the Fisher story, the modern high-school girl gave a speech, but the essence of the story, nearly forty years later, is the same.

Officials at Forest Hills High School in Ocala, Fla., said they had never seen anything like it. Miss Loung Le, eighteen-year old valedictorian of her graduating class, drew tears and a standing ovation from her audience when she said:

"My family and I fled Southeast Asia six years ago because we were pro-U.S.A., and had we remained we would have been executed.

"I owe my very presence on this stage tonight to you and this wonderful country. When we could no longer prevail against our enemies, you accepted over 100,000 of us to your shores, gave us freedom, a new start, and a new nation.

"There are some things worth dying for. The freedom you have here is one of those things. I have come to appreciate the United States as the greatest nation on earth. She is worthy of your fullest loyalty and greatest sacrifice.

"Treasure her. Love her. Defend her!"

Prose Selection

Thanksgiving Day
by DOROTHY CANFIELD FISHER

A new girl came into the Winthrop Avenue public school about the beginning of November, and this is how she looked to the other boys and girls in the seventh grade. She couldn't understand English, although she could read it enough to get her lessons. (This was a small public school in a small inland American town where they seldom saw any foreigners, and people who couldn't speak English seemed outlandish.) She wore the queerest-looking clothes you ever saw, and clumping shoes and great, thick, woolen stockings. (All the children in that town, as in most American towns, dressed exactly like everybody else, because their mothers mostly bought their clothes at Benning and Davis' department store on Main Street.) Her hair wasn't bobbed and curled, neither a long nor short bob; it looked as though her folks hadn't ever had sense enough to bob it. It was done up in two funny-looking pigtails. She had a queer expression on her face, like nothing anybody had ever seen—kind of a smile and yet kind of offish. She couldn't see the point of wisecracks but she laughed over things that weren't funny a bit, like the way a cheerleader waves his arms. She got her lessons *terribly* well, (the others thought somebody at home must help her more than the teachers like) and she was the dumbest thing about games—didn't even know how to play duck-on-a-rock or run-sheep-run. And queerest of all, she wore *aprons*! Can you beat it!

That's how she looked to the school. This is how the school looked to her. They had come a long way, she and her grandfather, from the town in Austria where he had a shop in which he repaired watches and clocks and sold trinkets the peasant boys bought for their sweethearts. Men in uniforms and big boots had come suddenly one day— it was in vacation and Magda was there—and had smashed in the windows of the shop and the showcase with the pretty things in it, and had thrown all the furniture from their home back of the shop out into the street and made a bonfire of it. And although Grandfather had not said a word to them, they had knocked him down, and hit him with their sticks till his white hair was all wet and scarlet with blood. Magda had been hiding in a corner and saw this; and now, after she had gone to sleep, she sometimes saw it again and woke up with a scream, but Grandfather always came quickly to say smilingly, "All right, Magda child. We're safe in America with Uncle Harry. Go to sleep again."

He had said she must not tell anybody about that day. "We can do something better in the New World than sow more hate," he said seriously. She was to forget about it if she could, and about the long journey afterwards, when they were so frightened and had so little to eat; and, worst of all, when the man in the uniform in New York thought for a minute that something was wrong with their precious papers and they might have to go back. She tried not to think of it, but it was in the back of her mind as she went to school every day, like the black cloth the jewelers put down on their counters to make their pretty gold and silver things shine more. The American school (really a rather ugly old brick building) was for Magda made of gold and silver, shining bright against what she tried to forget.

How kind the teachers were! Why, they *smiled* at the children. And how free and safe the children acted! Magda simply loved the sound of their chatter on the playground, loud and gay and not afraid even when the teacher stepped out for something. She did wish she could understand what they were saying. She had studied English in her Austrian school, but this swift, birdlike twittering didn't sound a bit like the printed words on the page. Still, as the days went by she began to catch a word here and there, short ones like "down" and "run" and "back." And she soon found out what *hurrah*! means, for the Winthrop Avenue School made a specialty of mass cheering and every grade had a cheerleader, even the first-graders. Magda thought nearly everything in America was as odd and funny as it was nice. But the cheerleaders were the funniest with their bendings to one side and the other and then jumping up straight in the air till both feet were off the ground. But she loved to yell "Hurrah!" too, although she couldn't understand what they were saying!

This is what they were saying—at least the six or seven girls who tagged after Betty Woodworth. Most of the seventh-graders were too busy studying and racing around at recess time to pay much attention to the queer new girl. But some did. They used to say, "My goodness, look at that dress! It looks like her grandmother's—if she's got one."

"Of all the dumb clucks. She doesn't even know enough to play squat tag. My goodness, the first-graders can play *tag*."

"My father told my mother this morning that he didn't know why *our* country should take in all the disagreeable folks that other countries can't stand anymore."

"She's Jewish. She must be. Everybody that comes from Europe now is Jewish. We don't want our town all filled up with Jews!"

"My Uncle Peter saw where it said in the paper we ought to keep them out. We haven't got enough for ourselves, as it is."

Magda could just catch a word or two, "country" and "enough" and "uncle." But it wouldn't be long now, she thought happily, till she could understand everything they said and really belong to seventh grade.

About two weeks after Magda came to school, Thanksgiving Day was due. She had never heard of Thanksgiving Day, but since the story was all written out in her history book she soon found out what it meant. She thought it was perfectly lovely! She read the story of the Pilgrim Fathers and their long hard trip across the ocean (she knew something about that trip) and their terrible first winter, and the kind Indian whose language they couldn't understand, who taught them how to cultivate the fields, and then—oh, it was poetry, just *poetry*, the setting aside of a day forever and forever, every year, to be thankful that they could stay in America! How could people (as some of the people who wrote the German textbooks did) say that Americans didn't care about anything but making money? Why here, more than three hundred years after that day, this whole school and every other school, everywhere all over the country, was turning itself upside down to celebrate with joy their great-grandfathers' having been brave enough to come to America and to stay here, even though it was hard, instead of staying in Europe, where they had been so badly treated. (Magda knew something about that, too.)

Everybody in school was to do something for the celebration. The first-graders had funny little Indian clothes, and they were going to pretend to show the second-graders (in Puritan costumes) how to plant corn. Magda thought they were delightful, those darling little things, being taught already to be thankful that they could go on living in America. Some grades had songs, others were going to act in short plays. The children in Magda's own seventh grade that she loved so were going to speak pieces and sing. She had an idea all her own, and because she couldn't be sure of saying the right words in English she wrote a note to the teacher about it. She would like to write a thankful prayer (she could write English pretty well now), and learn it by heart and say it, as her part of the celebration. The teacher, who was terrifically busy with a bunch of boys who were to build a small "pretend" log cabin on the stage, nodded that it would be all right. So Magda went away happily to write and learn it by heart.

"Kind of nervy, if you ask me, of that little Jew girl to horn in on *our* celebration," said Betty.

"Who asked her to come to America, anyhow?" said another.

"I thought Thanksgiving was for *Americans*!" said another.

Magda, listening hard, caught the word "American" and her face lighted up. It wouldn't be long now, she thought, before she could understand them.

No, no, they weren't specially bad children, no more than you or I—they had heard older people talking like that—and they gabbled along, thoughtlessly, the way we are all apt to repeat what we hear, without considering whether it is right or not.

On Thanksgiving Day a lot of those grown-ups whose talk Betty and her gang had been repeating had come, as they always did, to the "exercises." They sat in rows in the assembly room listening to the singing and acting of the children and saying "the first-graders are too darling," and "how time flies," and "can you believe it that Betty is up to my shoulder now? Seems like last week she was in the kindergarten."

The tall principal stood at one side of the platform and read off the different numbers from a list. By and by he said, "We shall now hear a prayer written by Magda Bensheim and spoken by her. Magda has been in this country only five weeks and in our school only three."

Magda came out to the middle of the platform, a bright, striped apron over her thick, woolen dress, her braids tied with red ribbons. Her heart was beating fast. Her face was shining and solemn. She put her hands together and lifted them up over her head and said to God, "Oh, thank you, thank you, dear God, for letting me come to America and nowhere else, when Grandfather and I were driven from our home. I learned out of my history book that Americans all came to this country just how Grandfather and I come, because Europe treat them wrong and bad. Every year they gather like this — to remember their brave grandfathers who come here so long ago and stay on, although they had such hard times. American hearts are so faithful and true that they forget never how they were all refugees, too, and must thankful be that from refugees they come to be American citizens. So thanks to you, dear, dear God, for letting Grandfather and me come to live in a country where they have this beautiful once-a-year Thanksgiving, for having come afraid from Europe to be here free and safe. I, too, feel the same beautiful thank-you-God, that all we Americans say here today."

Magda did not know what is usually said in English at the end of a prayer, so did not say anything when she finished, just walked away back where the other girls of her class were. But the principal said it for her — after he had given his nose a good blow and wiped his eyes. He looked out over the people in the audience and said in a loud, strong voice, "Amen! I say Amen, and so does everybody here, I know."

And then—it was sort of queer to applaud a prayer—they all began to clap their hands loudly.

Back in the seventh-grade room the teacher was saying, "Well, children, that's all. See you next Monday. Don't eat too much turkey." But Betty jumped up and said, "Wait a minute, Miss Turner. Wait a minute, kids. I want to lead a cheer. All ready?"

"Three cheers for Magda!"

"Hip! Hip!"—she leaned 'way over to one side and touched the floor and they all shouted, "Hurrah!"

She bent back to the other side, "Hurrah!" they shouted.

She jumped straight up till both feet were off the ground and clapped her hands over her head and "Hurrah" they all shouted.

The wonderful moment had come. The curtain that had shut Magda off from her schoolmates had gone. "Oh! Ach!" she cried, her eyes wide. "Why, I understood every word. Yes, now I can understand American!"

Poetry Selections

Foreigner

by SIV WIDERBERG

My papa is a foreigner
My mama is also a foreigner
Marianne and I are foreigners too
right now
though we're American

Because right now we're in England
Ha, ha!

Didn't think of that, did ya?
That Americans are foreigners too
as soon as they're out of the country

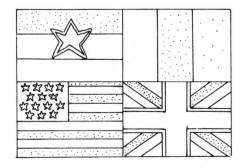

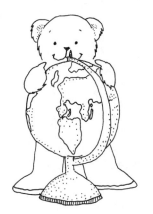

Manhattan

by MORRIS ABEL BEER

There's Asia on the avenue,
   And Europe in the street,
And Africa goes plodding by
   Beneath my window-seat.

This is the wondrous city,
   Where worlds and nations meet;
Say not romance is napping;
   Behold the city street!

249

Borders

by ARNOLD ADOFF

Great Grandma Ida came from a
   small village
in Poland
       on the Russian border
       to America,
       on a ship that   sailed
       for weeks,
       on the rough Atlantic
             Ocean:

to make a new place for her self;
to work in a factory; to find her
   father;
to find a man
 from a German town on the Polish
              border
to marry; to have and raise a
   daughter
       who would find and marry
       a man from a Russian town
           on the Polish
              border.

And in 1935 they would have a
   baby boy
       in a New York City hospital
who is daddy now to
         me.

Activities

Interview foreign students in your school. Find out why their families left their original countries. Why did they choose your town to settle in?

Show children what it might be like to visit or live in another country.

Exhibit foreign coins. Use the exchange rate in the newspaper to show the daily change of foreign money. Can your children convert drachmas, pesetas, francs, or yen into American dollars?

"Say something." Speak a foreign language. Ask a child, staff member or parent who speaks a foreign language to visit. Children can ask questions of the visitor. He or she answers in their own native language for the first few minutes.

Exhibit a slogan or sentence written in a foreign alphabet — perhaps in Russian, Greek, Arabic, or Hebrew.

Discuss which inventions originated in the United States.

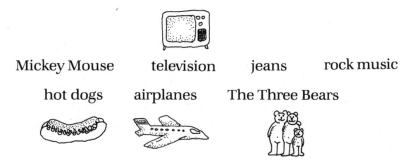

Mickey Mouse   television   jeans   rock music

hot dogs   airplanes   The Three Bears

Post a map of the world. Ask the children to point out where their families came from originally, including other towns in the United States.

Draw a line from the country of origin to your town. If you want to re-use the map you might want to use map pins (available in stationery shops) instead.

Creative Writing

Many of your grandparents, parents, friends—maybe even your-self—arrived from a foreign country to enter an American school. Write a letter to an imaginary friend back in your home country describing what you might have felt on the first day of school.

Have the children write a paragraph celebrating the American quality they most admire.

Treats . . . After School or in School

Roast turkey is traditionally served at an American Thanks-giving dinner, but we also eat many things that have been introduced to us by people who have immigrated to the United States.

Eating habits are often retained long after a family has arrived from another country or even another section of the United States.

Here are three easy to fix treats that were introduced by foreign-born Americans.

Pain au Chocolate (chocolate bread from France)

This is an after-school treat served in France. If you buy this from a bakery on the way home from school you will get a crisp bun with chocolate baked inside it. If you make it your-self when you get home you would make a chocolate sandwich. This is the way we did it at the Bailles in Nancy, France.

YOU NEED: A French roll or a five-inch piece of French bread. A chocolate bar.

HOW TO: Slice the bread in half, sandwich-style. Place choco-late on top of bread. Broil in oven for 2-3 minutes or until chocolate has melted. Bon appétit. Thank you, France.

Peter's Morgen Reis

Rice is a staple of many countries. In South Asia and the Far East rice is served with practically every meal from breakfast through dinner.

My husband was born in Austria, which is very far away from Asia, but his family eats a lot of rice as do many families in Austria. (*Morgen reis* means morning rice.)

YOU NEED: 1 cup cooked rice   1 teaspoon
   butter   brown sugar
   cinnamon   milk

HOW TO: Place a small bit of butter, brown sugar, and cinnamon on top of the rice. Pour milk just to cover on rice. Heat till butter has melted and rice is warm. Thank you, Austria. (*Makes one serving.*)

Fiji Ambrosia

If you travel anywhere in the South Seas you will be served lots of coconut. This tree provides shelter, food and even clothing in some parts of the world. If you look up Fiji on the map, you will find that it is a small group of islands in the South Pacific. Here is a favorite dish in the Fiji Islands:

YOU NEED: 1 banana   3 tablespoons honey
   1 cup grated coconut (available in
        baking section of the grocery store)

HOW TO: Slice banana crosswise and arrange one third of the slices on the bottom of a dish. Pour one third of the honey over the banana. Sprinkle one third of the coconut on the honey. Continue layering until all ingredients are in the dish, ready to eat. Thank you, Fiji.

Bulletin Board

Introduce children to foreign languages with this list of the phrase "I love you" written in many different languages. You could write on slips of paper and post them all over your classroom or library.

Amharic: Afekrishalehou

Arabic: Ana b'hibbik
   (Ana b'hibbak)

Armenian: K' ez kĕ sirem

Cambodian: Bon sro lanh oon

Catalán: T'estimo

Chinese: Wo ai ni

Danish: Jeg elsker Dig

Dutch: Ik houd van je

Farsi: Tora dust midaram

Finnish: Minä rakistan sinua

French: Je t'aime

Gaelic: Tá grá agam ort

German: Ich liebe dich

Greek: S'agapó

Hausa: Ina sonki

Hebrew: Ani ohev otakh
   (Ani ohevet otkhah)

Hindi: Maiñ tumheñ piyar
   karta huñ

Hopi: Nu' umi unangwa'ta

Hungarian: Szeretlek

Indonesian: Saja kasih saudari
   (Saja kasih saudara)

Italian: Ti voglio bene

Japanese: Watakushi-wa
   anata-wo aishimasu

Korean: Tangsinūl sarang hä yo

Lao: Khoi huk chau

Lingala: Nalingi yo

Lithuanian: Aš myliu tave

Mohawk: Konoronhkwa

Navaho: Ayór ánósh'ní

Norwegian: Jeg elsker Dem

Polish: Ja cię kocham

Rumanian: Te inbesc

Russian: Ya tebya liubliu

Serbo-croat: Ja tebe ljubim

Sioux: Techíhḣila

Spanish: Te quiero

Swahili: Ninikupenda

Swedish: Jag älska Dig

Tagalog: Iniibig kita

Thai: Chǎn ráte khun

Turkish: Ben sevi seviyorum

Urdu: Mujge tumae mahabbat
   hai

Vietnamese: Tôi yêu em

Visaya: Guihigugma co icaw

Welsh: Yr wyf yn du garu

Yiddish: Ich lib dich

Zuñi: Tom ho' ichema

*Note: The expressions in Italian and Spanish really mean "I want you". They use the verbs *volere* (Italian) and *querer* (Spanish) meaning "to want", "to desire", "to love" in preference to *amare* or *amar* whose only meaning is "to love".

Books about American Immigrants:

Ancona, George. *Dancing Is.* Il. with photographs. Dutton, 1981. All ages.
Photographs illustrate a variety of dances from around the world.

Anderson, Margaret J. *The Journey of the Shadow Bairns.* Random, 1980. M, U.
A thirteen-year-old travels with her four-year-old brother from Scotland to Canada in 1903.

Ashabranner, Brent. *The New Americans: Changing Patterns in U.S. Immigration.* Il. with photographs by Paul Conklin. Dodd, 1983. M, U.
An in-depth look at today's immigrants to America.

Beatty, Patricia. *Lupita Mañana.* Morrow, 1981. U.
A thirteen-year-old girl crosses the Mexican border and becomes an illegal alien to help her family.

Blaine, Marge. *Dvora's Journey.* Il. by Gabriel Lisowski. Holt, 1979. M.
Dvora's family leaves Russia in 1903 to immigrate to America.

Blumenthal, Shirley, and Jerome S. Ozer. *Coming to America: Immigrants from the British Isles.* Delacorte, 1980. M.
Describes immigration, from the seventeenth-century British colonists to the Irish of the 1840's. (One of a series.)

Bosse, Malcolm J. *Ganesh.* Crowell, 1981. U.
Jeffrey, aka Ganesh, has lived all his fourteen years in a small town in India. When he comes to a small town in the Midwest he is faced with blending one culture with another.

Branson, Karen. *The Potato Eaters.* Il. by Jane Sterrett. Putnam, 1979. U.
The O'Connor family tries to survive through the 1846 potato famine in Ireland. A sequel, *Street of Gold* (Putnam, 1981), tells of their arrival and struggle in New York.

Cohen, Barbara. *Gooseberries to Oranges.* Il. by Beverly Brodsky. Lothrop, 1982. M.
A picture-book presentation of a European girl's adjustment to her life in America.

Colman Hila. *Rachel's Legacy.* Morrow, 1978. U.
Rachel arrives in New York in 1908 and eventually develops her own clothing company.

Cooper, Terry Touff, and Marilyn Ratner. *Many Friends Cooking: An International Cookbook for Boys and Girls.* Il. by Tony Chen. Philomel, 1980. M, U.
An illustrated cookbook featuring food of many nations. Each recipe is accompanied by a short paragraph introducing the particular food.

Coutant, Helen. *First Snow.* Il. by Vo-Dinh. Knopf, 1974. P.
A Vietnamese girl sees her first New England snow while seeking to understand the death of her grandmother.

Cummings, Betty Sue. *And Now, Ameriky.* Atheneum, 1979. U.
An Irish immigrant's journey to America and her struggle to eventually own her own land.

Fiarrotta, Phyllis, and Noel Fiarotta. *The You and Me Heritage Tree: Children's Crafts from 21 American Traditions.* Workman, 1976. M.
Children's crafts selected from a variety of ethnic backgrounds. Clear, simple directions.

Fisher, Leonard Everett. *A Russian Farewell.* Il. by author. Four Winds, 1980. U.
Anti-Jewish persecution forces the Shapiro family to leave their homeland for America circa 1905.

Freedman, Russell. *Immigrant Kids.* Il. with photographs. Dutton, 1980. All ages.
Photographs show the children of poor European immigrants who came to America a century ago: the voyage, at home, at work, at school.

Fritz, Jean. *Homesick: My Own Story.* Putnam, 1982. M.
Jean, an American citizen, was born in China and arrives in America in the 1920's to adjust to a new life.

Geras, Adele. *Voyage.* Atheneum, 1983. U.
Vignettes of the passengers traveling from Europe to Ellis Island in 1904.

Heyman, Anita. *Exit from Home.* Crown, 1977. U.
A Yeshiva student gets involved with the 1905 Russian Revolution and is forced to emigrate.

Kessner, Thomas, and Betty Boyd Caroli. *Today's Immigrants, Their Stories: A New Look at the Newest Americans.* Oxford, 1982. U.
Immigrants since 1965 discuss their experiences in the United States.

Kherdian, David. *The Road from Home: The Story of an Armenian Girl.* Greenwillow, 1978. U.
The author's mother is expelled from Turkey. This book chronicles her family's wanderings until she leaves for America. *Finding Home* (Greenwillow, 1981) is the sequel set in America.

Lasky, Kathryn. *Night Journey.* Il. by Trina Schart Hyman. Warne, 1981. M.
Rachel's great-grandmother tells about her family's escape from Czarist Russia.

Levoy, Myron. *The Witch of Fourth Street and Other Stories.* Il. by Gabriel Lisowski. Harper, 1972. M.
Stories about European immigrants on New York's lower East Side.

Loescher, Gil, and Ann Dull Loescher. *The World's Refugees, a Test of Humanity.* Il. with photographs. Harcourt, 1932. U.
The history and present status of the world's refugees.

Lord, Bette Bao. *In the Year of the Boar and Jackie Robinson.* Il. by Marc Simont. Harper, 1984. M.
Shirley leaves China to make her home in Brooklyn, New York. She struggles with learning English and routs for her favorite baseball team; the Brooklyn Dodgers.

Madison, Winifred. *Call Me Danica.* Four Winds, 1977. M.
Danica's family leaves their small Croatian village for the adjustments to Canadian city life.

Marzollo, Jean. *Halfway Down Paddy Lane.* Dial, 1981. U.
Kate, a 1980's teen-ager, wakes up to find herself in a family of Irish immigrants in the year 1850.

McCunn, Ruthanne Lum. *Pie-Biter.* Il. by You-shan Tang. Design Enterprises of S.F., 1983. M.
Hoi, a Chinese immigrant working on the railroads in the 1860's, becomes an entrepreneur and a folk hero.

Meltzer, Milton. *The Chinese Americans.* Crowell, 1980. M, U.
An easy-to-read overview of the ridicule, abuse, and violence that the Chinese had to endure before banding together to fight for civil rights and economic freedom. (One of a series.)

Pellowski, Anne. *First Farm in the Valley: Anna's Story.* Il. by Wendy Watson. Philomel, 1982. M.
Polish immigrants in Wisconsin in the 1860's are depicted through episodic chapters describing a warm, close family.

Sandin, Joan. *The Long Way to a New Land.* Il. by author. Harper, 1981. P.
A Swedish family voyages to America in 1868, in an easy-to-read book.

Spier, Peter. *People.* Il. by author. Doubleday, 1979. All ages.
Celebrates the uniqueness of people in a glorious picture book.

Uchida, Yoshiko. *A Jar of Dreams.* Atheneum, 1981. M.
An eleven-year-old Japanese-American girl learns to accept the ways of a Japanese aunt.

Wartski, Maureen Crane. *A Boat to Nowhere.* Il. by Dick Teicher. Westminster, 1980. M.
This book tells the story of a teacher and his grandchildren who leave a Vietnamese village on a fishing boat.

Yep, Laurence. *Child of the Owl.* Harper, 1977. M, U.
Casey is a contemporary Chinese-American teen who is forced to confront her heritage when she goes to live with her grandmother in San Francisco's Chinatown.

——. *Dragonwings.* Harper, 1975. M.
Eight-year-old Moon Shadow joins his father in San Francisco's Chinatown in 1909.

A Traditional Christmas

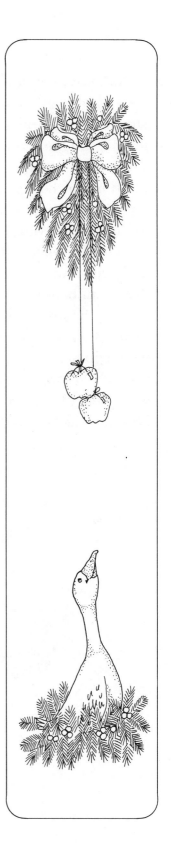

*Christmas is coming, the geese are
    getting fat,*
*Please to put a penny in an old
    man's hat;*
*If you haven't got a penny, a
    ha'penny will do,*
*If you haven't got a ha'penny,
    God bless you.*

                    — MOTHER GOOSE

Christmas arrives promptly every year
at Thanksgiving and lasts for six weeks. For
more than twenty years I have been reading
a yearly crop of new juvenile Christmas
books, but the mainstay of my Christmas
program has remained "The Christmas Apple," a story I have told to both religious
and secular groups.

Ruth Sawyer's story of Hermann Joseph, a generous man who deserves a miracle, is appropriate for most age groups. The shorter story can be adapted for any holiday, Thanksgiving or Easter, where feasting is a traditional activity.

If you are not in a position to hoard the library's entire collection of Christmas books for your program exhibit, you might substitute an exhibit of books suggested as holiday gifts, books suggested as leisure reading during Christmas vacation, or cookbooks suggested for holiday feasting. If you hold a pre-Christmas games workshop — and you would be doing a real service to harried gift-givers if you did — your book exhibit might include books about games.

"The Christmas Apple" deserves a special setting. Before you tell or read the story, turn the lights off and use the light of candles to set the mood of the story. The story is a very moving one and, although I usually like to tell a longer story first, the audience and you might enjoy being left with a feeling of awe, so present the Rettich story first, the poems, and then end with "The Christmas Apple."

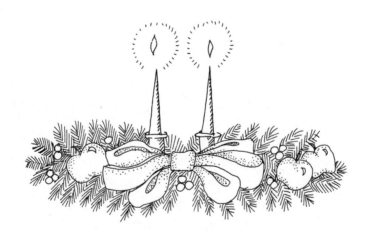

Prose Selections

The Christmas Apple
by RUTH SAWYER

Once on a time there lived in Germany a little clockmaker by the name of Hermann Joseph. He lived in one little room with a bench for his work, and a chest for his wood, and his tools, and a cupboard for dishes, and a trundle bed under the bench. Besides these there was a stool, and that was all—excepting the clocks. There were hundreds of clocks: little and big, carved and plain, some with wooden faces and some with porcelain ones—shelf clocks, cuckoo clocks, clocks with chimes and clocks without: and they all hung on the walls, covering them quite up. In front of his one little window there was a little shelf, and on this Hermann put all his best clocks to show passersby. Often they would stop and look and someone would cry: "See, Hermann Joseph has made a new clock. It is finer than any of the rest!"

Then if it happened that anybody was wanting a clock, he would come in and buy it.

I said Hermann was a little clockmaker. That was because his back was bent and his legs were crooked, which made him very short and funny to look at. But there was no kinder face than his in all the city, and the children loved him. Whenever a toy was broken or a doll had lost an arm or a leg or an eye, its careless mütterchen would carry it straight to Hermann's little shop.

"The kindlein needs mending," she would say. "Canst thou do it now for me?"

And whatever work Hermann was doing he would always put it aside to mend the broken toy or doll, and never a pfennig would he take for the mending.

"Go spend it for sweetmeats, or, better still, put it by till Christmastime. 'Twill get thee some happiness then, maybe," he would always say.

Now it was the custom in that long ago for those who lived in the city to bring gifts to the great cathedral on Christmas and lay them before the Holy Mother and Child. People saved all through the year that they might have something wonderful to bring on that day; and there was a saying among them that when a gift was brought that pleased the Christ child more than any other He would reach down from Mary's arms and take it. This was but a saying, of course. The old Herr Graf, the oldest man in the city, could not remember that it had ever really happened; and many there were who laughed at the very idea. But children often talked about it, and the poets made beautiful verses about it; and often when a rich gift was placed beside the altar the watchers would whisper among themselves, "Perhaps now we shall see the miracle."

Those who had no gifts to bring went to the cathedral just the same on Christmas eve to see the gifts of the others and hear the carols and watch the burning of the waxen tapers. The little clock-maker was one of these. Often he was stopped and someone would ask, "How happens it that you never bring a gift?" Once the bishop himself questioned him: "Poorer than thou have brought offerings to the Child. Where is thy gift?"

Then it was that Hermann had answered, "Wait; someday you shall see. I, too, shall bring a gift someday."

The truth of it was that the little clockmaker was so busy giving away all the year that there was never anything left at Christmastime. But he had a wonderful idea on which he was working every minute that he could spare time from his clocks. It had taken him years and years; no one knew anything about it but Trude, his neighbor's child, and Trude had grown from a baby into a little housemother, and still the gift was not finished.

It was to be a clock, the most wonderful and beautiful clock ever made; and every part of it had been fashioned with loving care. The case, the works, the weights, the hands, and the face, all had taken years of labor. He had spent years carving the case and hands, years perfecting the works; and now Hermann saw that with a little more haste and time he could finish it for the coming Christmas. He mended the children's toys as before, but he gave up making his regular clocks, so there were fewer to sell, and often his cupboard was empty and he went supperless to bed. But that only made him a little thinner and his face a little kinder; and meantime the gift clock became more and more beautiful. It was fashioned after a rude stable with rafters, stall, and crib. The Holy Mother knelt beside the manger in which a tiny Christ child lay, while through the open door the hours came. Three were kings and three were shepherds and three were soldiers and three were angels; and when the hours struck, the figure knelt in adoration before the sleeping Child, while the silver chimes played the Magnificat.

"Thou seest," said the clockmaker to Trude, "it is not just on Sundays and holidays that we should remember to worship the Christ Kindlein and bring Him gifts—but every day, every hour."

The days went by like clouds scudding before a winter wind, and the clock was finished at last. So happy was Hermann with his work that he put the gift clock on the shelf before the little window to show the passersby. There were crowds looking at it all day long, and many would whisper, "Do you think this can be the gift Hermann has spoken of—his offering on Christmas eve to the church?"

The day before Christmas came. Hermann cleaned up his little shop, wound all his clocks, brushed his clothes, and then went over the gift clock again to be sure everything was perfect.

It will not look mean beside the other gifts, he thought, happily. In fact he was so happy that he gave away all but one pfennig to the blind beggar who passed his door; and then, remembering that he had eaten nothing since breakfast, he spent that last pfennig for a Christmas apple to eat with a crust of bread he had. These he was putting by in the cupboard to eat after he was dressed, when the door opened and Trude was standing there crying softly.

"Kindlein—kindlein, what ails thee?" And he gathered her into his arms.

"'Tis the father. He is hurt, and all the money that was put by for the tree and sweets and toys has gone to the Herr Doktor. And now, how can I tell the children? Already they have lighted the candle at the window and are waiting for Kris Kringle to come."

The clockmaker laughed merrily.

"Come, come, little one, all will be well. Hermann will sell a clock for thee. Some house in the city must need a clock; and in a wink we shall have money enough for the tree and the toys. Go home and sing."

He buttoned on his greatcoat and, picking out the best of the old clocks, he went out. He went first to the rich merchants, but their houses were full of clocks; then to the journeymen, but they said his clock was old-fashioned. He even stood on the corners of the streets and in the square, crying, "A clock—a good clock for sale," but no one paid any attention to him. At last he gathered up his courage and went to the Herr Graf himself.

"Will Your Excellency buy a clock?" he said, trembling at his own boldness. "I would not ask, but it is Christmas and I am needing to buy happiness for some children."

The Herr Graf smiled.

"Yes, I will buy a clock, but not that one. I will pay a thousand gulden for the clock thou hast had in thy window these four days past."

"But, Your Excellency, that is impossible!" And poor Hermann trembled harder than ever.

"Poof! Nothing is impossible. That clock or none. Get thee home, and I will send for it in half an hour and pay thee the gulden."

The little clockmaker stumbled out.

"Anything but that—anything but that!" he kept mumbling over and over to himself on his way home. But as he passed the neighbor's house he saw the children at the window with their lighted candle and he heard Trude singing.

And so it happened that the servant who came from the Herr Graf carried the gift clock away with him; but the clockmaker would take but five of the thousand gulden in payment. And as the servant disappeared up the street the chimes commenced to ring from the great cathedral, and the streets suddenly became noisy with the many people going thither, bearing their Christmas offerings.

"I have gone empty-handed before," said the little clockmaker, sadly. "I can go empty-handed once again." And again he buttoned up his greatcoat.

As he turned to shut his cupboard door behind him his eyes fell on the Christmas apple, and an odd little smile crept into the corners of his mouth and lighted his eyes.

"It is all I have — my dinner for two days. I will carry that to the Christ child. It is better, after all, than going empty-handed."

How full of peace and beauty was the great cathedral when Hermann entered it! There were a thousand tapers burning and everywhere the sweet scent of the Christmas greens — and the laden altar before the Holy Mother and Child. There were richer gifts than had been brought for many years: marvelously wrought vessels from the greatest silversmiths; cloth of gold and cloth of silk brought from the East by the merchants; poets had brought their songs illuminated on rolls of heavy parchment; painters had brought their pictures of saints and the Holy Family; even the king himself had brought his crown and scepter to lay before the Child. And after all these offerings came the little clockmaker, walking slowly down the long, dim aisle, holding tight to his Christmas apple.

The people saw him and a murmur rose, hummed a moment indistinctly through the church and then grew clear and articulate: "Shame! See, he is too mean to bring his clock! He hoards it as a miser hoards his gold. See what he brings! Shame!"

The words reached Hermann and he stumbled on blindly, his head dropped forward on his breast, his hands groping the way. The distance seemed interminable. Now he knew he was past the seats; now his feet touched the first step, and there were seven to climb to the altar. Would his feet never reach the top?

"One, two, three," he counted to himself, then tripped and almost fell. "Four, five, six." He was nearly there. There was but one more.

The murmur of shame died away and in its place rose one of

wonder and awe. Soon the words became intelligible: "The miracle! It is the miracle!"

The people knelt in the big cathedral; the bishop raised his hands in prayer. And the little clockmaker, stumbling to the last step, looked up through dim eyes and saw the Child leaning toward him, far down from Mary's arms, with hands outstretched to take his gift.

The Christmas Roast

by MARGRET RETTICH
translated from the German by ELIZABETH D. CRAWFORD

Once a man found a goose on the beach. The November storms had been raging several days before. She had probably swum too far out, been caught, and then tossed back to land again by the waves. No one in the area had geese. She was a real white domestic goose.

The man stuck her under his jacket and took her home to his wife. "Here's our Christmas roast."

They had never kept an animal and had no coop. The man built a little shed out of posts, boards, and roofing board right next to the house wall. The woman put sacks in it and put an old sweater on top of them. In the corner they put a pot with water in it.

"Do you know what geese eat?" she asked.

"No idea," said the man.

They tried potatoes and bread, but the goose wouldn't touch anything. She didn't want rice either, and she didn't want the rest of their Sunday cake.

"She's homesick for the other geese," said the woman.

The goose didn't resist when they carried her into the kitchen. She sat quietly under the table. The man and the woman squatted before her, trying to cheer her up.

"But we aren't geese," said the man. He sat on a chair and tried to find some band music on the radio. The woman sat beside him, her knitting needles going clickety-clack. It was very cozy. Suddenly the goose ate some rolled oats and a little cake.

"She's settling down, our lovely Christmas roast," said the man. By next morning the goose was waddling all over the place. She stuck her neck through the open doors, nibbled on the curtains, and made a little spot on the doormat.

The house in which the man and woman lived was a simple one. There was no indoor plumbing, only a pump. When the man pumped a bucket full of water, as he did every morning before going to work, the goose came along, climbed into the bucket, and bathed. The water spilled over, and the man had to pump again.

In the garden there was a little wooden house, which was the toilet. When the woman went to it, the goose ran behind her and pressed inside with her. Later she went with the woman to the baker and then to the dairy store.

When the man came home from work on his bicycle that afternoon, the woman and the goose were standing at the garden gate.

"Now she likes potatoes, too," reported the woman.

"Wonderful," said the man and stroked the goose on the head. "Then by Christmas she will be round and fat."

The shed was never used, for the goose stayed in the warm kitchen every night. She ate and ate. Sometimes the woman set her on the scales, and each time she was heavier.

When the man and the woman sat with the goose in the evening, they both imagined the most marvelous Christmas food.

"Roast goose and red cabbage. They go well together," said the woman and stroked the goose on her lap.

The man would rather have had sauerkraut than red cabbage, but for him the most important thing was the dumplings. "They must be as big as my head and all the same size," he said.

"And made with raw potatoes," added his wife.

"No, with cooked ones," asserted the man. Then they agreed that half the dumplings should be made with raw potatoes and half with cooked ones. When they went to bed, the goose lay at the foot and warmed them.

All at once it was Christmas.

The wife decorated a small tree. The husband biked to the shop and bought everything they would need for the great feast. He also brought a kilo of extra-fine rolled oats.

"Even if it's her last," he said with a sigh, "she should at least know that it's Christmas."

"I've been wondering," began the woman, "how, do you think,

should we…I mean…we still have to….'' But she couldn't get any farther.

The man didn't say anything for a while. "I can't do it,'' he said finally.

"I can't either,'' said the woman. "I could if it were just any old goose. But not this one. No, I can't do it, no matter what.''

The man grabbed the goose and fastened her onto his baggage carrier. Then he rode his bicycle to a neighbor's. In the meantime, the woman cooked red cabbage and made the dumplings, one just as big as the next.

The neighbor lived far away, to be sure, but still not so far that it was a day's journey. Nevertheless, the man did not come home until evening. The goose sat contentedly behind him.

"I never saw our neighbor. We just rode around,'' he said ashamedly.

"It doesn't matter,'' said the woman cheerfully. "While you were gone, I thought it over and decided that adding something else to dinner would just spoil the good taste of the red cabbage and the dumplings.''

The woman was right, and they had a good meal. At their feet the goose feasted on the extra-fine rolled oats. Later all three sat together on the sofa in the living room and enjoyed the candlelight.

The next year, for a change, the woman cooked sauerkraut to go with the dumplings. The year afterward there were broad noodles to go with the sauerkraut. They were such good things that nothing else was needed to go with them.

And so time passed. Goose grew very old.

Poetry Selections

Country Christmas

by AILEEN FISHER

Let's hang up some suet
for juncos and jays,
let's put out some hay for the deer,
let's throw in some corn
where the cottontail stays,
this holiday season of year.

Let's scatter some millet
and barley and wheat —
it isn't much trouble or fuss
to give all the wild folk
a holiday treat
so they can have Christmas, like us!

The Christmas Exchange

by ARTHUR GUITERMAN

When Bill gives me a book, I know
It's just the book he wanted, so
When I give him a Ping-Pong set,
He's sure it's what I hoped to get.

Then after Christmas we arrange
A little Christmas Gift Exchange;
I give the book to him, and he
Gives back the Ping-Pong set to me.

So each gives twice — and that is
    pleasant —
To get the truly-wanted present.

268

Our Christmas Tree

by JACK PRELUTSKY

Daddy took me to the forest
for our Christmas tree today,
he said that we'd enjoy it
and we'd hardly have to pay.

We were wearing scarves and
  mittens,
all our very warmest clothes,
but our cheeks soon looked like
  cherries
and our fingers nearly froze.

We hunted through the forest
for a tree that was just right,
by the time we finally found one
we were both an awful sight,

I was shivering and shaking,
Daddy shook and shivered too,
I was colder than an iceberg,
Daddy's face was turning blue.

Daddy finally chopped that tree
  down,
but the way he did was dumb,
when it fell, it knocked him
  backwards
and he cut his nose and thumb,

Daddy also sprained his shoulder,
banged an elbow, scraped a knee,
as I helped him up, he muttered,
"Son! Next year we'll buy our tree."

269

Sharon Johnson's Plush Goose Puppet

This stuffed goose is easy to make and fun to play with. It is actually a puppet: by twisting the end of the wooden rod that runs through the goose's body you can make its head turn.

Materials:

1 piece white fake fur, 20″ x 20″
1 piece orange felt, 11″ x 16″
white felt (see pattern to determine how much is needed)
black felt for eyes (see pattern to determine how much is needed)
12 ounces Polyester fiber for stuffing
1 wooden rod, 18″ long, ½″ in diameter
1 wood screw, 2″-2½″ long, ⅛″ in diameter
thin cardboard

Instructions:

1. Using the dimensions given, draw all the patterns on a piece of paper and cut out the shapes. Place the cutouts of the two body pieces, the neck gusset, and the body gusset on the wrong side of the fake fur. Cut carefully around the pattern. (Note: For all pieces of the goose, work on the wrong side of the materials.)

2. Continuing to work on the wrong side of the fake fur, pin the two body pieces together along the goose's back from D to C, and then stitch along that line.

3. Pin the neck gusset to one of the body pieces from A to B1, and then stitch along that line. Repeat with other body piece.

4. Pin the body gusset to one of the body pieces from B2 to C, and then stitch along that line. Repeat with other body piece.

5. Turn the work right side out.

6. Drill a hole slightly smaller than ⅛″ in diameter about ¼″ from the top of the rod. Insert screw in hole so that the same amount is exposed on either side.

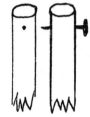

USE THIS PUPPET WHEN TELLING "THE CHRISTMAS ROAST"

7. Insert some polyester fiber stuffing in the top of the goose's head.

8. Insert wooden rod into the goose's body so that the end with the screw is in the head, with the screw crosswise to the beak. (The other end of the rod should come out of the body between the two gussets.)

9. Place stuffing in rest of head around rod. Stuff tightly.

10. Loosely place stuffing in the neck section from J to K.

11. Cut upper and lower beak pieces out of orange felt. Pin the pieces together along A to A1, easing the fabric to fit, and then stitch along that line. Turn beak right side out.

12. Cut lower beak pattern out of cardboard and insert as a stiffener within lower portion of felt beak. Stuff the beak tightly with stuffing.

13. Pin beak to head, attaching the middle of the upper beak (D) to the middle of the upper head (D) and attaching the middle of the lower beak (E) to the middle of the neck gusset (E). Ease the fabric to fit around the rest of the beak. Turn the fake fur under about 1/3″. Handstitch twice around beak to insure that it is securely attached.

270

14. Stuff the rest of the body tightly with stuffing. Pinch the tail at M and handstitch M to M tightly together so that tail curves under. The rod should come out of the body between the 2 gussets at L — stuffing should be packed tightly around it.

15. Handstitch the opening between the 2 gussets close (B1 to B2).

16. Cut out the four foot pieces out of orange felt. Pin two of the pieces together along FHG and then stitch along that line. Leave open FIG for insertion of leg.

Turn the foot right side out. Repeat for the other foot. Stuff each foot lightly with stuffing.

17. Cut out a leg piece out of orange felt. Pin the piece together from I1 to I and then stitch along that line. Turn the leg right side out. Repeat for the other leg.

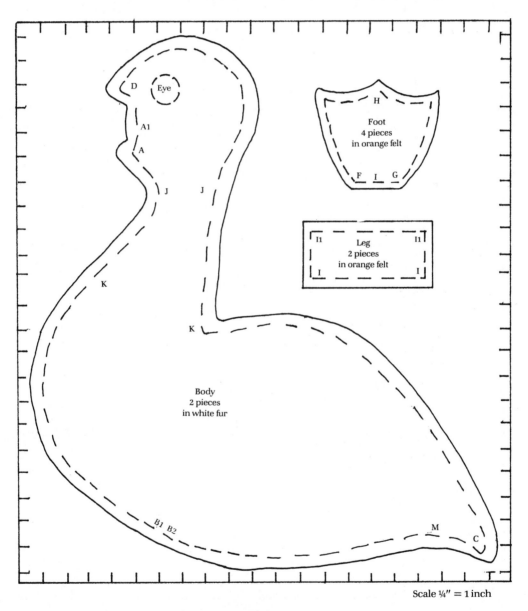

Scale ¼″ = 1 inch

271

18. Turn leg piece under ¼″ and insert that hem into foot opening at FIG. Handstitch leg to foot along that line. Repeat for the other leg and foot pieces.

19. Tightly stuff legs. Then attach legs in the middle of body seamline behind rod at B2. Turn leg fabric under ¼″ and hand stitch to body.

20. Cut out eye pieces out of black and white felt. Glue white piece in center of larger black piece. Then glue smaller black piece to the top of the white piece with one edge touching the edge of the black piece. Glue eyes to each side of head.

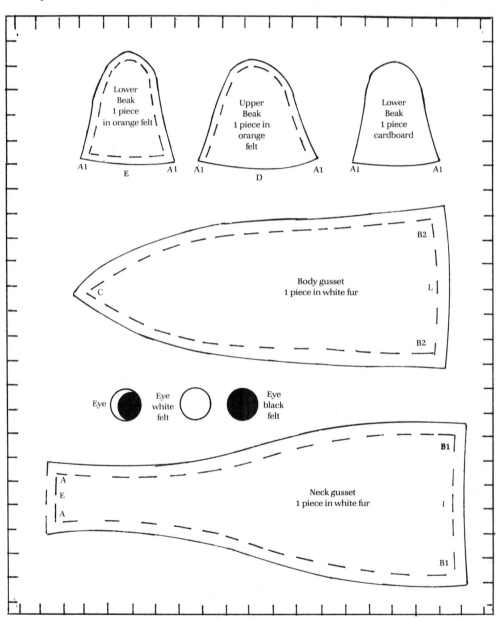

Christmas Treats

Shiny red apples to accompany "The Christmas Apple"

Sprinkle-covered cookies to accompany Kraus's *The Christmas Cookie Sprinkle Snitcher* (Windmill, 1969).

Candy Cane Cookies

YOU NEED: 1 cup shortening (half butter or margarine)
1 cup powdered sugar, sifted
1 egg
1½ teaspoon almond extract
1 teaspoon vanilla
2½ cups flour
1 teaspoon salt
½ teaspoon red food coloring
½ cup crushed peppermint candy
½ cup granulated sugar

HOW TO: Heat oven to 375°. Cream shortening, sugar, egg, and flavorings. Mix in flour and salt. Divide dough in half. Blend food coloring into one portion. Roll 1 teaspoon each of colored and plain dough into two 4-inch strips. Twist the two strips together and curve top to form a cane. Bake about 9 minutes. While warm, sprinkle cookies with combination of candy and sugar.

Or, if you don't feel like baking, use plain vanilla cookies. Children may use prepared frosting, or home-made, to frost the cookies. Add sprinkles before frosting sets.

Souvenir

After you have read Aileen Fisher's poem *Country Christmas* (see page 268), why not provide small plastic bags filled with bird seed (available in grocery stores) for each child to take home to offer to winter birds in their neighborhood?

Bulletin Board

Pin up Christmas cards with Christmas book annotations typed inside.

Creative Writing/Activities

Have the children rewrite *The Night Before Christmas*, in verse or narrative form, as it might take place at their own homes. If they don't celebrate Christmas, have them describe the scene at home before any major holiday.

Christmas Game Workshops

Christmas is coming *or* Christmas has just passed. Either way, it's time to hold a games workshop. Before Christmas you can hold a workshop for parents and after Christmas one for children. For both, the speakers will be children.

Any adult who has shopped for a children's game in a toy store has experienced the frustration of encountering shelf upon shelf of sealed boxes of games. How do you know what is inside these cellophane-sealed packages? The store clerk is often just as puzzled as the customer about the contents. Sometimes the best way to find out how these games work is from the people who play them: the children.

PRE-CHRISTMAS WORKSHOP

Have children bring their favorite board game or toy to the library. Make available lots of table space to exhibit the toys. Children stand behind their contribution. If several children bring the same game, they stand together.

Adults are invited to walk around and chat with the children about the games.

POST-CHRISTMAS WORKSHOP

Scout your workshop leaders from the first workshop. You need children who will be articulate and *nice* enough to teach younger children how to play games. Have participants sign up in advance so you will be sure to have enough playing space for each child. Include classic games such as chess, checkers, and Monopoly, as well as the more contemporary favorites such as backgammon and Dungeons and Dragons. Allow at least three hours for small groups to learn to play the games; a shorter time, say an hour and a half, is ample for a pre-school or primary-age workshop.

Make it clear in your promotion materials what age group of visitors you want to attract.

Hold another workshop for younger children's games, such as chutes and ladders, with older children again taking charge.

If you find that any games have become the rage in your community, set aside space for continuous play, and be sure to display game books near the playing area.

A List of Books for Christmas:

New Christmas books are published each year. This booklist includes some selected favorites. The books are generally used only during a short portion of the year, but if you are planning a Christmas program, reserve your exhibit books early. The same people that buy their Christmas presents in August seem to borrow Christmas books in September!

Bible. *The Story of Christmas: A Picture Book.* Adapted and il. by Felix Hoffman. McElderry, 1975. All ages.
  A picture-book version of the nativity.

Briggs, Raymond. *Father Christmas.* Il. by author. Coward, 1973. All ages.
  In comic-strip style, Father Christmas grumbles through Christmas Eve.

Carrick, Carol. *Paul's Christmas Birithday.* Il. by Donald Carrick. Greenwillow, 1978. P.
  A birthday party for a child whose birthday falls on December 24.

Climo, Shirley. *Cobweb Christmas.* Il. by Joe Lasker. Crowell, 1982. All ages.
  The Spiders decorate Tante's Christmas tree.

Costikyan, Barbara Heine. *Be Kind to your Dog at Christmas and Other Ways to Have Happy Holidays and a Lucky New Year.* Il. by Joyce Audy dos Santos. Pantheon, 1982. All ages.
  Christmas superstitions from around the world.

Davies, Valentine. *Miracle on 34th Street.* Il. by Tomie de Paola. Harcourt, 1975. M, U.
  New illustrations make this Christmas classic a good read-aloud.

de Paola, Tomie. *Clown of God.* Il. by author. Harcourt, 1978. P.
  An old juggler gives his only gift to the Christ child.

Devlin, Wende. *Cranberry Christmas.* Il. by Harry Devlin. Parents, 1976. P.
  Sister Sarah comes to visit for Christmas and Mr. Whiskers ends up entertaining with a festive skating party. The recipe for cranberry cookies would make a good treat to serve.

Dickens, Charles. *A Christmas Carol.* Il. by Trina Schart Hyman. Holiday, 1983. U.
  The classic tale illustrated with full-color paintings. (See also the version illustrated by Michael Foreman. Dial, 1983)

Domanska, Janina. *Din Dan Don, It's Christmas.* Il. by author. Greenwillow, 1975. All ages.
  Colorful pictures of an animal procession to Bethlehem based on a Polish Christmas Carol.

Gackenbach, Dick. *Claude the Dog: A Christmas Story.* Il. by author. Clarion, 1974. P.
  Although Claude gets many Christmas gifts, he gives them all to a less fortunate friend.

Gammell, Stephen. *Wake Up, Bear...It's Christmas.* Il. by author. Lothrop, 1981. All ages.
  Bear entertains a familiar stranger.

Gay, Michel. *The Christmas Wolf.* Il. by author. Greenwillow, 1980. P.
  Father Wolf goes to town to get toys for his wolf children and succeeds through a misadventure.

Gibbons, Gail. *Christmas Time.* Il. by author. Holiday, 1982. P.
  Why and how we celebrate Christmas with bright colorful pictures.

Goodall, John S. *An Edwardian Christmas.* Il. by author. McElderry, 1978. All ages.
  Wordless picture book shows preparations for an upper-class Christmas.

Henry, O. *The Gift of the Magi.* Il. by Erik Blegvad. Hawthorn, 1972. M, U.

The lovely short story about a couple who sacrifice their most treasured possessions to make each other happy.

Hoban, Lillian. *Arthur's Christmas Cookies.* Il. by author. Harper, 1972. P.

Arthur mistakenly uses salt instead of sugar in his cookies, but they make fine tree ornaments. Use this I-Can-Read book in a craft program.

Hoban, Russell. *The Mole Family's Christmas.* Il. by Lillian Hoban. Parents, 1969. P.

The mole family builds a chimney so that the "fat man in a red suit" will visit and bring a Christmas gift.

Kamerman, Sylvia E., ed. *On Stage for Christmas.* Plays, Inc. 1978. All ages.

A collection of thirty-five royalty-free plays suitable for lower grades through high school.

Kent, Jack. *Jack Kent's Twelve Days of Christmas.* Il. by author. Parents, 1973. All ages.

Lively cartoon drawings add to the enjoyment of this traditional carol.

Kraus, Robert. *The Christmas Cookie Sprinkle Snitcher.* Il. by Vip. Windmill, 1969. P, M.

The sprinkle snatcher is foiled by a young boy. Sprinkle-covered cookies would make a good treat after reading this story.

Laurence, Margaret. *The Christmas Birthday Story.* Il. by Helen Lucas. Knopf, 1980. All ages.

A retelling of the Bible story illustrated with stylistic drawings.

The Little Drummer Boy. Il. by Ezra Jack Keats. Words and music by Katherine Davis, Henry Onorati, and Harry Simeone. Macmillan, 1968. All ages.

Picture book based on the song about a little drummer boy who drums for the Christ child as an offering.

Livingston, Myra Cohn, ed. *Poems of Christmas.* McElderry, 1980. M, U.

Religious and secular poems.

Manushkin, Fran. *The Perfect Christmas Picture.* Il. by Karen Ann Weinhaus. Harper, 1980. P.

Mr. Green tries throughout the year to capture his large family in a picture.

Mikolaycak, Charles. *Babushka: An Old Russian Folktale.* Il. by author. Holiday, 1984. All ages.

Full color paintings show Babushka's search for the Christ child.

Moore, Clement. *The Night Before Christmas.* Il. by Tomie de Paola. Holiday, 1980. All ages.

The traditional poem illustrated with a colonial American setting.

Oakley, Graham. *The Church Mice Christmas.* Il. by author. Atheneum, 1980. P.

The church mice would like a Christmas party, but where will they get the money?

Parker, Nancy Winslow. *The Christmas Carol.* Il. by author. Dial, 1983. All ages.

"Fafa is no ordinary camel."

Pearson, Susan. *Karin's Christmas Walk.* Il. by Trinka Hakes Noble. Dial, 1980. P, M.

A little girl walks home thinking about her Uncle Jerry's Christmas visit.

Pearson, Tracey Campbell. *We Wish You a Merry Christmas.* Il. by author. Dial, 1983. All ages.

Exuberant pictures illustrate this Christmas carol.

Prelutsky, Jack. *It's Christmas.* Il. by Marylin Hafner. Greenwillow, 1981. All ages.

Funny poems for the beginning reader.

Rettich, Margret. *The Silver Touch and Other Christmas Stories.* Trans. from the German by Elizabeth D. Crawford. Il. by Rolf Rettich. Morrow, 1978. M, U.

A collection of contemporary family Christmas stories.

Robinson, Barbara. *The Best Christmas Pageant Ever.* Il. by Judith Gwyn Brown. Harper, 1972. M.

"The Herdmans were absolutely the worst kids in the history of the world" and they are going to take part in the Christmas pageant.

Rock, Gail. *The House without a Christmas Tree.* Il. by Charles C. Gehm. Knopf, 1974. M.

Addie's father refuses to let her have a Christmas tree in a sentimental family story.

Seuss, Dr. *How the Grinch Stole Christmas.* Il. by author. Random, 1957. P.

In nonsense verse, this picture book tells how a miserable creature tries to eliminate Christmas.

Stevenson, James. *The Night After Christmas.* Il. by author. Greenwillow, 1981. P.

A discarded teddy bear and doll find new homes.

Theroux, Paul. *London Snow: A Christmas Story.* Il. by John Lawrence. Houghton, 1980. M, U.

Two children search for their cantankerous landlord in a snowstorm. See also *A Christmas Card* (Houghton, 1978).

Thomas, Dylan. *A Child's Christmas in Wales.* Il. by Edward Ardizzone. Godine, 1980. M, U.

This distinguished prose poem with Ardizzone's illustrations is the perfect book for the Christmas season.

"Trosclair." *Cajun Night Before Christmas.* Ed. by Howard Jacobs. Il. by James Rice. Pelican Publishing (630 Burmaster Street, Gretna, Louisiana 70053), 1973. All ages.

Uses Cajun dialect for the classic poem.

Van Leeuwen, Jean. *The Great Christmas Kidnapping Caper.* Il. by Steven Kellogg. Dial, 1975. M.

A gang of mice who live in the Macy's toy department solve the mystery of the kidnapping of the store Santa Claus.

Varnum, Brooke Minarik. *Play and Sing — It's Christmas.* Il. by Emily Arnold McCully. Macmillan, 1980. All ages.

Follow the directions and you can play Christmas carols on any keyboard instrument.

Wells, Rosemary. *Morris's Disappearing Bag.* Il. by author. Dial, 1975. P.

Morris is not allowed to play with his sister's and brother's gifts until he promises to let them have a turn with a bag that makes them invisible.

Wiggin, Douglas. *Birds' Christmas Carol.* Il. by Jesse Gillespie. Houghton, 1941. M.

A sentimental Christmas story about the Birds who make a merry Christmas for the Ruggles family.

Williams, Vera B. *It's a Gingerbread House: Bake It! Build It! Eat It!* Il. by author. Greenwillow, 1978. P.

A Read-Alone book gives directions for making a gingerbread house.

Winthrop, Elizabeth. *A Child Is Born.* Adapted from the New Testament. Il. by Charles Mikolaycak. Holiday, 1983. M, U.

Zolotow, Charlotte. *The Beautiful Christmas Tree.* Il. by Ruth Robbins. Parnassus, 1972. P.

Mr. Crockett plants a Christmas tree in the city and it is a joy all year long.

Valentine's Day: Friends

"Good friends always stick together."
— HELME HEINE. *Friends*

I have been interested in national and regional holidays for a number of years. When I'm in a foreign country, I always ask about any local festivals. I am particularly interested in the customs used to mark a special day. I ask about special food, songs, or games traditionally played. I often ask how a holiday originated. At first I was surprised when people seemed to be completely ignorant of the reason for the celebration. Then I realized that we have our own share of celebrations whose origins are obscure.

Valentine's Day is not a legal holiday, but it is widely celebrated in the United States as a day for lovers and friends to exchange cards and small gifts. Ask ten people why we celebrate Valentine's Day and nine and a half people will plead ignorance. This is natural, since the way a traditional holiday is celebrated is much more important than why it is. Although there were two different

279

third-century Christian martyrs named Valentine, our Valentine's Day has nothing to do with these saints. A Roman festival called Lupercalia may be the basis for our western celebration. Names were drawn from a box and men and women were paired by chance. They exchanged gifts and often became friends and even marriage partners after this initial meeting at the Lupercalia feast.

In the United States, Valentine's Day has been celebrated with the exchange of greeting cards, handmade or commercially produced. Some cards are called comic Valentines and have funny or caustic messages on them, some contain flowery sentiments. Unsigned valentines are often sent by shy admirers. Since children are unlikely to be involved in a romantic love relationship, Valentine's Day has been extended to include the exchanging of cards between friends, teachers, and relatives.

Although the traditional classroom Valentine Box is a lovely and lively idea, I think a slight variation on the traditional Valentine's Day theme is more appropriate for elementary-school-age children. I've chosen to celebrate friends and friendship on February 14.

Making friends and maintaining friendships are often the central themes of a children's book. There are several picture books featuring the vagaries of friendship that would be appropriate for sharing aloud with a group of children.

In Marjorie Weinman Sharmat's *The 329th Friend*, a raccoon finds out that he can be his own best friend. In *My Friend Jacob* (Lucille Clifton) a retarded boy is befriended by a younger neighbor. Readers will discover that friends can be much older, like Sam Greene's sixty-year-old friend in *Thank You, Jackie Robinson* (see page 27), or competitive adversaries like Philip Hall in Bette Greene's novel *Get On Out of Here, Philip Hall*, or become friends simply because of propinquity like Jonah and his neighbor Goober in *Banana Twist*. The friendship in *The Fledgling*, by Jane Langton, is between a young girl and a goose.

The reading selection and poems have been chosen to show some of the more poignant aspects of friendship.

Prose Selections

from Rosie and Michael
by JUDITH VIORST

When my parakeet died, I called Rosie.

When my bike got swiped, I called Rosie.

When I cut my head and the blood came gushing out, as soon as the blood stopped gushing, I called Rosie.

She is my friend.

When my dog ran away,
I called Michael. When my bike got swiped,
I called Michael. When I broke my wrist and the bone was sticking out, as soon as they stuck it back in,
I called Michael.

He is my friend.

If Rosie told me a secret and people hit me and bit me, I wouldn't tell what Rosie's secret was. And then if people twisted my arm and kicked me in the shins, I still wouldn't tell what Rosie's secret was. And then if people said, "Speak up, or we'll throw you in this quicksand," Rosie would forgive me for telling her secret.

If Michael told me a secret and people clonked me and bopped me, I wouldn't tell what Michael's secret was. And then if people bent back my fingers and wrestled me to the ground, I still wouldn't tell what Michael's secret was.

And then if people said, "Speak up, or we'll feed you to these piranhas," Michael would forgive me for telling his secret.

If Rosie bought me an ice cream bar, it wouldn't be toasted almond. If Rosie bought me a shirt, it wouldn't be green. If Rosie bought me a book, it wouldn't be *How Your Sewer System Works*, or *Sven of Sweden*.

You can count on a friend.

If Michael bought me some candy, it wouldn't be licorice. If Michael bought me a scarf, it wouldn't be brown. If Michael bought me a book, it wouldn't be *Know Your Lungs*, or *Dances of Costa Rica*.

You can count on a friend.

Michael would try to save me if a lion attacked. He'd catch me if I jumped from a burning house. And if by mistake he missed the catch, he could have my stamp collection. He is my friend.

I'd never get my tonsils out if Rosie didn't, too.

I'd never move to China without Michael.

I'd give her my last piece of chalk.
I'd give him my last Chicklet.
Rosie is
Michael is
My friend.

I'm Not Oscar's Friend Anymore

by MARJORIE WEINMAN
SHARMAT

There's this kid Oscar who lives down the street. Once when I didn't know any better I was his friend. A couple of days ago he said something very fresh to me. So fresh I won't repeat it. So I said something fresh right back. And he said something fresher. And then we weren't friends anymore.

It only took about two minutes to make enemies with Oscar. But it will take forever to make up. Forever like never. Because I will never make up with Oscar. Oscar is the kind of guy who if he had a glass of grape juice he would spill half of it on me.

When we were friends I drew a picture of Oscar. I made a few mistakes but they can be fixed. We had a game where we've been keeping score for three months and my score so far comes to 265 and Oscar's comes to 73. But now Oscar's lost his chance to catch up. Oscar will be 73 forever and it will serve him right. What's so great about Oscar anyway? Every spring he gets poison ivy and smells of calamine lotion.

And he was always calling in the middle of dinner. But I was polite and talked to him. Have you ever tasted cold hot soup?

I bet Oscar misses me. When he wakes up in the morning I'm probably the first person he thinks of. He thinks about having a real good time playing with me.

Then he remembers that I'm not his friend anymore. So he pulls the covers back over himself and goes to sleep for another hour and has a terrible nightmare that I'll never make up with him. The only thing worse than a terrible nightmare is a true nightmare.

Oscar will most likely put on one brown sock and one black sock because his mind will be on me. And later on in the day he will discover that he is wearing his shirt inside out and he will try to figure out how it happened. He will be so mixed up he'll brush his hair and teeth without being reminded.

Oscar will watch cartoons on television and wonder why they are not as funny as they used to be.

Every time his doorbell rings he'll hope it's me. He'll run to answer it, but it will only be somebody like the Con Edison man to read the meter or the United Parcel man with a package for his mother.

This is the day the cleaning woman comes to Oscar's house. Oscar will follow her around and tell her his troubles. She'll give him a rag to help her dust and she'll listen while they both work. And the house will get clean. But it won't help Oscar. She'll tell him that next week when she comes, he and I will be all made up. But that's not true.

Because I am never making up with you, Oscar. I am your permanent ex-friend. Next year after it's been winter and spring and summer and fall again, I still won't be your friend.

Maybe you'll mope around the house so much that your mother will think you're sick and take you to the doctor.

You'll sit in the waiting room for two hours while little kids crawl all over you and somebody puts a sticky lollipop in your hair. Then the doctor will tell you that you're perfectly well but it's good that you came in because it's time for your booster shot.

Afterwards maybe your mother will take you for a chocolate soda. But you know what, Oscar? That soda will taste like virus medicine. You can count on it.

You didn't know when you were well off, Oscar. Without me you're a sinking ship.

Come to think of it, I'm not the kind of guy who would let a ship sink.

I'll let Oscar make up with me. And I'll even make it easy for him. I'll walk by his house and if he's lucky enough to be outside, I'll let him make up with me then and there. Here I come, lucky Oscar.

So where are you? Probably inside crying over that funny television program. Tough luck, Oscar. This was your big chance to get me back. And you blew it.

I could ring the doorbell. No, you might get the idea that *I* wanted to make up.

So that's it, Oscar. You missed your chance to be my friend again. You'll just have to play with Roger and I know you can't stand him. Or Ginger, if you can put up with her bragging. Your brother Bruno is around, but he's only three years old and very boring. And there's always Mike. If you like pests. Boy, are you stuck, Oscar.

I'm glad I'm home. That was a dumb idea, walking by Oscar's house.

I think I'll call up one of my many friends to play with me. I've got a list of friends *that* long. Jennifer went to visit her grandfather in Waterville, Maine. That takes care of her.

And there's Wallace. But he's still working on his ant colony and he always dumps his extras down my back.

What about that new kid on the street? I wonder if he tries out that stranglehold as a habit or it just happened the four times I've seen him.

Well, there's always Roger, Mike, and Ginger. If you're hard up. Maybe I'll give Oscar one chance over the telephone.

"Hello, Oscar. I'll let you be my friend again. What? Don't you remember? A couple of day ago. Sure, a big fight. Never mind. Just come over and see my new train. Five minutes? Okay. Good-bye."

Oscar can't remember anything unless I remind him. Yes, sir, without me Oscar is a sinking ship.

Poetry Selections

My Four Friends

by JACK PRELUTSKY

I live in an apartment house
next to a vacant lot,
my buddies live there also,
the four best friends I've got.

There's Tony and there's Lumpy
and there's Harvey and there's Will,
and we all hang out together
in the middle of our hill.

Tony's always cheerful,
I think he's really neat
although he wears thick glasses
and is clumsy on his feet.

Lumpy causes trouble,
he's the terror of the block,
he gets away with plenty
'cause he's just too small to sock.

Harvey's mean and nasty,
he's selfish as a pig,
but no one ever hits him
'cause Harvey's just too big.

Will is sort of special,
he acts like a chimpanzee.
I like Will an awful lot
'cause Will's a lot like me.

Sometimes
   we have races,
and sometimes
   we play ball,
but mostly
   we're just buddies
doing nothing
   much at all.

Moochie

by ELOISE GREENFIELD

Moochie likes to keep on playing
That same old silly game
Peeka   Boo!
Peeka   Boo!

I get tired of it
But it makes her laugh
And every time she laughs
She gets the hiccups
And every time she gets the hiccups
I laugh

I Have a Friend

by KARLA KUSKIN

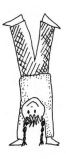

I have a friend who keeps on standing on her hands.
That's fine,
Except I find it very difficult to talk to her
Unless I stand on mine.

Susanne

by SIV WIDERBERG
translated from the Swedish by VERNE MOBERG

I've been at Susanne's
for several days
Slept there
Eaten there
Played there
Done my homework there

Pretty soon Susanne will come over to my place
Then *I'm* going to ride *my* bike the whole time
and let Susanne run along beside

Treat

Taffy

Taffy candy is the perfect treat for bringing people together. You need to have at least two people to make it. If you are not friends before you begin, you will surely be friends after you have spent an afternoon pulling and eating.

YOU NEED: (for each two people)

1 cup sugar

¾ cup corn syrup

½ cup water

¼ teaspoon cream of tartar

1 teaspoon flavoring
  (vanilla or peppermint)

1 tablespoon butter

food coloring (optional)

HOW TO: Grease a small dish for each person and set aside.

Combine sugar, corn syrup, water, and cream of tartar in a saucepan. Stir constantly until mixture comes to a boil and sugar has melted. Continue to cook without stirring for thirty minutes more or until temperature of mixture registers 250° on a candy thermometer. (If you don't have a candy thermometer, test by dropping some of the mixture into a cup of cold water. If it forms a hard ball, it is ready.)

Remove from heat and stir in flavoring and butter and a few drops of food color if you wish. Divide taffy into the greased dishes and wait until it is cool enough to handle. This takes about fifteen to twenty minutes. (Read while the candy is cooling.)

When taffy is ready, remove jewelry from hands, wash, dry, and grease hands with butter. Using the tips of your fingers and thumbs, start pulling taffy. As your taffy becomes satiny and translucent, combine it with a friend's, pull into long strips, and cut into bite-size pieces with greased scissors. Any candy that is not eaten can be stored, the pieces individually wrapped in plastic wrap.

Bulletin Board

Post valentines to book characters.

Dear Beast of Monsieur Racine,

I love looking at the details of your drawings, the leaking coffee pot, the blank pictures on the walls, the handless policeman.

Best of all I like the surprise ending.

Love,

Beast Lover

Ungerer, Tomi. *The Beast of Monsieur Racine.* (Farrar, 1971)

Dear Bunnicula,

Our family owns a rabbit. After I read your book, I went outside to see if our rabbit had fangs. She didn't.

Kisses from

Harold, a dog

Howe, Deborah, and James Howe. *Bunnicula: A Rabbit-Tale of a Mystery.* Il. by Alan Daniel. (Atheneum, 1979)

Dear Figgs & Phantoms,

Mysteries are my favorite books, but you are more than a mystery. I love the way you use words and I love the characters Truman, the Human Pretzel, Romulus the Walking Book of Knowledge, and Remus, the Talking Adding Machine.

Happy Valentine's Day

from (a friend)

Raskin, Ellen. *Figgs & Phantoms.* Il. by author. (Dutton, 1974)

Creative Writing/Activities

Your Friend

Have the children write a description of a friend: a person, a pet, or an inanimate object. It can be a physical description, but ask them to be sure to discuss the personality traits of their friend. What do they particularly like or dislike about their friend?

Valentine

Have the children make a valentine for their favorite book character.

Portrait

Have the children draw a portrait of a friend. Complete this sentence as a caption for the portrait. "My friend is…"

Books about Friends:

Ames, Mildred. *The Silver Link, The Silken Tie.* Scribners, 1984. U.
> Two prep school students, each trying to bury a memory from the past, seem linked by psychic powers.

Angell, Judie. *Tina Gogo.* Bradbury, 1978. M.
> Tina, a foster child, learns to adjust to Sarajane and her family.

Bargar, Gary W. *Life. Is. Not. Fair.* Clarion, 1984. M.
> In a story set in 1959, Louis Lamb befriends a black classmate and discovers that life is not fair.

Bawden, Nina. *The Robbers.* Lothrop, 1979. M, U.
> Would you steal to keep a friend?

Benchley, Nathaniel. *Kilroy and the Gull.* Il. by John Schoenherr. Harper, 1977. M.
> Morris, a gull, helps Kilroy, a whale, to escape from the humans.

Bonsall, Crosby Newell. *Mine's the Best.* Il. by author. Harper, 1973. P.
> Two boys argue about whose balloon is best, then band together against a girl.

Bosse, Malcolm J. *Ganesh.* Crowell, 1981. U.
> Jeffrey/Ganesh comes to mid-America from India. He persuades his new friends to support him in a hunger strike to save his aunt's house.

Buchwald, Emilie. *Floramel and Esteban.* Il. by Charles Robinson. Harcourt, 1982. M.
> An adventurous cow finds a friend and learns to become a musician...honest.

Bunting, Eve. *The Empty Window.* Il. by Judy Clifford. Warne, 1980. M, U.
> C.G. is afraid to visit his terminally ill best friend.

Byars, Betsy. *The Cybil War.* Il. by Gail Owens. Viking, 1981. M.
> Simon is in love with Cybil, but Tony makes a friendship difficult.

————. *The Pinballs.* Harper, 1977. M.
> Children in a foster home begin their stay as enemies and end up as friends.

Caines, Jeannette. *Just Us Women.* Il. by Pat Cummings. Harper, 1982. P.
> A little girl looks forward to a relaxed trip with her aunt.

Carle, Eric. *Do You Want to Be My Friend?* Il. by author. Crowell, 1971. P.
> A mouse searches for an animal friend in an early I-Can-Read book.

Clifton, Lucille. *My Friend Jacob.* Il. by Thomas di Grazia. Dutton, 1980. M.
> Sam's best friend is the retarded boy next door.

Cohen, Barbara. *Thank You, Jackie Robinson.* Il. by Richard Cuffari. Lothrop, 1974. M.
> Sam Greene's best friend is a sixty-year-old black man who is a baseball fan too.

Cummings, Betty Sue. *Turtle.* Il. by Susan Dodge. Atheneum, 1981. M, U.
> A great read-aloud tells the story of a friendship between an older woman and a turtle from both their viewpoints.

Danziger, Paula. *The Pistachio Prescription.* Delacorte, 1978. M, U.
> Cassie downgrades herself, but her friend Vicki supports her in her endeavors.

Daugherty, James. *Andy and the Lion.* Il. by author. Viking, 1938. All ages.
> Andy befriends a lion and becomes a hero.

Delton, Judy. *Kitty in the Middle.* Il. by Charles Robinson. Houghton, 1979. M.
> Three girls find the fourth grade at St. Anthony's an exciting year.

Ehrlich, Amy. *Leo, Zack, and Emmie.* Il. by Steven Kellogg. Dial, 1981. P.
> The new girl in Room 208 can wiggle her ears and run like a football player.

Fenton, Edward. *The Refugee Summer.* Delacorte, 1982. M, U.
> Five children summer in a small town in Greece.

Fox, Paula. *A Place Apart.* Farrar, 1980. U.
> Hugh is only friends with Victoria when she is useful.

Friends Are Like That! Selected by the Child Study Children's Book Committee at Bank Street. Il. by Leigh Grant. Crowell, 1979. P.
> A collection of short stories emphasizing friendship for young children.

Gaeddert, Lou Ann. *Your Former Friend, Matthew.* Il. by Mary Beth Schwark. Dutton, 1984. M.
Matthew suddenly seems to be more interested in his newly found chums than in his old friend Gail.

Gantos, Jack. *The Perfect Pal.* Il. by Nicole Rubel. Houghton, 1979. P.
Vanessa tries all kinds of animals to find the perfect pal and finally finds Wendall.

Garrigue, Sheila. *Between Friends.* Bradbury, 1978. M.
Jill finds friendship with a retarded girl down the street.

Goffstein, M. B. *Neighbors.* Il. by author. Harper, 1979, M, U.
A lonely woman tries to befriend her new neighbor.

Gormley, Beatrice. *Best Friend Insurance.* Il. by Emily Arnold McCully. Dutton, 1983. M.
Maureen buys insurance from a salesman in hopes of finding a perfect friend in 24 hours.

Greene, Bette. *Get On Out of Here, Philip Hall.* Dial, 1981. M.
Beth's friends are less loyal after she makes a few "leadership" mistakes.

Greene, Constance C. *I Know You, Al.* Il. by Byron Barton. Viking, 1975. M.
Al's friend tells this story of their friendship as Al meets her mother's new boyfriend and prepares for her father's wedding. A sequel to *A Girl Called Al* (Viking, 1969).

Guy, Rosa. *The Friends.* Holt, 1973. U.
Phyllisia is ashamed of her friend Edith and insults her in front of others but learns that true friendship takes courage.

Hamilton, Virginia. *Zeely.* Il. by Symeon Shimin. Macmillan, 1967. M.
Geeder has a crush on six-and-a-half-feet-tall Zeely, who she believes is a Watusi queen.

Hanlon, Emily. *It's Too Late for Sorry.* Bradbury, 1978. U.
To please Rachel, Kenny befriends Harry, a retarded teen-ager, but Phil pushes Kenny to abandon him.

Hautzig, Deborah. *Hey, Dollface.* Greenwillow, 1978. U.
Are Val and Chloe too close?

Heide, Florence Parry. *Banana Twist.* Holiday House, 1978. M.
Jonah does not like Goober, but if you keep bumping into someone, well (sigh), you have to be friends.

Heine, Helme. *Friends.* Il. by author. McElderry, 1982. All ages.
"Good friends always stick together."

Hoban, Russell. *Best Friends for Frances.* Il. by Lillian Hoban. Harper, 1969. P.
Frances doesn't want to play with her younger sister, Gloria, and Albert won't play with Frances, but all three end up friends.

Hughes, Monica. *The Keeper of the Isis Light.* Atheneum, 1981. M, U.
Olwen lives alone on the planet Isis with her friend and companion Guardian, a robot.

Hurwitz, Johanna. *Busybody Nora.* Il. by Susan Jeschke. Morrow, 1976. P.
A little girl makes friends with everyone in her apartment house…even with Mrs. Mind-Your-Own-Business.

———. *The Hot and Cold Summer.* Il. by Gail Owens. Morrow, 1984. M.
Rory has always been best friends with Derek until a girl named Bolivia comes to spend the summer.

———. *The Law of Gravity.* Il. by Ingrid Fetz. Morrow, 1978. M.
Margot and her friend Bernie use New York City as their playground.

Kerr, M. E. *The Son of Someone Famous.* Harper, 1974. U.
Two friends, Brenda Belle, and Adam, write in alternate chapters about their friendship.

Langton, Jane. *The Fledgling.* Harper, 1980. M.
Georgie learns to fly with her friend Prince Goose.

Lindgren, Astrid. *Ronia, the Robber's Daughter.* Trans. from the Swedish by Patricia Crampton. Viking, 1983. M.
Ronia meets Birk, the son of her father's enemy, and they become best friends.

Lowry, Lois. *Autumn Street.* Houghton, 1980. M, U.
Streetwise Charles and sensitive Elizabeth try to cope with a world of adults during World War II.

Marney, Dean. *Just Good Friends.* Addison-Wesley, 1982. M.
A thirteen-year-old boy's best friends are two girls.

Marshall, James. *George and Martha.* Il. by author. Houghton, 1972. All ages.
Five short, illustrated stories featuring two hippopotami. See also *George and Martha Rise and Shine* (Houghton, 1976) and *George and Martha Tons of Fun* (Houghton, 1980).

Miles, Betty. *The Trouble with Thirteen.* Knopf, 1979. M.
Annie and Rachel are best, best friends but Rachel is moving away.

Myers, Walter Dean. *The Young Landlords.* Viking, 1979. M.
A group of friends become the owners of an apartment house and find out that being a landlord brings work and problems.

Paterson, Katherine. *Bridge to Terabithia.* Il. by Donna Diamond. Crowell, 1977. M.
Jess, a practical boy, meets imaginative Leslie. They invent a mythical kingdom and enjoy their secret until tragedy changes everything.

Peck, Richard. *Dreamland Lake.* Holt, 1973. U.
When two boys discover a body in the woods, a friendship ends.

Sharmat, Marjorie Weinman. *I'm Not Oscar's Friend Anymore.* Il. by Tony DeLuna. Dutton, 1975. P.
A boy tells about his fight with his best friend and then discovers that Oscar doesn't even remember the fight.

———. *The 329th Friend.* Il. by Cyndy Szekeres. Four Winds, 1979. P.
Emery Raccoon discovers that he is his own best friend.

Springstubb, Tricia. *Give and Take.* Atlantic/ Little, 1981. U.

Insecure, overweight Naomi and strikingly handsome Polly are best friends when dating begins to be a serious business.

Stevenson, James. *Wilfred the Rat.* Il. by author. Greenwillow, 1977. P.
A rat finds two friends, a squirrel and a chipmunk, and joins them despite the fact that he's been offered a job in an amusement park.

Turkle, Brinton. *Thy Friend, Obadiah.* Il. by author. Viking, 1969. P.
A Quaker boy makes friends with a gull on the island of Nantucket.

Viorst, Judith. *Rosie and Michael.* Il. by Lorna Tomei. Atheneum, 1974. All ages.
A boy and girl explain why they are such good friends.

Weiss, Nicki. *Maude and Sally.* Il. by author. Greenwillow, 1983. P.
Sally and Maude are best friends, but what about Emmylou?

Wells, Rosemary. *When No One Was Looking.* Dial, 1980. M, U.
Would you kill so that your best friend could win a tennis match?

Wittman, Sally. *A Special Trade.* Il. by Karen Gundersheimer. Harper, 1978. All ages.
A little girl and an older neighbor grow up and change together.

Yolen, Jane. *The Transfigured Hart.* Il. by Donna Diamond. Crowell, 1975. M.
Two very different children become friends because of their interest in a white deer.

Zolotow, Charlotte. *Say It!* Il. by James Stevenson. Greenwillow, 1980. All ages.
A mother finds a lovely way to say I Love You.

———. *The Unfriendly Book.* Il. by William Pène Dubois. Harper, 1975. P.
Bertha is constantly criticizing Judy's friends in this small picture book.

———. *Janey.* Harper, 1973. P.
Memories of a best friend.

Index

86 1725

Bauer, Caroline Feller.
  Celebrations : read-aloud holiday and
theme book programs / by Caroline
Feller Bauer ; drawings by Lynn Gates
Bredeson. -- [Bronx, N.Y.] : H.W.
Wilson, c1985.
  xviii, 301 p. : ill. ; 27 cm.
  ISBN 0-8242-0708-4

  1. Children--Books and reading.
2. Libraries, Children's--Activity
programs. 3. Activity programs in
education. 4. Holidays. I. Title